D1052628

HEALING VOICES

Toni Ann Laidlaw
Cheryl Malmo
and Associates

HEALING VOICES

Feminist Approaches to Therapy with Women

Jossey-Bass Publishers · San Francisco

HEALING VOICES
Feminist Approaches to Therapy with Women
by Toni Ann Laidlaw, Cheryl Malmo, and Associates

350 Sansome Street
San Francisco, California 94104

Library of Congress Cataloging-in-Publication Data

Laidlaw, Toni Ann, date.
Healing voices: feminist approaches to therapy with women / Toni Ann Laidlaw, Cheryl Malmo and associates.
p. cm.—(The Jossey-Bass social and behavioral science series)
Includes bibliographical references.
ISBN 1-55542-225-X
ISBN 1-55542-418-X (paperback)
1. Feminist therapy. 2. Psychotherapy. I. Malmo, Cheryl, date. II. Title. III. Series.
RC489.F45L35 1990
616.89'14—dc20 89-43458
CIP

Manufactured in the United States of America

The paper used in this book meets the State of California requirements for recycled paper (50 percent recycled waste, including 10 percent post-consumer waste), which are the strictest guidelines for recycled paper currently in use in the United States.

JACKET DESIGN BY CHARLOTTE KAY GRAPHIC DESIGN

FIRST EDITION
HB Printing 10 9 8 7 6 5 4 3 2
PB Printing 10 9 8 7 6 5 4 3 2

Code 9019
Code 9216 (paperback)

The Jossey-Bass
Social and Behavioral Science Series

Contents

Preface

The issue of women's psychological health has received a great deal of attention during the past few years, primarily because of the women's movement. This attention has resulted in revelations of how mental health services have both misunderstood women's needs and done serious and even irreparable damage to those who have turned to them for help or relief. As a result, interest is growing in the burgeoning field of feminist therapy, whose primary purpose is to offer women counseling or therapy that recognizes their particular concerns as women and enhances the quality of their lives. While a number of books have attempted to define feminist therapy, less attention has been paid to the variety of healing techniques used by feminist therapists. *Healing Voices: Feminist Approaches to Therapy with Women* presents a rich and diverse selection of these therapeutic healing techniques.

Each therapist in the book was chosen because of her particular approach to healing work and her special skills in guiding her clients toward health and wholeness. Although this book focuses on therapists' work with their female clients, the techniques described can be and have been used successfully with men as well. Most of the therapists included here have a feminist orientation, bringing to their work an awareness of how women have been devalued and limited in our society, often from earliest childhood.

Since an important component of feminist therapy is helping women recognize that they are the experts when it comes to their own experience, and because discovering their own voices within the therapeutic relationship is empowering, we have also included the clients' voices. Clients have much to teach therapists and others about the dynamics of therapy and the therapeutic relationship. Their responses to and insights about their own therapeutic processes are essential to a full understanding of the contribution of therapy, feminist and otherwise, to the mental health field. *Healing Voices* is among the first books about the practice of therapy that systematically includes the clients' perspectives. The clients in this book are women who have experienced some form of childhood trauma, ranging from unhealthy female socialization to emotional and physical neglect to psychological, physical, and sexual abuse.

This book was conceived as a way for feminist therapists to share in some detail the different kinds of healing work they are doing with their clients and for clients to share their experiences of working with feminist therapists. The book will be of interest to practitioners, individuals already in therapy, and those who are curious about or considering entering therapy. Teachers and students in various mental health fields, including counseling and clinical psychology, social work, psychiatric nursing, and psychiatry, will find the book a useful resource.

Healing Voices assumes, in general, a feminist perspective. However, the therapists who write about their therapeutic practice here are doing a particular kind of inner healing work that is not common to all feminist therapists. They view the healing process as transformative in that it is more than cumulative or cognitive. The therapists also recognize how past events influence present feelings, thoughts, and behavior, and in their work they help their clients reclaim and heal their lost and damaged childhood selves. The healing they refer to involves an inner change made up of two parts: the identification and expression of feelings and the reframing of destructive and unhealthy beliefs. The therapists describe a range of techniques that can aid this type of healing, and the clients and workshop participants describe their experiences of healing using the various techniques.

Overview of the Therapists'/Facilitators' Contributions

In Chapter One, Toni Ann Laidlaw and Cheryl Malmo discuss the emergence and development of feminist therapy over the past two decades and describe the important ways in which it differs from other therapeutic perspectives. They define their notion of psychological healing and acknowledge past and contemporary practitioners who have contributed to their understanding of the dynamics involved in the healing process.

The four chapters in Part One focus on women's emergence from isolation and their movement toward connection with other women and with their inner selves. In making these changes, women challenge the rules and prescriptions that have limited and distorted their sense of who they are.

In Chapter Two, Laidlaw describes the emotionally crippling process of female socialization. Outlining her workshop on compulsive eating and body image, she uses consciousness-raising exercises and guided fantasies to examine the nature of this problem and help workshop participants develop strategies for change.

Maggie Hodgson explains in Chapter Three how the tradition within Native communities to respect Elders and to put the welfare of the extended family and the community ahead of the individual has hidden, until recently, the problems of alcoholism and child sexual abuse. She discusses the necessity for non-Native caregivers to understand the extended family system and community-minded culture of Natives if they are to work successfully with Native individuals. She also believes that Native caregivers must get help for their own problems as survivors of incest and alcoholism before they work with others who have these problems.

In Chapter Four, Cathy Mayhew describes a parenting workshop she has developed for adult children of alcoholics (ACOAs). Basic to Mayhew's approach is an understanding that ACOAs suffer from unresolved grief related to childhood losses and that this grief must be worked with before her clients can improve their parenting skills. She describes techniques she uses to help ACOAs through this grieving process, including discussion, visualization, guided fantasy, writing, and play.

A founding member of Support, Education and Prevention of Sexual Abuse of Children (SEPSA), Maureen McEvoy describes in detail in Chapter Five the SEPSA group model for survivors of sexual abuse. Her focus in this chapter is on the importance of reconstructing and honoring incest survivors' personal boundaries. After outlining how she structures a therapy group, she describes specific exercises for teaching survivors healthy ways to establish boundaries and thus keep themselves safe in relationships.

Part Two includes three chapters that describe how our senses and the unconscious mind can facilitate the therapy process. Judy Weiser's chapter (Chapter Six) emphasizes the importance of clients reexperiencing the past unfiltered in order to get as close as possible to the moment when a childhood trauma was originally encountered. She shows how photographs can bridge the intervening years and connect the clients with information nonverbally stored within. Once clients reexperience the original feelings and thoughts that accompanied the trauma, the healing process can truly begin.

In Chapter Seven, Yvonne Rita Dion Buffalo discusses healing stories that speak to the spirit, an integral part of some Native traditions. She illustrates different kinds of stories that can be used to bring unconscious conflict and resistance to a conscious level in order to aid personal transformation and promote health and balance. Buffalo shares personal stories to illustrate her own transformation.

Jungian dreamwork from a feminist perspective is the theme of Bonnelle Lewis Strickling's chapter (Chapter Eight). She focuses her discussion on the dreams and analytic work of one of her clients, explaining the use of the positive transference process between the client and herself as an integral part of the healing work that was accomplished.

Part Three includes three chapters dealing with different ways of working therapeutically with feeling and memory that is stored in the body at the time of a trauma. Naida D. Hyde describes in Chapter Nine the psychotherapeutic use of naturally occurring imagery for healing survivors of incest. She takes the reader on a journey through this process, which involves using relaxation techniques and either guided or nondirected imagery to find and heal the lost inner child damaged by the incest trauma.

In Chapter Ten, Malmo explains how hypnosis is compatible with a feminist approach to therapy when control of both the hypnosis and the hypnotherapy is turned over to the client. Describing step by step the affect bridge technique for tracking feelings or bodily sensations, she explains how it is used to uncover repressed memories of traumatic events in childhood.

Joan Turner's chapter (Chapter Eleven) on touch therapy focuses on how meaningful and relevant body sensations and experiences are to psychological healing. As illustration, Turner offers both (1) accounts of her own experience of her body and of her personal growth and change and (2) descriptions of her work with her clients.

Part Four includes three chapters that show how different techniques can be used together to aid psychological healing. Jan Ellis explains in Chapter Twelve how metaphors, drawings, and music may be used therapeutically to facilitate healing. In the chapter, she outlines a four-stage journey through the therapeutic process—getting safe, taking risks, encountering rage and despair, and getting free—that she typically undertakes with clients who are either cancer patients or incest survivors.

The focus of Diane Lépine's chapter (Chapter Thirteen) is the working out of guilt experienced by incest survivors who in childhood acted out their sexual abuse on other children. She illustrates her strategies for dealing with this guilt, including educational interventions and the use of gestalt chair work, writing, and hypnosis.

In Chapter Fourteen, Malmo describes why and how women become dissociated from themselves as a means of coping with various childhood traumas. She presents her model for working with different child and adult ego states common to many women; this model is based on the feminist principle of equality and the notion that seemingly self-destructive behaviors must be understood as coping strategies. Malmo shows how ego-state therapy can be easily integrated with numerous other therapeutic techniques.

About the Client/Workshop Participant Sections

Following each therapist's or facilitator's description of her work is an account written by one of her clients or a workshop participant describing her experience in the workshop or in therapy. The structuring of the book in this way is a metaphor for feminist therapy, which is based on the belief that the client/participant is the expert on her own experience and that, in the therapeutic relationship, it is she who has the final word. This said, some comments about the value of these contributions to the book seem in order.

The writings of these women illuminate how the various aspects of the healing process may be experienced. We learn about their fear of being exposed in therapy or in groups, their fear of being judged, and their need to be respected and validated. We learn, too, about the importance of their finding safety and trust in the therapeutic relationship, as well as their finding a safe place within themselves from which to begin their healing work. Some document the unfolding of the therapeutic process as they uncover lost memories, face the painful and sometimes horrific realities of the past, and find the words they need to fill their silence. Some share how they developed unhealthy and self-destructive coping strategies in order to survive traumatic experiences. Others describe their initial despair and confusion or their excitement and joy upon discovering and building a relationship with their inner child. We learn how different women developed creative strategies to help themselves heal, and we are moved by their stories. And we gain a sense of the courage, strength, beauty, and growing empowerment of these women. By the end of the book, we have a clear sense of what "Simone" means when she says: "This journey hurts and it's hard work, but it heals."

Each of the clients and workshop participants who contributed to *Healing Voices* was given the option of identifying herself or remaining anonymous. For those who chose to remain anonymous, fictitious names have been placed in quotation marks; naturally, author biographies are not included for them.

Acknowledgments

We wish to thank a number of people who helped us through the various stages of preparing this book. We appreciate Marlene Kadar's confidence in our work and her enthusiasm as she encouraged us to undertake this project. Sylvia Vance assisted us in making editorial decisions, and to her we owe a great deal of thanks. Eva Radford was generous with information and suggestions regarding production, promotion, and distribution of the book, and to her we also owe our thanks. We are grateful to Gracia A. Alkema, senior editor at Jossey-Bass, for her sincere interest in and enthusiasm about our work and for her invaluable assistance during the later stages of the project. The emotional support we received from our partners, Eric Hanley and Ray Harper, is also greatly appreciated.

We are indebted to the Ontario Arts Council for its financial support in getting the book underway and to The Women's Press in Toronto for its recommendation of the same. Robert Fournier, associate vice-president of research, and Ken Leffek, dean of graduate studies, both at Dalhousie University, were generous with funding for the typing and printing of the manuscript, and to them we are also indebted.

Finally, we wish to thank all the contributors to the book for their inspiration and cooperation on this project. It has been for us a celebration of the healing relationship between feminist therapists and their clients and of our mutual growth as we learn from one another.

January 1990

Toni Ann Laidlaw
Halifax, Nova Scotia

Cheryl Malmo
Edmonton, Alberta

The Authors

Toni Ann Laidlaw and Cheryl Malmo met in 1969 in graduate school, where they were studying applied psychology. While there, together they discovered feminism. They were both so excited by its relevance to their lives that they found themselves reading feminist literature as much as possible and using what they learned to critique the psychology books they were required to study. As a result, each threw out her original thesis topic and actively pursued research on the psychology of women.

What began as a collegial and social relationship at the beginning of graduate school flourished during two years in a consciousness-raising group. Their friendship has deepened over the past twenty years in the special way in which so many women's friendships do. They have shared many experiences in that time, including the struggles of single parenthood and watching their children grow. Central to their continuing friendship is their shared identity as feminist psychologists and psychotherapists.

Being feminist psychologists means to Malmo and Laidlaw that they acknowledge and reject the stereotyping, devaluing, and abuse of women; recognize how limiting and debilitating this is; and understand its damaging psychological effects on women. They bring this awareness and their commitment to change to their work as teachers, therapists, and writers.

Because most feminist literature deals with change at a social and political level, Laidlaw and Malmo thought it important to share with others what they believe are the significant—and indeed necessary—kinds of personal change that are taking place among women in feminist therapy. It is for this reason that they undertook the creation of this book. They also saw the book as an opportunity for feminist therapists to share their knowledge and skills and learn from one another and for clients to share their experiences of different kinds of feminist therapy. Malmo and Laidlaw agree that the conceptualizing and co-editing of this book has both challenged and enriched them; the experience has deepened their friendship as well as augmented their professional lives.

Toni Ann Laidlaw received her M. Ed. degree (1969) from the University of Calgary and her Ph.D. degree (1978) from the University of Alberta, both in educational psychology. She is professor in the School of Education at Dalhousie University, Halifax, Nova Scotia, teaching in the areas of counseling, developmental psychology, and women's studies. In addition, she has a small private practice in feminist therapy. She has been an active member of the feminist community, both on and off the campus. She is past president of the Dalhousie Women Faculty Association, past vice-president and president *pro tem* of the Dalhousie Faculty Association, and former chair of the Presidential Advisory Committee on Sexual Harassment. In the community, in addition to radio, television, and speaking engagements, she has facilitated a number of workshops focusing on women's issues and has been a board member of Bryony House, the Halifax transition house for battered women. Her diverse interests in feminism have led to a number of exciting and varied projects, including coproduction of a thirteen-part community television series on Nova Scotia women. In 1988 she was one of four feminist academics to travel to Nigeria to help establish women's studies programs at the universities at Ile/Ife and Ibadan. Her most recent publication is *No Place Like Home: Diar-*

ies and Letters of Nova Scotia Women, 1771–1938 (1988, with M. Conrad and D. Smyth).

Cheryl Malmo has been a feminist psychotherapist in private practice in Edmonton since 1975 and is an instructor with the Women's Program at the University of Alberta in Edmonton. She obtained her M.Ed. degree (1972) and her Ph.D. degree (1983), both from the University of Alberta in educational psychology. She was once a sessional lecturer in the Department of Family Studies, Faculty of Home Economics, and she has taught summer school sessions for the School of Education and the Maritime School of Social Work at Dalhousie University. She has taught numerous workshops for the Faculty of Extension's Women's Program, including "Second Look" (a course for women who wish to make personal and/or career changes in their lives), "Compulsive Eating and Body Image," and "Feminist Counseling." For the past several years she has been involved in training professionals in Edmonton, Calgary, and Halifax to work with survivors of sexual violence and to use hypnotherapy with women. Over the years Malmo has been interviewed on radio and television talk shows about various issues regarding women's mental health. She was featured on three programs in the *About Women* series on Access Network, an educational television channel. She wrote a course, "Issues and Strategies for Counseling Girls and Women," for Athabasca University.

About the Professionals

Yvonne Rita Dion Buffalo is a graduate student in medical anthropology at the University of Alberta. About herself she writes: "North American Indian scholars have recently been challenging the portrayal of their indigenous culture by the dominant Western culture as worthless and inferior. As a Plains Cree Indian woman, I find this recent phenomenon both stimulating and exciting, particularly in my field of medical anthropology. My interest in holistic healing and health issues for Native women comes partly from my personal struggles. For instance, I spent most of my younger years in various homes and convents. The people who ran these institutions taught me to feel ashamed about my culture and myself. When I got out on my own I was unequipped to cope with life. Needless to say, my teen years were filled with trauma and heartache. I was fortunate, however, to find employment with various Native and non-Native leaders in the 1960s. This experience changed my life. Since then I have continued to upgrade my education, work, and life skills. A major focus of my studies has been holistic healing. At the same time I have been working to reclaim and revive meaningful childhood experiences from within my Native culture—rituals, ceremonies, and stories passed on to me by my family and my ancestors. I have begun to understand the meaning and power of my experiences and have been able to incorporate and adapt various practices to my life as a Native woman living in an urban setting in the 1980s. In addition, I am finding alternative ways of responding to "immobilizing" experiences. I plan to go to China to examine the concept of energy flow (referred to as chi) in Chi Quong, Tai Chi, and Feng Shui. I hope to incorporate this knowledge into what I know about North American Native medicine and to develop some strategies to use for healing Native women."

Jan Ellis was born in California and is the eldest of three sisters. She grew up in the vast wasteland of suburban Los Angeles. Fortunately, it was the post-Sputnik era, and she got a decent education. A scholarship got her to the University of California, Santa Barbara. She transferred to the University of California, Berkeley, in time for the student riots and received her B.A. degree (1971) in psychology. She moved to Winnipeg in 1971 and now considers Canada her home.

Ellis began to suspect she was a feminist when she faced blatant sex discrimination in working as a personnel manager. She *knew* she was a feminist when she started to leave her now ex-husband's laundry and papers on the floor and place bets with her friends on how many days he would step over them before berating her for being a poor housekeeper. She finally realized she was a radical when she was given a bullhorn at a pro-choice rally. After a series of jobs, such as adolescent group home director and birth control research assistant, and a disastrous two years in pre-med, she found a plum position as a mental health educator. When she wasn't busy training average people to lead public educational groups on stress reduction, she went to workshops to learn therapy skills from the best clinicians she could find. Upon finding herself teaching the seminar on humanistic therapies in her night graduate school course, she finally let go of the last academic "should" (you should have a Ph.D. to be a therapist), hung out her shingle in 1978, and has been in full-time private practice ever since. Ellis is now expert in the treatment of incest/abuse trauma and of disorders of the immune system.

Maggie Hodgson is of Carrier Indian French ancestry. She is executive director of Nechi Institute, a Native addictions and family violence counseling, training, and research center in St. Albert, Alberta. Hodgson has worked in the human services field for eighteen years within the Native and non-Native world in the areas of community development, justice, and addictions. She worked as a paralegal community developer in Saskatchewan for six years and was the first formal family court worker with Native People for Native Families in Crisis, a position she held for four years. She also has worked as a consultant to the province of Alberta on Native child welfare and as a consultant to Health and Welfare Canada on Native mental health and Native addictions.

Hodgson is coauthor of *My Spirit Weeps* (1988), a book on Native child sexual abuse. She presented at an international conference on Native addictions in Oslo, Norway. She actively promotes the prevention of family violence in Native communities across Canada and is an avid promoter of therapy for professionals in the human services. Her motto, "walk your talk," reflects the Native philosophy of giving back to the community what you gain for yourself.

Naida D. Hyde received her master's degree in psychiatric nursing from Boston College and her Ph.D. degree in clinical psychology from the University of Windsor. She is currently a registered psychologist in private practice in Vancouver. Over the past ten years she has specialized in working with incest survivors, helping them heal their invisible wounds. In addition, much of her professional time has focused on training professionals to work with survivors. Among her published articles on these topics are "Uncovering the Repression: Some Critical Considerations in the

Psychotherapy of Women Incest Survivors" (*Alberta Psychology,* 1987), "Covert Incest in Women's Lives: Dynamics and Directions for Healing" (*Canadian Journal of Community Mental Health,* 1986), and "Long-Term Effects of Childhood Sexual Abuse" (*British Columbia Medical Journal,* 1984). She is presently completing the certification program of the Academy for Guided Imagery in San Francisco.

Diane M. Lépine was formerly a teacher in Alberta and Africa. Later she obtained a master's degree in counseling psychology, and she now works as a chartered psychologist. Her research has been in the area of incest, and her primary professional interest is in working with women. She has been a counselor and a counseling coordinator at the Sexual Assault Centre in Edmonton, where she worked with individuals and facilitated therapy groups for incest survivors. As well, she has tutored a course on issues and strategies for counseling girls and women for Athabasca University. Currently, she is an instructor for the Women's Program, Faculty of Extension, University of Alberta, where she teaches workshops entitled "Compulsive Eating and Body Image" and "From Striving to Thriving." She now spends most of her working time in private practice, which she enjoys tremendously.

Maureen McEvoy has been an educator and counselor in the area of child sexual abuse for over eight years. Her clinical work includes counseling individuals and facilitating therapy groups for those who experienced child sexual abuse. McEvoy has lectured extensively on the prevention and treatment of child sexual abuse. She has provided numerous professional development seminars on prevention programs, such as The C.A.R.E. Kit and FEELING YES, FEELING NO, to school districts throughout British Columbia. She has served as consultant to the (Canadian) National Film Board, Pacific Region, and as coordinating producer for a television series on child sexual abuse on The Knowledge Network. Most recently she provided the research for the National Film Board, Studio D's film on incest "To a Safer Place," which was released in 1987. In 1982 McEvoy participated in the development of the incest therapy program at the Ottawa Sexual Assault Support Centre. After moving to Vancouver she cofounded the Support, Education and Prevention of Sexual Abuse (SEPSA) nonprofit group, whose purpose is to increase public awareness of child sexual abuse; provide long-term counseling and support for survivors and offenders; and educate children, parents, and professionals about prevention programs.

Cathy Mayhew is the founder of Recovery Counselling Services, a resource designed to meet the special needs of adult children of alcoholics and survivors of sexual and physical abuse in childhood. She is an innovator in this field and has developed a parenting group for adult children of alcoholics. Her interest in parenting represents a deep concern for children that is reflected in her sensitivity to the child within every individual. She brings to her work a depth of understanding based on her own recovery. She combines this personal approach with a solid clinical background and is a skilled individual, family, and group counselor. Mayhew holds a master's degree from the University of British Columbia in social work. Her ten-year professional history includes work in hospital settings and employee assistance programs, and she has a strong background in prevention. She has developed expertise in dealing with addictions as well as with child sexual abuse, and she recognizes the self-help movement as an important part of recovery.

Bonnelle Lewis Strickling received her Ph.D. degree from the University of British Columbia in philosophy. Her doctoral thesis was on emotions. Trained as a Gestalt therapist, Strickling has developed strong Jungian interests. She is coordinator of the Department of Philosophy at Vancouver Community College, Langara Campus; in addition, she has a private practice in psychotherapy in which she sees individuals and facilitates groups. Born in West Virginia, she emigrated to Canada in 1971 and is now a Canadian citizen. She is a member of the board of directors of the C. G. Jung Society of Vancouver and of the Canadian Society for Women in Philosophy. Her other publications include "Self-Abnegation" in *Feminist Perspectives in Philosophy* (1988, M. Griffiths and M. Whitford, eds.) and "Simone de Beauvoir and the Value of Immanence" (*Atlantis,* 1988).

Joan Turner has a private practice in therapeutic massage/counseling and body work. She offers workshops on such topics as coping with stress, and she often speaks on women's issues. Much of Turner's teaching is based on her life experiences: professional training in social work, therapeutic massage, breath, and voice; numerous workshops on Gestalt therapy, traditional Chinese medicine, and so on; and active use of her body/mind in a variety of sports, yoga, and Tai Chi. For almost twenty years and until recently, she was associate professor, School of Social Work, University of Manitoba. In 1983 she co-edited (with L. Emery) *Perspectives on Women.* Turner and Emery are working on an anthology, *Living the Changes,* about contemporary Canadian women. Turner is owner of Bold Print, the Winnipeg women's bookstore.

Judy Weiser, a psychologist, art therapist, and social worker, is director and training coordinator of the PhotoTherapy Centre in Vancouver. Specializing in the nonverbal and visual aspects of communication and behavior (including cultural differences), she has been a consultant and therapist in private practice for over twenty years. Weiser specializes in working with many culturally different, disadvantaged, disabled, and "hard-to-reach" populations, including street kids, teens and families with alcohol- and/or drug-related problems, the deaf, and Native people. Fluent in sign language, she is also a professional photographer with many gallery exhibits and photographic publications to her credit. In the past few years she has limited her practice in order to conduct PhotoTherapy workshops and training events worldwide. Editor of *Phototherapy Journal* and secretary of the International Photo Therapy Association, Weiser has written numerous articles and several book chapters on this topic, and she has a full-length book in progress. She has been featured in a variety of publications, including *LIFE, MacLean's, The New York Times, National Globe and Mail, U.S.A. Today,* and in interviews on NBC and CBC.

About the Clients, Workshop Participants, and other Contributors

Janie-Rae Crowley is a married mother of two children. She is forty years old and lives in Edmonton, where she works as a nurse.

She is an adult child of an alcoholic who has been in recovery for three years.

Leah Minuk is a thirty-four-year-old lesbian with two children—a twelve-year-old daughter and a five-year-old son. She works outside her home and spends what time she has left playing with her children, volunteering in her co-op, enjoying her friends, and trying to heal her long-standing wounds. Of her life she says, "It is not easy, but it holds a lot of promise."

Jenny Nash was born in England in 1940. She went to Canada in 1967 to join some Canadian friends she had met while they were traveling in England. She began working as a child care counselor in 1970 and is grateful to many of these young people, who taught her a great deal and helped her grow and mature. She now works in Vancouver as a systemic family therapist and considers art and photo therapy a rich tool. Married and the mother of an eight-year-old child, she believes that life begins at forty—her age when she gave birth.

Patricia Perry was educated at the University of Alberta. She lives and works in Bonnyville, Alberta, where she teaches high school English; writes songs, plays, poetry, and stories; and produces variety shows. She is unstintingly supported in these endeavors and in her quest to slough off the difficulties of the past by her husband of twenty years, Ian, with whom she is enjoying raising three daughters.

Carol Rose is a Winnipeg child care educator, workshop leader, and spiritual counselor. Together with Lu Ann Lynde, she developed "Motherpath Cards," depicting images of Biblical women, which she uses in workshops throughout North America. The mother of four sons and a daughter, Rose is married to a rabbi/theologian who is also a family therapist.

Betsy Warland is a writer and editor who lives on Salt Spring Island, just off the coast of Vancouver. Her recent books are *serpent (w)rite* (1987) and *Double Negative* (1988, with D. Marlatt). She has also written a forthcoming book of theorograms, *proper deafinitions.*

Chris Watson describes herself as leading a cautious, single life as a high school English teacher and mother to her thirteen-year-old son. She is particularly cautious about men. She still sees and talks to her father, but their relationship is guarded and polite. Periodically, she sees him as the middle-aged man he was and not as the old man he is; when that happens she gets angry and writes a lot. She still has nightmares and flashbacks, but they are no longer devastating to her. About herself she says, "I have my son and my friends and my job and my self, and I'm okay." In her life, Chris has taken a few very blatant risks; writing in this book was one of them.

"Eve," "Madeleine," "Michaela," "Phyllis," "Rebecca," and **"Simone"** have chosen to use these pseudonyms to protect their identities.

May this poem be to victims of abuse an image of hope and to therapists an image of the joyful end to which their valuable work is directed.

Little one,
little pretty one,
so sad.

Leap,
eyes alight,
into my outstretched arms.

I will hold you,
I will protect you,
I will love you.

I will love you.
I will love you.

Together we will whirl,
inscribing radiant circles
under an ecstatic sun.

—Patricia Perry

1

Introduction: Feminist Therapy and Psychological Healing

Toni Ann Laidlaw
Cheryl Malmo

Feminist therapy evolved from the feminist consciousness of those of us in the mental health field who experienced a discrepancy between our own experiences as women and those described by the psychological theories we were required to learn and apply. We observed that the oppression of women was as present and as damaging in our own profession as it was in society at large. (Among the works that most influenced our thinking at that time were Weisstein, 1971, and Chesler, 1989, which first appeared in 1972.) Excited by the possibilities for change offered by feminist analysis, we used that analysis as a model for critiquing traditional psychological theories and research. This critique exposed the pervasiveness of androcentrism and sexism throughout the body of psychological literature, and existing approaches to therapy were no exception.

We came to recognize that traditional psychoanalysis begins from an androcentric position by assuming that a woman embodies all that a man does not. Since male characteristics are the ones that are valued, women are, by definition, inferior. Those qualities that Freud ascribed to womanhood—passivity, masochism, and narcissism—become our biological handicaps. Behavioral therapy with its focus on learned behaviors disregards the personal or emotional meanings that we give to our experiences as women and ignores the social context in which those experiences occur. While humanistic therapy acknowledges the importance of giving meaning to our lives, its emphasis on freedom and free choice makes us entirely responsible for all that happens to us. Psychiatry, arguably the most influential of all therapies, and certainly the one most available in Canada and Great Britain where, if a patient is referred by a medical doctor, its costs are covered under Medicare and the National Health Service, is based on a medical model. Consequently attention is focused on "cures," and inordinate emphasis is placed on "correct" diagnoses as defined by the *Diagnostic and Statistical Manual of Mental Disorders,* Third Edition (see Caplan, 1987, for a feminist critique of the DSM-III). From this perspective, women who seek relief from emotional trauma are referred to as patients and are characterized as sick and in need of medication and other medical interventions. Throughout treatment, the process of psychotherapy tends to be minimized. As with the previous models, the impact of cultural norms, social expectations, and political structures on the lives of these women are largely ignored (see Burstow and Weitz, 1988, for a critique of Canadian psychiatry).

Angered by the sexist assumptions and detrimental consequences of these therapies, we began to listen seriously to ourselves, our friends, and our clients to learn the truth about women's experiences. And as we listened and learned, we began to understand that women were reacting in large part to unhealthy and destructive circumstances in their lives and in the process were developing unhealthy coping strategies in order to survive.

At the same time, women's liberation activists were providing safe places for women to meet and share their experiences. As a result of this sharing, the various kinds of violence toward women—sexual harassment, battering, rape, and incest—and the extent to which they were occurring were gradually uncovered. Initially, many feminists believed that these problems could be solved, in time, through collective political action. However, as women risked breaking the silence about the violence that they had endured, it became clear that changes had to be accomplished internally as well as externally. The psychological dimension needed to be dealt with in its own right. Thus, disclosure and validation of women's experiences were only the first step toward inner change; all of the psychological damage that women had suffered needed to be healed.

As women began feeling safe in disclosing their pain to other women, they also looked for alternative therapeutic resources that would not only validate their experiences but also support their struggle to heal. Female therapists who identified themselves as feminist were sought out with a sense of great urgency. And the more we, as therapists, listened to and worked with these women, the more we began to understand what they needed from us in order to become psychologically healthy and strong. It was through this collaborative process that feminist therapy was born. (Our description of feminist therapy is derived from our ongoing experience with clients as well as our continuing study, teaching, and writing in this area. Some aspects of feminist therapy discussed here are taken from Pyke, 1983; Sturdivant, 1980; Collier, 1982; and Malmo, 1985.)

As feminist therapists, we are trained in a variety of traditional theoretical orientations and come from a variety of disciplines. However, we differ from our nonfeminist colleagues in a number of significant ways. First and foremost, feminist therapists understand that women constitute an oppressed group in our culture. (Understanding sexism, feminists also have an understanding of people who are oppressed by classism, racism, homophobia, ageism, and prejudice based on religious or ethnic affiliation.) We understand, also, the psychological effects of this oppression on women. Those of us who are old enough may have taken part in women's consciousness-raising groups in the 1960s and early 1970s where we dissected every part of our own and the other group members' experiences as girls and women, learned to accept, value, and speak for ourselves, learned to receive as well as to give support, and learned to initiate change, both personally and politically. It was in such a consciousness-raising group that we, the senior authors, first explored together what it meant to be women in a patriarchal culture.

In the therapeutic relationship, feminist therapists welcome their clients' inquiries about their values, orientation, and methods, encouraging them to be educated and conscientious consumers. At appropriate times, feminist therapists share with their clients stories about their own experiences to assist the clients' process. By being open about their values and orientation, by making well-timed self-disclosures, and by encouraging the client to take an active part in making decisions about the course of therapy, feminist therapists step out from behind the professional mask of neutrality and become real people. In doing so, they demystify the therapeutic process and minimize the professional distance and power imbalance between themselves and their clients.

Feminist therapists reject stereotypes of women and men as limiting, distorting, and unhealthy and recognize the many ways that stereotypes are learned. They also have developed a fine tuning for detecting at a glance when women are being devalued or are devaluing themselves and know effective methods for teaching women to trust and value themselves and to develop self-esteem. Feminist therapists also employ consciousness raising, known in therapeutic circles as reframing, resocialization, or reparenting, to put women's personal experience into a larger perspective.

In therapy, feminist therapists assume an equal relationship with their clients, valuing and respecting them as partners of equal worth. While the therapist has a certain expertise (knowledge and skills) and can provide a safe place for therapeutic work, the client is the expert on her own experience, and is the best judge of what is right for her. Further, the client is in charge of the therapeutic process in that she controls or has final say over the content of a therapeutic session, the choice of method (insofar as the therapist is able to comply), and the pacing of therapeutic work. Feminist therapists act as facilitators or guides and as companions or witnesses in the clients' therapeutic journey. As such, they validate the clients' experiences, encourage them to fully examine their feelings, beliefs, intentions, and behavior, and support their movement toward healthy growth and change.

Feminist therapists understand that anger is a particularly difficult feeling for women because they have been taught that anger is not appropriate if one is to be feminine. They also understand that self-nurturing is a difficult issue for women because of their socialization to always put others' needs first. Knowing that their clients may have been taught to devalue women in general, feminist therapists teach the valuing of female friends. They encourage their clients to make friends if they don't have any and to share personal intimacies with their friends, as they are ready.

Finally, feminist therapists reject the adjustment model of mental health, which encourages women to conform to social expectations or norms. They are committed to a form of therapy that incorporates both internal and external change. In keeping with this commitment, they support their clients' attempts not just to identify and express their perceptions, feelings, thoughts, and intentions but also to act on them in whatever ways seem appropriate, comfortable, and healthy. Feminist therapists consider it appropriate to give their clients additional kinds of support besides emotional support. They often refer clients to appropriate community resources, write letters and appear in court on their behalf, and accompany their clients to appointments when necessary. In other words, feminist therapists act as their clients' advocates. In addition, they are often involved in their own communities on behalf of women, educating the public and people in positions of power about women's needs and experiences. In these many ways, feminist therapists facilitate and support the empowering of women.

While feminist therapy was developing and flourishing, there was a growing interest in the concept of psychological healing within the larger therapeutic community. The practice of healing work in psychology has its roots in the psychodynamic traditions of Sigmund Freud (Fine, 1973; Freud, 1973; Harper, 1959) and Carl Jung (Harper, 1959; Jung and Kerenyi, 1973; Whitmont and Kaufmann, 1973). (It is important to point out that we recognize and reject those aspects of the theories that we discuss throughout this chapter that are sexist and androcentric. What we are doing is identifying the parts of the theories that we find valuable.) It is our view that healing work is accomplished in psychotherapy when the client is engaged fully, when communication is established with both her conscious and unconscious mind, when both left-brain and right-brain functions are engaged, when both cognition and feelings are involved. In healing work, change takes place on an intrapsychic level, involving an inner shift or a resynthesis after new material (coming either from the client's unconscious memory or from the therapist's reframing of an experience) is introduced and integrated.

Since much of women's psychological pain is rooted in early experience, healing work involves, in part, a journey back to childhood, sometimes to very early childhood, to a time when the original traumas took place. Freud and Jung clearly recognized the importance of childhood experiences in the development of the adult psyche. They also understood that painful experiences from childhood may need to be repressed or denied by the conscious mind and, therefore, become buried in the unconscious mind. Though hidden, these memories retain the power to motivate and even to determine behavior. Freud often worked with dreams, free association, and hypnosis to gain entry into the realm of the unconscious, and Jung often worked with fantasies, dreams, metaphors, and physical symptoms to communicate with the psyche. Both considered it imperative for therapists to work with the memories and traumas of the child who inhabited the adult psyche in order to develop the patient's health and wholeness. Jung explains as follows: "Now it is an axiom of psychology that when a part of the psyche is split off from consciousness it is only apparently inactivated; in actual fact it brings about a possession of the personality, with the result that the individual's aims are falsified in the interests of the split-off part. If, then, the childhood state of the collective psyche is repressed to the point of total exclusion, the unconscious content overwhelms the conscious aim and inhibits, falsifies, even destroys its realization. Viable progress only comes from the cooperation of both" (Jung and Kerenyi, 1973, p. 83). In feminist healing work, the client is encouraged to re-experience the memories and feelings associated with that early trauma, in safety and with her therapist as a supportive guide, in order to heal the split.

One of the ways in which feminist therapy differs from traditional psychoanalytical therapies is that it espouses change rather than adjustment to a societal standard. In this respect, it identifies with humanistic or third-force psychology, which also put forth the notion that the goal of therapy was a change of consciousness, a change of feelings toward oneself, and a change in one's relationship to society. How various Eastern and Western philosophies support the ideas of change and liberation is the theme of much of the writing of Alan Watts (1961, 1969). As it developed, humanistic psychology (Sutich and Vich, 1969) acknowledged in different ways the importance of engaging a part of the mind other than that used for conscious thinking and decision making in order to facilitate psychological change. Specifically, transcendental meditation (Bloomfield, 1976), rolfing (Feitis, 1978; Rolf, 1977), primal scream therapy (Janov, 1970, 1971), rebirthing (Orr and Ray, 1977), encounter groups (Schutz, 1967, 1973), Gestalt therapy (Kempler, 1973; Perls, 1969; Stevens, 1971; Yontef, 1976), transactional analysis (Berne, 1964; Harris, 1976; Holland, 1973), and ego-state therapy (Watkins, 1978; Watkins and Watkins, 1979) developed over time as methods of treatment that engage a part of the mind other than rational thinking and that precipitate powerful change. Among these, Gestalt therapy, transactional analysis, and ego-state therapy developed approaches to treatment that acknowledge the importance of working to uncover and eventually integrate into the whole the parts of the psyche that have become dissociated during childhood.

Milton Erickson (Erickson, 1986; Haley, 1985; Rosen, 1982; Rossi, 1986) has taught us about the therapeutic conditions under which emotional healing and inner change can take place. He has demonstrated that this healing takes place naturally, if therapists both permit it and provide the right emotional setting. Once the stage has been set (trust established), the role of the therapist is to facilitate, guide, and observe the change process. Ernest Rossi (1986) is breaking new ground by integrating the fields of physiology and psychology in such a way that therapists can now understand how emotional healing and inner change actually occur at a cellular level.

Different aspects of this approach to healing are presently being practiced within a variety of cultures. Since North American Natives are finally being heard by the larger culture, they have shared with us a variety of their traditional healing methods, which stress health and balance and incorporate a spiritual dimension (Allen, 1983; Jilek, 1982; Lincoln, 1983). The work of the Swiss analyst Alice Miller (1983a, 1983b, 1985) alerts us to the systematic destruction of the child's spirit that takes place when children are not loved unconditionally. Miller explains that the origins of violence are rooted in these conditions. She insists that the therapist must always be the advocate for the inner child in all adult patients.

Many feminist therapists are attracted to these developing practices of psychological healing. In a medical context, the term *healing* implies a process that occurs from within the organism even though the cause of the damage may be external. And it is in this sense that we understand it as therapists. Whereas we recognize that much of women's pain is a result of circumstances external to them and that these circumstances must be changed, we believe that women must be assisted to recover from the psychological damage that is so common to their experience. In order to facilitate the process, the therapist acts as guide and supporter. But it is the client who has everything she needs inside her to find the answers that are meaningful to her, to express herself fully, to recognize her worth, to heal. It is precisely this kind of internal change that gives women the strength to make personal changes in their lives and to work collectively toward social, economic, and political change. Psychological healing is essential for the empowerment of women.

What follows are examples of how some feminist therapists have integrated their feminism with healing practices to bring about inner change in their clients and workshop participants and of how these women experience that change.

References

Allen, P. G. *Studies in American Indian Literature.* New York: Modern Language Association of America, 1983.

American Psychiatric Association. *Diagnostic and Statistical Manual of Mental Disorders.* (3rd ed.) Washington, D.C.: American Psychiatric Association, 1980.

Berne, E. *Games People Play.* New York: Grove Press, 1964.

Bloomfield, H. H. "Application of the Transcendental Meditation Program to Psychiatry." In V. Binder, A. Binder, and B. Rimland (eds.), *Modern Therapies.* Englewood Cliffs, N.J.: Prentice-Hall, 1976.

Burstow, B., and Weitz, D. (eds.). *Shrink Resistant: The Struggle Against Psychiatry in Canada.* Vancouver, B.C.: New Star Books, 1988.

Caplan, P. J. "The Psychiatric Association's Failure to Meet Its Own Standards: The Dangers of 'Self-Defeating Personality Disorder' as a Category." *Journal of Personality Disorders,* 1987, *1* (2), pp. 178–182.

Chesler, P. *Women and Madness.* (Rev. ed.) Garden City, N.Y.: Doubleday, 1989.

Collier, H. *Counselling Women.* New York: Free Press, 1982.

Erickson, M. H. *Mind-Body Communication in Hypnosis.* New York: Irvington, 1986.

Feitis, R. (ed.). *Ida Rolf Talks About Rolfing and Physical Reality.* New York: Harper & Row, 1978.

Fine, R. "Psychoanalysis." In R. Corsini (ed.), *Current Psychotherapies.* Itasca, Ill.: Peacock, 1973.

Freud, S. *An Outline of Psycho-Analysis.* London: Hogarth Press and Institute of Psycho-Analysis, 1973.

Haley, J. *Conversations with Milton H. Erickson.* Vol. 1: *Changing Individuals.* New York: Triangle Press, 1985.

Harper, R. A. *Psychoanalysis and Psychotherapy.* Englewood Cliffs, N.J.: Prentice-Hall, 1959.

Harris, T. A. "Transactional Analysis: An Introduction." In V. Binder, A. Binder, and B. Rimland (eds.), *Modern Therapies.* Englewood Cliffs, N.J.: Prentice-Hall, 1976.

Holland, G. A. "Transactional Analysis." In R. Corsini (ed.), *Current Psychotherapies.* Itasca, Ill.: Peacock, 1973.

Janov, A. *Primal Scream.* New York: Putnam, 1970.

Janov, A. *The Anatomy of Mental Illness.* New York: Putnam, 1971.

Jilek, W. G. *Indian Healing.* Surrey, B.C.: Hancock House, 1982.

Jung, C., and Kerenyi, C. *Essays on a Science of Mythology.* Princeton, N.J.: Princeton University Press, 1973.

Kempler, W. "Gestalt Therapy." In R. Corsini (ed.), *Current Psychotherapies.* Itasca, Ill.: Peacock, 1973.

Lincoln, K. *Native American Renaissance.* Berkeley: University of California Press, 1983.

Malmo, C. L. *Psychology 343: Issues and Strategies in Counselling Girls and Women.* Athabasca, Alta.: University of Athabasca Press, 1985.

Miller, A. *The Drama of the Gifted Child.* New York: Farrar, Straus & Giroux, 1983a.

Miller, A. *For Your Own Good: Hidden Cruelty in Child-Rearing and the Roots of Violence.* New York: Farrar, Straus & Giroux, 1983b.

Miller, A. *Thou Shalt Not Be Aware: Society's Betrayal of the Child.* New York: Farrar, Straus & Giroux, 1985.

Orr, L., and Ray, S. *Rebirthing in the New Age.* Millbrae, Calif.: Celestial Arts, 1977.

Perls, F. S. *Gestalt Therapy Verbatim.* Lafayette, Calif.: Real People Press, 1969.

Pyke, S. "Workshop on Feminist Therapy." Presentation at Women and Therapy Conference, Toronto, 1983.

Rolf, I. P. *Rolfing: The Integration of Human Structures.* New York: Harper & Row, 1977.

Rosen, S. *My Voice Will Go with You: The Teaching Tales of Milton H. Erickson.* New York: Norton, 1982.

Rossi, E. L. *The Psychobiology of Mind-Body Healing.* New York: Norton, 1986.

Schutz, W. C. *Joy: Expanding Human Awareness.* New York: Grove Press, 1967.

Schutz, W. C. "Encounter." In R. Corsini (ed.), *Current Psychotherapies.* Itasca, Ill.: Peacock, 1973.

Stevens, J. O. *Awareness: Exploring, Experimenting, Experiencing.* Moab, Utah: Real People Press, 1971.

Sturdivant, S. *Therapy with Women: A Feminist Philosophy of Treatment.* New York: Springer, 1980.

Sutich, A. J., and Vich, M. A. (eds.). *Readings in Humanistic Psychology.* New York: Free Press, 1969.

Watkins, J. G. *The Therapeutic Self.* New York: Human Sciences Press, 1978.

Watkins, J. G., and Watkins, H. H. "Theory and Practice of Ego-State Therapy." In H. Grayson (ed.), *Short Term Approaches to Psychotherapy.* New York: Human Sciences Press, 1979.

Watts, A. W. *Psychotherapy East and West.* New York: Ballantine Books, 1961.

Watts, A. W. "Oriental and Occidental Approaches to the Nature of

Man." In A. J. Sutich and M. A. Vich (eds.), *Readings in Humanistic Psychology*. New York: Free Press, 1969.

Weisstein, N. "Psychology Constructs the Female: Or the Fantasy Life of the Male Psychologist." In M. Garscoff (ed.), *Roles Women Play: Readings Toward Women's Liberation*. Belmont, Calif.: Brooks/Cole, 1971.

Whitmont, E. C., and Kaufmann, Y. "Analytical Psychotherapy." In R. Corsini (ed.), *Current Psychotherapies*. Itasca, Ill.: Peacock, 1973.

Yontef, G. M. "Gestalt Therapy: Clinical Phenomenology." In V. Binder, A. Binder, and B. Rimland (eds.), *Modern Therapies*. Englewood Cliffs, N.J.: Prentice-Hall, 1976.

PART ONE

BREAKING THROUGH THE BARRIERS

2

Dispelling the Myths: A Workshop on Compulsive Eating and Body Image

Toni Ann Laidlaw
Workshop Participant: "Michaela"

> Food is a metaphor through which women speak of their inner experiences.
>
> —*Susie Orbach* (in Lawrence, 1987, p. 7)

The current feminist movement has put to rest any lingering doubts that women in our society constitute an oppressed group. As concerned women, we have talked to each other, compared experiences, and recognized with much anger and a growing sense of power the shared consequences of this oppression. We have come to understand through these experiences, which are continually verified through feminist theory and research, that much of the pain in our lives is a direct consequence of this oppression and not the result of private failings or personal inadequacies—that the personal really is political. Yet, in spite of this growing consciousness, women of all ages continue to make negative judgments about their bodies and to characterize their relationship with food as a personal problem.

As women, we have access to food in a way in which we do not have access to power, including power in our day-to-day lives.

As Sheila Kitzinger has pointed out, the connection between love and food is basic for us (Cline and Lean, 1987). It begins when mothers give birth and put the baby to the breast. When they offer food, they offer themselves. They are continually reinforced in the belief that they are the nurturers and are therefore responsible, through feeding, for the health of their families. Food becomes a metaphor for expressing their love and concern. While this provides them with a potential source of power, however indirect, it also makes them vulnerable. To refuse their food is to reject them.

We have also discovered that food is one of the few instant gratifiers both permitted and readily available to women. It can comfort us, if only temporarily, when we cannot comfort ourselves or when there is no one to comfort us. In fact, eating is sometimes the best thing that happens to a woman in her day. But the relationship of food to our bodies also becomes a source of great stress. There is good reason for this. Since we are judged by our bodies, we come to perceive them as a potential asset or experience them as the basis for rejection. To attempt to approximate the continually changing requirements for beauty is to be given the promise of another source of indirect power. Yet the current image of the "beautiful" female in our society, defined not by ourselves but by others, is a dangerous one of almost unattainable thinness. In addition, our bodies are made so public, so overly visible that in many ways they become our greatest vulnerability. It is primarily girls and women who are battered, raped, and sexually assaulted.

Thus, food becomes not only a potential source of power for women but also a means by which we are made profoundly vulnerable. As a symbol of love, it becomes dangerous for us while remaining nourishing and good for others. As a source of comfort, its effects are short-lived, because food can never feed the emotional hungers that remain repressed. Eating behaviors that mask the real emotional needs eventually become compulsive, because the feelings are never acknowledged and the real needs are never satisfied. At the same time, the pressures to be thin encourage self-deprivation through dieting. A fundamental danger with dieting is that it takes control out of our hands and puts it in the hands of "experts" who tell us what is best for us. As a consequence, we come to judge ourselves according to how many pounds we have gained or lost.

This preoccupation with food and dieting and weight usurps our energies, often resulting in increased feelings of inadequacy and failure.

In the cases of anorexia (deliberate starvation) and bulimia (a pattern of self-induced vomiting following an eating binge), women's health is seriously jeopardized, often resulting in permanent damage or death. For bulimics and anorexics, controlling food intake (and output) becomes a primary means of having control in the world. Bulimic women, like compulsive eaters, use food for comfort and to mask feelings. But they also take very seriously the message that they must conform to an image of thinness in order to be valued as women and so attempt to control their weight through dieting, induced vomiting, and the use of laxatives. Anorexic women deny that they have any feelings (or need for food) at all and take literally the image of thinness as power. They are controlling, in an extreme way, external influences and their own development into womanhood. It is these women who are the most ritualistic in their eating behaviors and whose compulsive behaviors include fanatical exercising, also intended to control weight.

The problems that women have in relation to food and their bodies have reached epidemic proportions. Surveys indicate that up to 80 percent of female students on university campuses have borderline to severe eating disorders. There is evidence that dissatisfaction with body size and a perceived need to diet can begin in girls as early as seven years of age, affirming that eating disorders are rooted in childhood and that they are significantly related to female socialization. Yet we persist in viewing our relationship to food as individual, personal, and private. Why have eating disorders become the norm for North American women? When did we learn these patterns, and why do we find them necessary?

For a number of years, I have held workshops for women on compulsive eating and body image. I limit the size of each workshop to sixteen participants in order to maximize the opportunity for individual participation and discussion within a group context. The purpose of these workshops is threefold. First, they help women recognize that there is a connection between women's oppression in general and their own relationship to food and body image in particular. To do this, they need to understand what the connections are, where they come from, and why they persist. Second, participants require a safe environment in which to explore the meanings that "fat" and "thin" have for them emotionally, stripped as much as possible from gender stereotypes and social expectations. Finally, the workshops offer an opportunity for women to strategize together ways of initiating feelings of self-acceptance apart from body weight and food consumption or deprivation.

The women who attend these workshops have ranged in age from their late teens to their late sixties. In addition to the wide age range, there is a diversity of body size that has often surprised and even upset some participants at the beginning of the workshop. "If I looked like you, I wouldn't be here!" or "I feel even more uncomfortable being so big when you look so normal. Are you here to learn about fat people?" These kinds of comments often provide the first step toward an awareness that body size in itself is not an indicator of self-acceptance or a healthy relationship with food. What all the women do share is a fearful relationship with food and the experiences of eating compulsively. In their words, "I find myself eating when I'm not hungry." "I'm so busy eating that I don't even taste the food." "I was so upset I ate everything in sight. It didn't matter what it was."

The workshop begins with each of us sitting in a circle and introducing ourselves. Once this is done, I invite each participant to tell us her strongest hope and her biggest fear about the day. These are recorded on flip charts. Hopes range from learning more about eating compulsively to losing weight once the workshop is over. Fears tend to focus on emotional concerns, including being judged, being afraid to share personal experiences, and feeling rotten about themselves at the end of the day. It is important to go over these lists with the participants, letting them know which expectations are reasonable and which ones aren't.

At this point, I introduce rules for communicating during the workshop. These rules go a long way toward alleviating many of the fears expressed by participants. They include speaking only for ourselves, which means using "I" and not "you" or "we" or abstractions. In addition, it is important to be nonjudgmental. The goal is to understand one another, not to judge or to give advice. Giving advice assumes superiority and power over others, which reinforces a sense of inadequacy and makes others feel both closed and defensive. It is also important that everyone have an opportunity to speak and that no one person dominate the discussion. But it is made clear that each woman must take responsibility for whether she speaks. Finally, confidentiality is essential so that people can feel safe about sharing their feelings and experiences in the group.

Gender-Role Tracing

Once the communication rules have been discussed, the participants break into groups of four for a gender-role tracing exercise. The purpose of this exercise, which was developed by Rosemary Liburd, is to identify and examine the messages that we as women get about what it means to grow up female in this society. Each of the groups generates a list of messages received in one of four age groups: childhood (up to age eleven), adolescence (ages twelve to nineteen), young adulthood (ages twenty to thirty-five), and older adulthood (ages thirty-six and up). The messages should include expectations and rules about activities and behaviors that each woman has personally experienced and that were deemed appropriate or inappropriate for proper femininity. These messages usually come from important people in our lives, including parents, siblings, friends, teachers, lovers, and spouses, and from society in general, including the various media, schools, churches, hospitals and other institutions, and the workplace. There are no right or wrong answers. What matters is that the experiences be as concrete as possible and that each member of the group share as many as she can recall for her age group. One member of the group acts as recorder, and the lists of messages are kept on flip-chart paper to be shared with the whole group later.

When the lists are completed, the groups go through them again and consider the hidden messages underlying the overt message. For example, an overt message during childhood might be that "girls should wear dresses and look pretty." The hidden message might be that how girls look is more important than what they do or that girls are objects for the viewing of others. When the hidden messages have been determined, members of the group assign a value—positive, negative, or mixed—to each message, depending on how they experienced it. A mixed message is one that has both positive and negative components to it. It often involves a double-bind situation, where there is a hidden and quite different message beneath the surface one. For example, the message in adolescence that "nice girls should not go out at night alone" is mixed. It is positive in recognizing the physical dangers that put females at risk in this society but negative in assuming a double standard for girls and boys. It also implies that it is a girl's sexuality that needs protecting rather than her person. And it disregards the option of teaching girls how to protect themselves, implying that they will be safe only under parental or male protection. When the individual groups have completed this part of the exercise, we return to the whole to share our findings. If time permits, I encourage members to add their experiences to groups in which they did not participate—their overt messages, the hidden messages, and their valuation of them.

The most significant result of this exercise is that it vividly demonstrates the extent to which female socialization is unhealthy for women. For example, two recurring messages that women often receive in both childhood and adulthood are that we must serve others and that we should put other people's feelings before our own. "Girls should take care of their younger sisters and brothers." "Be obedient." "Don't be selfish." "Girls should always be nice." "It's important to be understanding." "Girls should be self-sacrificing." The impact of these messages is that as children many of us experience what can only be described as emotional neglect. We are expected to care for others at the expense of ourselves. In the words of Tevlin and Leiblum (1983), "Men assert and request; women accommodate and comply" (p. 137). Because a large number of our personal needs are not met in childhood, we don't expect them to be met in adulthood. Quite simply, we don't know how to ask for what we have never been given. In time, many of us are unable to even identify what our own needs might be. In this way, we develop a passive stance toward others and continue to feel emotionally deprived. "A woman who cannot act assertively—who cannot refuse an unreasonable request or ask for what she wants—has little control over her life" (Muehlenhard, 1983, p. 153).

Closely tied to this is the message that most women receive early on that anger (or at least its expression) is forbidden to us if we are to become successfully feminine. "Girls should be polite." "Girls should not talk back." "Girls should not cause trouble." "Act like a lady." "Don't swear." "Don't fight." The effect of these messages is that most of us learn to suppress our anger—first we learn not to express it and eventually, not to feel it at all. When we do express anger, often in spite of ourselves, it tends to come out inappropriately and destructively. Thus, we come to fear our anger, a fear that is reinforced by our observations of men's rage and violence. As a result, we limit our expression of normal feelings and develop fears that we will lose control of this forbidden aspect of ourselves.

Women are also frequently taught that the appropriate way to respond to members of the opposite sex is with deference. "Let him win." "Hide your intelligence." "Boost his ego." "Talk about the things he wants to talk about." "You don't need an education like your brothers do." As a result, we become alienated from ourselves and learn to live our lives vicariously through men (and later, too, through our children). And while all people need to feel a sense of belonging, women, in particular, have an overdeveloped need for approval by others in order to feel validated. As we learn to value men and to devalue ourselves, we are also taught to devalue other women. "Females are scatterbrained and silly." "Women are only interested in makeup and clothes." "All other women are the competition." "Girls can't be trusted." Thus, we come to view other females with suspicion or contempt, and by distrusting and undervaluing the companionship and support of other women, we isolate ourselves even further. In addition, we cut off the possibility of positive collective action.

In order to be "successfully" socialized, most women are encouraged and, indeed, expected to give inordinate attention to personal appearance. This is often done to the exclusion of developing physical and intellectual competences that would increase self-esteem and expand employment opportunities. "Girls should be pretty." "Girls should look feminine." "Girls should be clean and neat." "Girls should wear dresses." "Girls shouldn't be chunky." "Girls should be slim and dainty (or sexy)." "The best thing about you is your curly blond hair." As women, we come to experience ourselves as objects rather than subjects and to expect others to perceive us in the same way. A woman "has to survey everything she is and everything she does because how she appears to others, and ultimately how she appears to men, is of crucial importance for what is normally thought of as the success of her life. Her own sense of being in herself is supplanted by a sense of being appreciated as herself by another" (Berger, 1972, p. 46). Because so much of what is defined as successful for women depends on our physical appearance, we judge our worth largely on that basis. And because we can never achieve the ever-changing ideal, our appearance, and most particularly our body, is never acceptable as it is.

With respect to sexuality, we are given extremely conflicting or ambivalent messages. As children, we are told not to touch "down there," but we may also be seen as cute if we act flirtatiously. In adolescence, the conflicting messages continue. We are expected to be popular with boys. "Girls should always have a boyfriend or a date." However, we are expected to remain chaste. "Good girls don't have sex." "Save yourself for marriage." According to Tevlin and Leiblum (1983), feminine fulfillment is supposedly achieved not through sex but rather through the "gentle affection and verbal intimacies of 'romantic love' and the eventual roles of wife and mother" (p. 131). Tied to this message, then, is the implicit belief that marriage will turn a girl's life around, that finding the "right" man and having babies will answer everything. Once we are married, the assumption is that our sexual needs should conform or defer to those of our partners. As of 1987, only ten states in the United States fully recognized spousal rape as a crime, and nine states continued to maintain by law the wife's obligation to submit sexually to her husband (Estrich, 1987). While spousal rape has been recognized in Canadian law since 1983, many women realize that in order to maintain their marriages (and thus their economic and social position in the community), they will have to be sexually available to their spouses on a regular basis irrespective of their own needs or wishes (Cole, 1989).

The importance of remaining pure and sexually naive until marriage is coupled with the observation that as females we are never safe. "The world is dangerous for you." "Don't wear seductive clothing." "Females need protection." "Don't go out on your own." On the one hand, we are told that our sexuality, as a commodity, is one of the few things of value that we have, and, on the other, we learn that it is the very thing that makes us vulnerable. Since the pervasive sexual ideology in our culture is one of male dominance and female submission, sexuality is closely tied to male power and female powerlessness (Cole, 1989). The epidemic proportion of girls and women who experience sexual violence during their lifetime is shocking testimony to this fact. And while men learn through socialization to become unemotional, independent, unconnected to their own feelings and therefore to the feelings of others, women are socialized to be responsible for others and therefore for relationships. In this way, men are "let off the hook" for aggressive or violent behavior and women are blamed for the violence, including sexual violence, that men perpetrate against them.

Thus, through the gender-role tracing exercise, participants learn the extent to which the socialization to be feminine is a psychologically crippling process. They learn that as females they have been taught to be passive, dependent, and selfless, to defer to men at the expense of devaluing themselves and other women, to care for and nurture others without nurturing themselves, to be dissociated from their bodies and their feelings, to be objectified, and to assume responsibility for the sexual denigration and violence done to them. If they are well socialized, they risk serious psychological consequences (as well as social, political, and economic ones). If they are able to resist, they still face personal and societal recrimination, discrimination, and censure, which can be devastating to their psychological well-being.

The gender-role tracing exercise serves a number of other important functions in addition to establishing that much of female socialization is harmful to women. It clearly demonstrates that many of the experiences of growing up female are shared despite differing ages, home communities, educational backgrounds, color, or class. Participants invariably express surprise at the number of their experiences that are shared. Equally enlightening is the recognition that members of the group experience almost all of these messages as negative or mixed. In my many years of running workshops, only once has a small group identified more than three messages as positive. Interestingly, three of the four women in the group were over fifty-five years of age, and their positive messages related to their present experiences rather than to past ones. "I don't have to be available sexually any more." "My husband is dead, my children have their own families, and now I can finally concentrate on me." "I'm free to come and go without having to answer to someone." Even then, there was some discussion in the total group as to whether some of the messages might not be construed as mixed.

Body Image

The next part of the workshop focuses on our meanings of and feelings about body size. This is accomplished through a relaxation exercise followed by the Fat and Thin Fantasy described by Orbach (1978, pp. 140–142). During this fantasy, participants imagine what it is like to live in, first, a very fat body, then, a very thin body.

> Imagine yourself at a party. . . . You are getting fatter. . . . You are now quite large. . . . What does it feel like? . . . Take a note of your surroundings. . . . How do you feel about them? . . . What kind of party is it? . . . What kinds of activities are going on? . . . Notice whether you are sitting or standing or moving about. . . . What are you wearing and how do you feel about your clothes? . . . What are they expressing? . . . Observe all the details in this situation. . . . How are you interacting with the other people at the party? . . . Are you on your own or talking, dancing, eating with others? . . . Do you feel like an active participant or do you feel excluded? . . . Are you making the moves to have contact with others or are the other people at the party seeking you out? . . . Now see what the "fat" you is saying to the people at the party. . . . Does it have any specific messages? . . . Does it help you out in any way to be fat in this situation? . . . See if you can go beyond the feelings of revulsion you might have to locate any benefits you see from being this size at the party. . . . Now imagine all the fat peeling and melt-

> ing away and in the fantasy you are as thin as you might ever like to be. . . . You are at the same party. . . . What are you wearing now? . . . What do these clothes convey about you? . . . How do you feel in your body? . . . How are you getting on with the other people at the party? . . . Do you feel more or less included now? . . . Are people approaching you or are you making the first moves? . . . What is the quality of your contact with others? . . . See if you can locate anything scary about being thin at the party. . . . See if you can get beyond how great it may feel and notice any difficulties you might be having with being this thin. . . . Now go back to being fat at the party . . . now thin again. . . . Go back and forth between the two images and particularly notice the differences. . . . When you are ready, open your eyes.

Once the participants have completed this exercise, they discuss it in pairs and then with the whole group.

This guided fantasy accomplishes a number of things. Women will be conscious of their negative feelings toward being fat and their positive feelings toward being thin. The exercise allows them to share these feelings with others who will neither ridicule them nor judge them on the basis of their body size. Comments on being very fat include "I looked revolting in my dress." "My legs were continually chafed and sore." "I was afraid to go near the food table." "No one asked me to dance." "I felt so big, I couldn't move." Some of the feelings about being thin include "I was the most popular person in the room." "I ate whatever I wanted to." "My dress looked wonderful, and I felt so light I could almost float."

But the most important aspect of the fantasy is that it allows women to get in touch with personal meanings of fat and thin that they are often unaware they have. They discover their feelings of safety around being fat. "People liked me for who I was and not for how I looked." "I was seen as warm and friendly, with a good sense of humor." "People couldn't push me around." "People took me seriously." "I could sit quietly and chat with someone if I wanted to." "No one expected too much of me." "People were careful of my feelings." The fantasy also exposes their fears of being thin. "I felt weak and vulnerable." "I was seen as a little piece of fluff." "Other women were threatened by me." "Men were constantly coming on to me." "I felt like I had to be witty and clever all the time because I was constantly on show." "No one took me seriously." "I would have to be sexual."

Typically, women are very surprised at how safe they feel with extra pounds. It is as though they had a buffer between their vulnerable selves and the world. At the same time, they are astounded to learn of the dangers that they associate with thinness. Perhaps for the first time, they become consciously aware of their emotional needs and how those needs are tied to body image. They also begin to realize that until they come to understand and accept their needs and learn to use their voice to speak their feelings and to assert themselves, they will continue using their bodies to communicate in indirect but safe and familiar ways.

Identifying Feelings

Once the personal meanings of fat and thin have been fully explored, the next step is to have the women get in touch with how they are using food to handle their feelings or meet their emotional needs. The guided fantasy below was designed by Cheryl Malmo. Following a relaxation exercise, the women are asked to relive in their imaginations the last time they ate food compulsively. They are instructed to pay attention to the feeling they experienced in their body prior to eating and to explore this feeling fully. I explain that their body is giving them a message and that it's important for them to listen carefully and to understand. They are then encouraged to imagine giving voice to this feeling and expressing it directly to the appropriate person.

> Now, I'd like you to remember a time recently when you ate food compulsively . . . a lot of food . . . cakes, cookies, doughnuts, chocolate bars, candy, toast, apples, whatever . . . food that you ate too quickly without really enjoying or even tasting what you ate . . . food that you weren't really hungry for and didn't feel good about eating the way you did. . . . Where are

> you? . . . What time of day is it? . . . Is anybody with you, or are you alone? . . . What has happened that you have a strong feeling about, or even just a little niggling feeling about? . . . What is your feeling? . . . What is the incident that triggered the feeling? . . . Recall it in detail. . . . How did you express your feeling? . . . Did it show on your face? . . . In your voice? . . . In your posture? . . . In your behavior? . . . Or were you successful at hiding the feeling completely? . . . Can you feel a sensation now in some part of your body where the feeling resides? . . . It may feel like a lump in your throat, a pressure in your chest, the beginnings of a headache, a heavy ball in your stomach, a tenseness in your limbs. Whatever your feeling is, let it be there. It is part of you and is important to pay attention to. . . . What is this sensation trying to tell you? . . . Give it a voice. . . . Speak in the first person, using "I," for the part of you that feels something. For example, if you have a pressure in your chest, it might be appropriate for it to say: "I am tight. I am dark and heavy, I make this woman hurt but I am trying to protect her." There is no right answer here. Just speak for your feeling from the point where you are aware of it in your body, saying what seems right for you. . . . Who might you have expressed this feeling to? . . . What did you do instead? . . . In your fantasy, try expressing the feeling to the appropriate person. . . . What happens? . . . How do you feel? . . . In a moment, when I tell you, I want you to open your eyes and come back to this room. But first let the experience of the fantasy sit with you and feel its effects. . . . Now open your eyes.

In the large group, the women share the various feelings that they experienced and that they attempted to numb or repress by means of their compulsive eating. A whole range of feelings are identified, including boredom, frustration, fear, hurt, anger, guilt, and joy. The women become conscious, perhaps for the first time, that an important feeling preceded their compulsive eating episode. And they also become aware that they are all using food as a means of handling their emotional needs. Further, they come to understand that the gender-role messages that they have internalized since childhood have led to their present inability to identify their feelings and express them directly. In other words, compulsive eating, like addiction to alcohol or drugs, is a symptom of other problems and needs to be understood as such.

Strategies for Change

In the final stage of the workshop, we consider some direct and healthy ways to handle feelings or to meet emotional needs as alternatives to compulsive eating. This is accomplished by first replacing old, destructive, and limiting messages from both childhood and adulthood with positive and healthy ones. For example, the women might wish to replace the message "Don't get angry" with "I have a right to express all of my feelings, including anger." Another message, "Sex is for men," might be replaced with "My sexuality is my own, and I can take pleasure in it on my own terms." And the message "Fat is ugly" may be changed to "My fat is an important part of me and is taking care of me right now. I need to appreciate and respect this."

One result of women not accepting their bodies as they are is that they typically have deprived themselves not only of food through dieting but also of many experiences. Life is put on hold until an acceptable weight is reached. The women are asked to make a commitment to be less judgmental and punitive and more accepting and nurturing toward themselves. Some choose to start accepting themselves by planning activities previously denied because they were embarrassed by their bodies—swimming, walking, dancing, eating out, shopping for clothes, initiating sexual activity. Others decide to begin valuing themselves by recognizing their own needs and finding ways to meet them—locking the door for a long, luxurious bath; creating a private space for themselves in their home; taking a course; changing their job; and so on. And some women resolve to stop dieting, which they experience as punitive and which assumes a judgmental attitude. It is these women who are most likely able to understand that the urge to eat compulsively is a signal that they need to attend to their emotional hungers. To assist in their understanding, I help the women reframe their symptom (the urge to eat compulsively) from a "negative threat to a positive challenge" (Rossi, 1986, p. 120). Finally, I encourage any women who are interested to form support groups to meet regularly following the workshop. A bibliography containing references on eating disorders written from a feminist perspective is provided for all participants.

When running these workshops, it is important for the facilitator to be aware that while female socialization is pervasive and affects all workshop participants one way or another, some women will be doubly burdened by certain cultural attitudes and practices that reinforce emotional connections to food. Also, many women will have been traumatized by physical, psychological, and/or sexual abuse, by living with a parent who was a practicing addict, or by having been somehow abandoned. If these women have developed compulsive eating as one of their coping strategies, they will need intensive therapy to heal from their traumas before they will be able to safely let go of their compulsive eating behavior. There may also be women who grew up in poverty or wartime conditions who will have particular experiences about food deprivation that will need to be dealt with separately. In short, the facilitator must be aware and help the participants to understand that the problems associated with compulsive eating and body image are rarely simple, and solutions will not be found in the workshop. But with the validation and support of other group members, a movement toward change can be accomplished by those women who resolve to become more accepting of themselves—their bodies and their feelings.

Workshop Participant's Voice: "Michaela"

Although in the past my weight had fluctuated up and down, as is the case with many other women, I reached a point in my life when my weight seemed to stabilize. The problem was I was heavier than I wanted to be, I was very unhappy with my physical appearance, and I did not feel good about myself, all of which was nothing new. By the same token, I also decided that I was tired of wishing that I was thinner; tired of feeling guilty about what I ate; tired of hating myself after I ate; tired of complaining about my weight; tired of vowing that tomorrow I would start the diet that was going to change my life. What I really wanted was to start feeling good about myself and to accept myself as I was. The task was to find a way to achieve this.

I realized from my previous experiences with weight loss groups and private nutrition counseling, and the diets that accompany such organizations, that they were not for me. I was well informed about good nutrition, and approaches emphasizing weight loss would have nothing new to offer me, except perhaps another diet. Although I had lost weight on such diets in the past, I had not maintained the weight loss. Moreover, at this stage I was less interested in losing weight, which tends to be the main goal of these approaches, and more interested in becoming comfortable with myself, and to begin to like myself and my body.

What I needed was a different approach, one that I was comfortable with, as well as one that would help me gain a better understanding of myself and enable me to feel better about myself. I knew that Toni conducted workshops that used a feminist analysis to explain compulsive eating and women's body image. Since I am a feminist, it made sense to me that Toni's workshop would likely fit my needs.

Although it is true that I wanted to become comfortable with my size, in many respects I entered the workshop hoping for that elusive magic wand that would immediately make me feel better about myself. Needless to say, this did not happen. However, I did learn several important things. First of all, it became apparent to me, through exercises such as the gender-role tracing exercise, just how pervasive and powerful women's socialization under patriarchy has been regarding our perceptions of our bodies. My weight, and my obsession with it, no longer seemed to reflect a character flaw within me. Rather, I began to understand how my idea of what I *should* look like had developed over the years, and how early this shaping had begun.

Secondly, I realized that I was using food as a source of comfort and/or escape. Binge eating became a way for me to deal with emotional issues in my life. Knowing this has enabled me to begin to deal more directly with some of these issues. I would also like to point out that thinking about my compulsive eating in this way further reinforced the notion that there was nothing inherently wrong with me; for example, that I had no self-control or that I lacked willpower.

Finally, rethinking and redefining my fat and my shape has helped me view myself and my size more positively. Consequently, I do feel better about myself. I no longer think of myself as fat, obese, huge, or overweight, descriptors that have negative and undesirable connotations for me. Instead, I think of myself as large, strong, nurturing, and round, descriptors that I find to be positive and quite appealing. This type of cognitive restructuring has turned out to be a most practical and useful strategy for me, especially on a day-to-day basis. For example, when I am shopping for clothes, thinking of myself as round, as opposed to fat, has reduced the feeling of intimidation I sometimes experience when I enter a women's clothing store. In addition, in the broader sense, redefining my physical shape has helped me to accept myself, as I am.

Thus, my exposure to a feminist approach to compulsive eating and body image has led me to a different understanding about my weight, about myself, and about my relationship with food. I have stopped thinking of food in terms of "good" and "bad," and if I want a certain food, I eat it. Food and eating have become something to be enjoyed, without recrimination.

Moreover, a feminist analysis has enabled me to redefine and reclaim my body and to reject the value system under patriarchy, which not only defines a woman's worth by her body but also defines what her body should attempt to look like. Whenever I am exposed to people who are obsessed with thinness and dieting, I realize that my value system is different from theirs. I no longer experience pain or shame when other people quite blatantly indicate that I am too fat, that I should have more self-control, or that I should go on a diet. I do not feel bad about myself, and I refuse to be obliged to offer explanations or excuses for my size. Nor do I vow, once again, that tomorrow I, too, will start a diet.

Today I am quite comfortable with myself and my body. In

the grander scheme of things, I have developed a greater appreciation for the role that female socialization has played in determining my image of myself. As well, I have gained some very practical skills. These skills have helped me deal with the more subtle, and sometimes not so subtle, day-to-day events that continue to tell me that women should be thinner than we are, no matter what our size.

References

Berger, J. *Ways of Seeing*. New York: Penguin Books, 1972.

Cline, S., and Lean, C. (producers). "Just Desserts: Women and Food." *Ideas* (a regular radio program). Canadian Broadcasting Corporation. Toronto, Oct. 19 and 26, 1987.

Cole, S. G. *Pornography and the Sex Crisis*. Toronto: Amanita, 1989.

Estrich, S. *Real Rape*. Cambridge, Mass.: Harvard University Press, 1987.

Corporation. Toronto, Oct. 19 and 26, 1987.

Lawrence, M. (ed.). *Fed Up and Hungry: Women, Oppression and Food*. London: Women's Press, 1987.

Muehlenhard, C. L. "Women's Assertion and the Feminine Sex-Role Stereotype." In V. Franks and E. D. Rothblum (eds.), *The Stereotyping of Women: Its Effects on Mental Health*. New York: Springer, 1983.

Orbach, S. *Fat Is a Feminist Issue: A Self-Help Guide for Compulsive Eaters*. New York: Berkeley Books, 1978.

Rossi, E. L. *The Psychobiology of Mind-Body Healing*. New York: Norton, 1986.

Tevlin, H. E., and Leiblum, S. R. "Sex-Role Stereotypes and Female Sexual Dysfunction." In V. Franks and E. D. Rothblum (eds.), *The Stereotyping of Women: Its Effects on Mental Health*. New York: Springer, 1983.

3

Shattering the Silence: Working with Violence in Native Communities

Maggie Hodgson
Client: "Phyllis"

For the past eighteen years, I have worked in Indian communities in Canada as a Native counselor and as a trainer for human service programs. The groups of Native people that I have worked with include the Carrier from northern British Columbia, the Shushwap from central British Columbia, the Cree from central Alberta and Saskatchewan, the Blackfoot from southern Alberta, and the Metis from British Columbia, Alberta, and Saskatchewan. The issues facing both women and men in these communities include:

- Cultural loss as a result of historical events
- High death rate related to violence
- Very high rate of alcoholism and drug abuse in both our male and female populations
- A tendency to believe the myth that addictions cause violence
- Loss of two generations of parenting because children were placed in residential schools between 1900 and 1960
- Physical and sexual violence experienced within the residential schools

- Unresolved grief resulting from a sense of abandonment when sent to residential schools

For those who may be unfamiliar with residential schools, in 1900, the federal government of Canada determined that the most effective way of "civilizing" Native children was to remove them from their parents' homes. At the age of five, the children were placed in government educational institutions that were staffed by priests and nuns. In some instances, they were moved as far as five hundred to one thousand miles from their communities. Police assisted with the removal of the children from their homes, if necessary, and parents who tried to hide their children were jailed by government agents. Some children never saw their parents again.

Because the goal of these policies was to integrate Native children into white culture, it became illegal for Native people to practice their indigenous religion and ceremonies. At the residential schools, the children were not allowed to speak their own Indian languages nor were they permitted to talk to their brothers or sisters if they were housed in separate dormitories. Initially, educational instruction was provided for approximately two hours each day. The children spent the remainder of the day doing farm work or cooking. By 1950, the children were in school for the full day. The practice of removing Native children from their homes and putting them into residential schools stopped in 1975. While it is the case that many Native people received an education that they were later able to utilize, most felt abandoned by their parents and suffered the loss of family, Native values, and cultural practices. In my view, the healing from this and other forms of violence in Native communities is still in the early stages.

The reality in many Indian communities is that over the last ten to fourteen years we have been addressing the disease of alcoholism. As our people recover from their addiction, they start to break the "Don't talk" rule associated with alcoholic, dysfunctional families. Our care givers are our first generation of people who are free from the oppression of boarding school and the alcoholism that is a response to that oppression. The difficulty is that there is still an unwritten rule in many of our communities, and that is "Don't talk about violence."

There are two further unspoken rules surrounding alcoholism that profoundly affect the disclosure of active violence. They are: "Don't trust" and "Don't feel." These are not cultural rules; they are rules that exist in any alcoholic home. Many of the Native service givers as well as the clients have been raised with these three rules, resulting in a strong prohibition against talking about violence. Many believe the primary myth that alcoholism is responsible for physical and sexual violence. This myth has to be dispelled because drinking is too often used as an excuse for violent behavior. Therefore, we recommend in our workshops that victims and perpetrators of violence be treated for their substance abuse before they are treated as survivors or perpetrators.

The incidence of suicide is very high in pockets of communities. The death rate in Native communities is approximately five to twenty times higher than the national average, depending on the community. When our children were removed from their homes of origin from 1900 to 1960 to attend boarding or residential schools, they experienced loss of parents, extended family, survival skills, and language, and were often subjected to physical, emotional, and sexual abuse. This created a state of alienation and despair in which the values of *community-mindedness,* which comes with an extended family system, were lost. These lost values were never replaced with the values of the nuclear family system.

Native communities that have actively addressed alcoholism and suicide have healed by redeveloping a sense of community and extended family. Two Indian communities that have moved from 100 percent alcoholism to 85 and 95 percent sobriety are actively dealing with the issue of survivors of violence. In both communities, there is a movement to rebuild healthy family members through the therapeutic process and to actively rebuild that sense of community-mindedness that comes with an extended family system. In both communities, the women are the leaders of this movement. They are utilizing their traditional forms of healing to complement the therapeutic process adapted from the white culture. Whereas in the past we were enveloped ("closed up") by the residential school system, now we are redeveloping ("unfolding") our own cultural traditions, beliefs, and values. We must also unfold the sexual abuse that exists in our communities.

An important cultural belief in the Native community is that we must respect our Elders. Unfortunately, this respect has been confused with condoning abuse by older people. Consequently, when an older person is the perpetrator of physical, emotional, or sexual abuse, our community is more reluctant to disclose that violence. This is not because violence is cultural but because respecting Elders is. The power of the extended family to suppress the disclosure when the abuser is an older person is very great. A way to address this issue is to take the perspective that we respect people who act in a respectful way. Reporting all perpetrators of sexual violence to the authorities and referring them to therapy shows respect for them: It allows the abusers to get help, and it also protects innocent victims.

The residential school experience is unfolding in a very painful but healing way. When 135 former residential school students were interviewed in one Indian community, 650 acts of buggery were uncovered, resulting in fourteen charges being laid and two victim-impact statements being made. We know from research that there is a risk that the male victims will become perpetrators of physical, emotional, or sexual abuse. Long-term planning for community safety requires a comprehensive program that involves the whole community, because it is the whole community that has been profoundly affected by violence. Service givers must have expertise in dealing with extended family systems, as well as with all forms of violence. Unfortunately, the churches have not come forth to acknowledge the involvement of their clergy and nuns in this abuse or to take financial responsibility for the rehabilitation of the survivors.

Developing mutual respect between non-Native and Native care givers who deal with violence in our communities is imperative. This process is difficult for the non-Native clinicians who believe that they know what is best for Natives. It is also difficult for the Native care givers who doubt their own capacity to learn or who do not trust their insights about the most effective methods of dealing with the violence.

Many Native service givers report that clients are disclosing to them abuse that they have experienced or violence that is affecting a child or an extended family member. They need information and training and, therefore, request and host workshops on family violence. The identified purpose of the workshops is to teach these Native care givers to identify signs and symptoms of abuse and to inform them of reporting procedures. Initially, workshop participants often ask questions about clients "out there" and later identify themselves as survivors of abuse. Non-Native psychologists and social workers often question how Native professionals can be social workers in Native communities if they are untreated themselves. It is important to identify our Native care givers who are untreated for the violence that they have experienced and refer them to a treatment program for survivors.

A primary difficulty that Native care givers have in dealing with abuse disclosures and reports is that they are often relatives of the abusers. Because reporting the abuse may result in the abuser being incarcerated, the extended family may place the care giver under immense social pressure to avoid dealing with the violence through the legally required route. One Elder, the deceased Abe Barnstick, said, "Our greatest strength as an Indian community can be our greatest weakness." Our strength is in the extended family. When we utilize that energy to suppress disclosure and to prevent possible treatment because our immediate relative is the abuser, it becomes a weakness. There is an additional problem when the care giver comes from an alcoholic home and may herself have been abused. Like the client, she, too, may have difficulty withstanding the pressure of the extended family. It is imperative that our Native service givers receive treatment as soon as they identify themselves as survivors of violence so that they can receive the help they need and support to assist them to cope with the social isolation that can evolve.

The most effective approaches to therapy with Native community members who have been abused are physical body work, drawings, and visualization. One of the reasons for the use of body work is that repressed fear is held in the body, and communication of this fear can be processed in body work. Silence can be broken in a less threatening way through the use of drawings and visualization. In these ways, a voice is found within the silence, and powerlessness can be transformed into empowerment.

In one Indian community where there is no available therapist, women have set up a support group for women survivors of sexual assault and incest. The group incorporates Indian dancing, singing, sweat lodge healing ceremonies, dieting, and exercising into their program. They are working to rebuild their self-image at all levels: spiritual, physical, emotional, and mental. Their greatest strength is their community-mindedness built on self-help and peer support. In keeping with the Native way, what they receive is given back to the community as their spirits touch the community in a healing way.

Client's Voice: "Phyllis"

"I am not a good wife, I am not a good mother, and I am not a good human being." These were the first words I spoke to a psychiatrist after attempting suicide in 1965, at age twenty-two. I had no previous exposure to therapy, and this was the beginning of a new path. That path was to take me through a number of therapeutic experiences, some bad, some good.

I was raised in the small town of Fraser Lake in northern British Columbia and had never heard about what a therapist was. I had only heard of "head doctors" who hospitalized people who were said to be "not playing with a full deck." But I knew I was in the right place when I was hospitalized in the University of Alberta's psychiatric ward after my suicide attempt in 1965. It gave me time out, and I learned that I could have "a full deck" and still get treatment. I had not slept for six months and was severely anorexic. I also learned the word *depression:* I was depressed, and there was treatment for my condition.

After two weeks in the hospital, I was discharged and assigned a male psychiatrist who spoke English with an accent. I had trouble understanding him. In retrospect, I think he believed I suffered from an antidepressant pill deficiency. He gave me pills to wake me up from a sleeping pill-induced state. His therapy consisted of saying "humph, humph, humph," at least ten times a session as he smoked his pipe. The best thing about that process was that I had someone to listen to me. He took careful notes about my "unsubstantiated fears," as he referred to them, and he continued to prescribe pills for me for six months. At the end of that time, I indicated that while I wanted to continue in therapy, the pills made it extremely difficult for me to care for my nine-month- and two-year-old sons. His response was, "I am the doctor, and if you do not want to take the medication for your paranoia and depression, please leave." So I did. I went up the hall to another psychiatrist's office and indicated that I needed help but did not feel I needed pills. That psychiatrist accepted me and my diagnosis of not needing pills.

The therapeutic approach of the second psychiatrist included listening and making the odd comment. The most meaningful suggestion he made was that I should do volunteer work, which I did. The most important benefit I received was that when I disclosed I had been sexually abused, the therapist did not fall over and die at the news. But he did not respond with any other comments either. I was left to assume I was okay because he did not respond negatively to my disclosure. Another benefit for me was that he honored my ability to identify what I needed. He followed my recommendation and did not insist I take pills.

In 1974 I entered group therapy. The participants were all women, with a male and a female therapist. The techniques utilized were Gestalt, visualization, transactional analysis, and art work. I was arguing with myself on the pros and cons of working on my anger at my dad for having sexually abused me. I felt caught about the issue; caught between my desire to heal and my good Catholic upbringing, which told me, "Honor your father," "Love your neighbor as yourself," "Forgive us our trespasses as we forgive those who trespass against us."

In my wisdom, I went to a good priest for confession, and I said, "How can God forgive me my sins if I cannot forgive my father?" Father Kroetch responded, "Do not judge yourself, that is God's job. God gave you feelings of anger and hate as a gift. Allow them out when you are ready. But do not judge yourself for having God-given emotions." I went to my growth group scared, but with a new resolve. I decided that night I would deal with my rage toward my dad.

My rage was expressed through a bioenergetic process of physical pushing and kicking and vocal release through swearing, yelling, and screaming. The group stayed close and supported my work. After that piece of work, I realized I could now love God because I had started to love myself. I felt a release of an imaginary green smelly fluid from my vaginal area when I was working. That fluid was my fear and anger. In the following months, I processed my anger toward my mom for not having been there to protect me.

A number of different techniques were used in the group. For me, visualizing feelings in sizes, colors, and textures worked well because I could not "feel." But I could move toward that end first by visualizing the feeling, then touching the feeling, and finally using a Gestalt process to give the feeling or, in my case, lump, a voice. I discovered that the purpose of the lump was to block the feeling that was there. The use of transactional analysis, which was more of an intellectual process, helped me put my thoughts together. This group was a good place for me to start dealing with and releasing pain.

When I returned to therapy in 1980, I knew I had the ability to verbalize. However, I tend to keep pain and stress locked in specific parts of my body, such as in my bladder area. I chose a therapist who specialized in body work because it was easier for me to release pain through body work than just by a verbal process. I also trusted this therapist to honor my limits. I had in the past experienced a therapist's anger for "not trying or wanting to change." This happened usually when I hit an impasse and they became frustrated with me. I understood it was their issue, but I did not want to pay $75.00 an hour to someone who would not work with me, where I was at. Another important issue for me was that the therapist I chose this time had an awareness of and acknowledged the element of healing the spirit. This therapist understood and encouraged me to integrate Native ceremony into my healing process.

In 1984, I went back to therapy again. In these sessions, my focus was dealing with fear of abandonment, and through this I received assistance in dealing with another important issue—how could I as a Native and sexual abuse survivor stand up to report sexual abuse in my extended family? My home of origin was a Native extended family system where there was extreme alcoholism and violence. How could I report this violence and still maintain my extended family relationships? How could I break that family violence rule "Do not talk about abuse"? Unfortunately, that rule fits to a *T* the children of alcoholics' rule "Do not talk about alcoholism." Given that I was raised in both an abusive home and a home that had active alcoholism, I was a prime candidate for maintaining silence when there was abuse going on in my extended family. Another rule that made it difficult for me to honor my willingness to change was that under no circumstances were we as Indian people to call the police on one of our own. Even worse than calling the police was to call the social worker.

I therefore had these rules to cope with when I decided to report an extended family member in 1984 for having abused his daughter. The perpetrator's wife was very angry with me. And my own family verbally disapproved of me "not minding my own business." I was threatened physically, and I was ostracized. I was hurt and angry because my extended family system had more of a vested interest in protecting the perpetrator and their fear than they did in protecting the child who was the recipient of the abuse. My therapist assisted me by having me look at my family map to identify who in my extended family could support me through the trauma of reporting a relative. This process was very therapeutic, because it provided me with the opportunity to face and process my greatest old fear about reporting my father when I was a child. "What would happen? I'll bet my family will hate me if I break up the family" was my fear. This fear had reemerged when I heard about the abuse in my extended family. I continued to identify potential supporters for breaking the "Don't talk" rule about violence and alcoholism to prepare for the inevitable time when I would hear of more abuse in my family.

A relative who was very dear to me was accused of raping his cousin. He was a police officer, and the police could not or would not get enough evidence to lay charges. My nephew chose to resign from the police force instead. The social service investigation was thwarted by my nephew's grandmother telling the rape complainant, "If ______ goes to jail, I will come to kill you myself." The grandmother had raised the complainant as her own from her toddler days. The pressure was too great for that girl to consider following through with charges, because her surrogate mother, who was one of the highest respected Elders in the community, threatened to kill her. She did not follow through with the charges. My nephew admitted to us he had raped the girl. We had an unwilling complainant, the RCMP [Royal Canadian Mounted Police] who "accepted" his resignation, an Elder grandmother who was following the unwritten rules not to contact the police or social workers. Three extended family members, age nineteen, nineteen, and thirty-three, and myself met with our relative to request he get treatment for, first, his alcoholism; second, the abuse he had suffered; and, third, his responsibility in raping his cousin. He agreed. However, he did not follow through and pursue treatment, even with our support. There were no formal charges.

During this process, my therapist helped me to identify my resources and to release my anger, fear of family social isolation, and frustration with the final results. The difference was I was mobilizing my extended family to start breaking the "Don't talk" rule. We now had three in our peer support system. An Elder who is now deceased once said, "As an Indian community, sometimes our greatest strength is our greatest weakness." Our extended family can help each other, but sometimes we use that energy to cover up alcoholism and violence out of what we see as loyalty to the family. When we allow that to happen, our system is our greatest weakness. But it has the potential of being our greatest strength if we honor *all* ages of our family.

The process of awareness is difficult. I have worked with a part of myself that was a catatonic baby within my visualized internal world. My baby stored the need to escape numerous incidents of sexual violence: sexual abuse by my father, sexual abuse by other drunken men in our home, witnessing my brother brutally beat my sister-in-law, and having been brutally raped as a young teenager. Waking up that baby, named "Putchie," has meant waking up memories only "Putchie" had. Each new memory is usually unwrapped from a current activity in my daily life that triggers my memory of witnessing extreme violence.

How did I remember the violence I witnessed? I went to church, and our good Catholic priest was giving a sermon on love. His sermon went something like this. "Love? What is love these days? You cannot even tell the difference between men and women by their dress and hair. The only way you tell the difference is if you punch a man, he'll punch you back and if you punch a woman, she'll say punch me again. You women deserve everything you get." I promptly stood up and walked out of the church. I walked home in a rage, and having experienced many arguments with that priest, I felt there was no use trying to convince him single-handedly of the unhealthy attitude he had and promoted about women. I stormed around my house for about five minutes and then took a bristol board poster off the wall and wrote on the back of it what the priest had said. Then I said to myself, he owes the women of this parish an apology. I put that on the board, too, and added, "If you agree, phone me at ______ ." Yes, I went back to church and picketed with a picture of Elvis Presley on one side of the poster and my comments on the other. The first person to come out of the church was my husband, who is a member of the military and lives by the rule that you do not challenge the system. He said in a very confused, embarrassed, soft, enquiring voice, "What are you doing, my girl?" Then he took off home.

I tried to see the archbishop the next day to complain, and he would not see me. When I asked who his boss was, I was told his boss was the Pope. I thought I had a better chance of laying a complaint with God than with the Pope. At least with God I would be guaranteed a hearing. I went before the parish council, who listened politely and indicated, "Thank you. We will discuss it next month." One female member on the council felt more should be done. My response was, "You can do what you want. If he does not apologize to the women of this parish by next Sunday, I'll have CBC and CTV's cameras out there viewing the women from the battered women's shelters picketing, and we will picket until he apologizes." The priest apologized the next Sunday. I said to myself, "Well, that was a pretty big mad for just one male chauvinist. What else is going on?"

In my next session with my therapist, I explored my anger at having witnessed sexual abuse. I dealt with the rage of seeing my sister-in-law being beaten all over her body and miscarrying pregnancy after pregnancy. I was angry at having witnessed many Catholic priests sexually abuse girls I went to school with. I had felt powerless to stop it for fear I would be abused myself if I tried to tell them not to sexually assault my friend. Therapy helped me to view my experiences from a new perspective. It taught me to learn about my patterns of behavior and why I feel sad, angry, or happy, or why I sometimes shut down my feelings. That priest was my catalyst for introspection.

Another important aspect of my therapy includes semiannual fasting of four days and four nights without food and water. These fasts are conducted with the guidance of an Elder. My fasting opens up my spirit more each year. It opens up my mind to seeing my patterns more clearly. My fasting opens up my spirit to healing and seeing the God in me and the spirit in others, and gives me insight into my direction in life. My fasting and participation in sweat lodge ceremonies assist me to cleanse the toxins from my body, toxins that are stored from keeping old anger and fear in my body. My release of these emotions becomes a thorough cleansing process: cleansing all parts of me—body, emotions, mind, and spirit. When I fast, it is in the country, by water and on Mother Earth. The Elders say, rain cleanses the earth, and our tears cleanse our soul. In this healing process, I learn my spirit touches yours. Yes, my greatest strength is my greatest strength, my love for myself, my extended family, and God. I become healthier every day as I continue in therapy. My therapist's spirit touches mine as she walks with me on my path to being a whole person and a professional in the human services field.

4

Reparenting the Self: A Parenting Group for Adult Children of Alcoholics

Cathy Mayhew
Group Participant: Janie-Rae Crowley

During my eight years as a social worker for the city of Edmonton, Alberta, I regularly offered a parenting course to the public. The course taught active listening, basic communication skills, and the use of natural and logical consequences as a method of disciplining children. As a result of feedback, I expanded the course to include more time for sharing of experiences. In one of these groups, eight out of nine parents talked about being abused as children. In all cases, these parents had come from alcoholic homes. Perhaps because I, too, was an adult child of an alcoholic, I began to think about how a parenting group could address the depth of pain that I was hearing. I was also concerned about how parents could apply the methods I was teaching when they were in so much pain.

An opportunity arose for me to design a parenting group for adult children of alcoholics (ACOAs) at the Alberta Alcohol and Drug Abuse Commission (AADAC), an alcoholism outpatient treatment facility in Edmonton. I decided to expand my original course to include such topics as "What is a normal family?" "What are the characteristics of ACOA parents?" and "How do the coping strategies developed by ACOAs in childhood affect parenting?'' The participants responded with enthusiasm, and, as in previous groups, the skill that seemed to have the most impact was active listening. But I was struck once again by the struggle that parents went through in trying to apply this and other skills and by the deep feelings of failure they experienced when they made a mistake. They seemed to feel a tremendous pressure to make up for their feelings of inadequacy as parents. They feared that their mistakes would condemn their children to the kind of childhood pain that they themselves had experienced.

Other problems also became evident. An emphasis on skill development seemed to reinforce controlling behaviors in parents who had developed those characteristics in order to survive in an alcoholic home. I worried that natural and logical consequences, a common method for disciplining children, would be used in a punitive way by these parents if they didn't know how to ''let go'' of overly controlling behavior. However, letting go of control and focusing on the self rather than on parenting skills was a difficult and scary process. One woman expressed her dilemma in this way: ''I have been to countless parenting groups, but I have never been to one where I was encouraged to develop my own style. How do I know what is right for my own family when I've never been parented myself?'' Adult children of alcoholics have an intense desire not to repeat what they experienced in childhood but lack an inner sense of what would be better. Because they have had to suppress the pain of childhood in order to survive, it seems that the most valuable skill that parents need, the ability to empathize with their child's pain, is missing.

As a result of the concerns expressed by ACOA parents, I developed a new format for teaching parenting skills. This format focuses entirely on the parents' reclaiming their own childhood as a way to develop these skills. And it is this parenting course that I will describe in this chapter. One of the significant components of this group is an emphasis on grief as a healing mechanism.

Grief and the Alcoholic Home

Growing up with alcoholism has been compared to living with an ''air raid a day.'' When an alcoholic parent is drinking, moods can change rapidly so that children learn to expect dramatic shifts in parental behavior. Over the course of a single evening, an alcoholic parent may alternatively be violent, overindulgent, and totally indifferent toward the children (Liepman, Taylor White, and Nirenberg, 1986). Even if one of the parents is nondrinking, his or her behavior can be equally unpredictable. Constant worry about the alcoholic spouse can lead to irritability and a tendency to overreact to normal childhood behavior (Wilson and Orford, 1978). Alternatively, the nondrinking parent's constant preoccupation with the alcoholism may result in his or her becoming emotionally unavailable to the children. The children soon learn that neither parent can be depended on to regularly meet their needs, experiencing the "consistency inconsistency" that Ackerman (1978) maintains is characteristic of parenting in an alcoholic family. Middleton-Moz and Dwinell (1986) explain what happens to children in such families: "Living with both the constant unpredictability of the alcoholic parent and the detachment/derangement of the co-dependent parent, who is preempted by stress, is difficult enough for an adult who has a fully developed defense system. A child will have to employ massive amounts of energy merely to survive. This puts normal development on hold; there is no energy left to invest in development. The end result is a child who often feels thirty years old at five and five years old at thirty" (p. 4). In order to deal with a situation where their needs for protection and care are not being met, children learn to rely on themselves. They learn to act like adults while they are still children. These children don't experience childhood, they survive it.

As parents, adult children of alcoholics continue to act like adults while feeling inside like children. Faced with the model provided by their parents, they resolve not to repeat that experience with their own children yet find to their bewilderment that they don't know how to change it (Perrin, 1984; Treadway, 1986). Faced only with their knowledge of what not to do, they believe that there is a "right" way to be a parent and search desperately for an answer. Rummer (1985) describes the feelings that accompany that search: "At any moment, I might trip up and be unmasked for what I [am]: the little girl clomping around in my mother's heels, a six-year-old cleverly masquerading in a woman's body, never giving up the hope that someday the grown-ups [will] let her in on the secret she was supposed to know, and what she was supposed to do with that knowledge, once she got it" (p. 27).

In other words, being in a perpetual state of crisis and being forced to develop coping strategies to handle the crises results in a loss of childhood for the children of alcoholics. "I feel like I was never a kid. What happened to my childhood?" is the poignant question often asked by ACOAs who have come for treatment.

People experience a sense of loss whenever they are deprived of something that they have had and valued or something that was needed, wanted, or expected (Whitfield, 1987). The emotional process of working through a loss is called "grief work," and the multitude of feelings that loss evokes is called "grief" (Middleton-Moz and Dwinell, 1986). Grief is a natural response to loss and as such contains within it the potential for growth. The ability to grieve is so fundamental to human growth, and loss such a common experience, that interference with the grieving process can have a major impact on all areas of life. It is precisely this mechanism that is so gravely affected by the unhealthy rules that operate in an alcoholic home (Black, 1981). In an unsafe environment where individuals cannot express their feelings or trust that they will be comforted, grief, like all other feelings, will be repressed. It is in this way that adult children of alcoholics are doubly victimized by their childhoods. First, they are not allowed to experience the feelings of being a child in a safe environment; second, they are not allowed to express the grief that results from such a loss. Consequently, unresolved grief can become a major factor in their adult lives.

Bowlby (1980) explains that the symptoms of unhealthy adult mourning include unconscious yearning for the lost person, unconscious reproach against the lost person combined with unconscious and often unremitting self-reproach, compulsive caring for that person, and persistent disbelief that the loss is permanent. Bowlby's description sounds remarkably similar to a description of adult children of alcoholics. Further, these characteristics explain the persistent belief on the part of adult children of alcoholics that someday their alcoholic and codependent parents will respond in the way they desire.

Unresolved Grief and Parenting

The idea that one will never be lovingly parented is too painful to bear, so it is denied. "Never is a difficult reality for any of us to countenance, and hence, we bargain, cajole, manipulate and deny in the hope that that which has been lost can be reclaimed if we are only good enough, or clever enough to find the magical combination" (Middleton-Moz and Dwinell, 1986, p. 120). This denial of pain and unresolved grief not only interrupts healthy development but also has a major impact on the way adult children of alcoholics relate to their own children. For many ACOAs, the attempt to create a perfect environment for their children is an attempt to deny the reality of the loss of their own childhood. This denial may then result in overprotectiveness or overinvestment in their own children.

A confusion of boundaries between themselves and their children may also be a problem for ACOAs. For example, the unresolved grief of a parent's childhood losses can be activated by his or her children's losses. Consequently, ACOAs either tend to overreact to their children's losses or sadness or tend to keep emotionally distant from their children. In the words of one woman, "I often feel that all those unresolved tears of my own childhood are just below the surface. I have built a wall to protect the tears from coming out, but I live inside that wall and my husband and my children cannot touch me. I want to cry with my children, I want to play their games, I want to hold them on my lap as my parents never did to me, but I am afraid" (Middleton, 1985, p. 37).

Another consequence of unresolved grief can be overpermissiveness toward children. For example, when children protest limit setting by crying, the parents' own pain can be triggered. Then, in order to relieve this pain, the parents may comfort their children inappropriately, giving in to their demands to stop the crying. On other occasions, they may try to talk their children out of their sadness by intellectualizing about the feeling. Sometimes parents completely ignore their children's losses in an attempt to avoid their own unresolved losses. Thus, by failing to deal with their children's grief, they are passing on the same pattern of denial that they feared and hated as children. Their denial of grief plays the same role in their homes that alcoholism played in their own upbringing. Grief is a central issue in the family, but it is never acknowledged and never dealt with. This is why Middleton (1985) calls alcoholism "the gift that keeps on giving."

Because of the impact that unresolved grief can have on parent-child relationships, it follows that dealing with childhood losses is a key to improving parenting skills in adult children of alcoholics. Middleton (1985) states that grief resolution results in parents becoming more open with their children. Once the grief is expressed, the walls can begin to come down, and feelings of fear are replaced with feelings of warmth. Grief resolution is so important, Middleton maintains, that until it occurs, skills learned in parenting classes cannot be used to good effect.

Pilot Parenting Course

Using Middleton's assumption that grief resolution is essential in order for ACOAs to learn parenting skills, I designed (with the help of Mark Haden, an employee at Alcohol and Drug Programs in Vancouver) a parenting course for adult children of alcoholics that focuses on grief resolution as a way to improve parenting skills.

The initial group was composed of ten members. Seven were recruited through referrals from Alcohol and Drug Program counselors in Vancouver, and three were self-referrals resulting from an announcement at a self-help group for adult children of alcoholics. Screening was done over the phone to ensure that group members were over eighteen, parents, and adult children of alcoholics. Participants who were recovering alcoholics were expected to have been sober for a minimum of six months. Two exceptions were made to this procedure. One member with four months of sobriety was included at the recommendation of her counselor. She had previously attended a traditional parenting class and dropped out after four sessions, stating that she preferred a skill-development approach. One non-ACOA participant was included because his spouse was attending and it was decided that it would be beneficial for both parents to attend together. He was also a recovering alcoholic, and although he completed the group, he was not included in the study that we did on the results of the group. His spouse was one of two participants who withdrew after two meetings. Both participants who withdrew were mothers and recovering alcoholics who stated that time restraints and baby-sitting problems prevented them from attending. Six adult children of alcoholics—three males and three females—completed the course. Their mean age was 36.1 years. All but one were recovering alcoholics. They had experienced an average of sixteen years as children in an alcoholic home.

Using the model established by Middleton-Moz and Dwinell (1986), we assumed that the grieving process would involve accessing painful childhood memories and experiencing the feelings that had been repressed as a result of the denial system within alcoholic homes. The image of the "child within" was used to represent those childhood feelings. "Nurturing the child within" meant encouraging the open expression of feelings associated with those memories. In this way, a model of healthy grieving was established within the group. At no time were parenting skills discussed. The focus of the group was the needs of the parents rather than the needs of their children.

Group members were told that grieving over their childhood losses and learning to nurture the "child within" would probably improve their parenting skills. The first two sessions concentrated on identifying the losses experienced in an alcoholic home, and the theme of grief resolution was introduced. This theme continued to be emphasized in group discussions in other sessions as appropriate. Each session usually began with a brief discussion followed by an experiential exercise. The remaining time was spent sharing and exploring in greater depth the feelings generated by the exercise. The exercises were designed to allow participants to reexperience the feelings that they had had as children and to find ways to comfort themselves. Emphasis was placed on learning how to identify and express the feelings that originated in childhood. These feelings were identified as belonging to the "child within," and methods such as guided fantasies, role plays, and written exercises were used to help participants gain access to those feelings.

In order to measure whether completion of the course had resulted in any change in parenting skills, we administered the Hereford Parent Attitude Survey (Hereford, 1963) on the first and last evenings of the group. This test measures such things as confidence in the parental role, understanding of how parents influence their child's behavior, openness between parent and child, and the ability to establish a trusting relationship. It has the advantage of being a standardized test so that there is a normative population of parents from nonalcoholic homes with which to make comparisons.

Analysis of the pre- and post-test scores of participants who had completed the course demonstrated that the group participants significantly improved their ability to accept the feelings of their own children. The greatest change in scores was noted with parents who had the lowest initial skill levels. Since parental acceptance has been shown to be the most important factor in the adjustment of children (Martin, 1975), this is a very encouraging result. Although the design of the group was quasi-experimental, it points the way toward further research on the impact of grief resolution on parenting skills.

Content of Group Sessions

In the first two sessions, participants concentrate on identifying the losses experienced in an alcoholic home, and the theme of grief resolution is introduced. Session one begins with introductions, followed by discussion of participants' and leaders' expectations and participants' fears in the group and ways of dealing with these fears. The participants are then given a writing exercise in which they are asked to respond to the following statements and questions:

1. Identify a loss you experienced in childhood—for example, loss of a pet, death of a grandparent, moving from one place to another.
2. How did you learn about the loss?
3. What was your reaction?
4. How did other family members respond to you?
5. How did other family members react to the loss?
6. What did this experience teach you about loss?

When the participants have completed the exercise, they share their responses in the group. Typically, ACOAs have had many losses, most of which were denied. The purpose of the exercise is to help them to identify what a loss is and to make them aware of how denial happens.

Session two begins with a discussion of the grieving process. The leaders introduce the idea that denial is the first stage of grieving. Through the discussion, it becomes apparent that most participants are still in a state of denial because they haven't had support to move through the next stages. The leaders stress the need for support; that is, that grieving can't be done alone and that it is the group that will serve as support. The participants are then taken through a guided fantasy in which they are introduced to a safe place from which to gain access to childhood memories. They are asked to imagine looking through a photo album of their childhood and letting it drop open at a picture of themselves as a child. They are then asked to get to know this child and to focus on how the child feels. Before ending the fantasy, participants are given the option of saying good-bye to the child or of keeping the child with them. The reason for this is that parting with the child can bring back the pain of abandonment that the ACOA feels so acutely. This exercise requires ample time for group discussion and sharing.

Session three involves another guided fantasy, in which the participants are once again taken to their safe place and then introduced to a higher self—a person who represents unconditional love and who they could be or would be if they were fully evolved. In the fantasy, they experience being approached and nurtured by the higher self. Next they are instructed to call the child to join them. They are now guided through the experience of nurturing their own inner child while at the same time being nurtured by their higher self. The exercise is followed by group sharing. Because many ACOAs have never been adequately parented or nurtured, they may feel afraid or rejecting of the child. The higher being allows them to understand and experience a part of themselves as nurturer. At the same time that they are nurturing, they are also being nurtured. Without this support from the higher being, nurturing the inner child would feel a lot like being a single parent, like being expected to take care of all of the emotional demands of a child without any support. This exercise is especially important for women, who typically do most of the nurturing of children in a family whether or not they are single parents and who rarely receive adequate nurturing themselves. Learning that they can receive the nurturing they missed by giving it to themselves is essential. As one participant put it, "My child has been waiting all her life for a parent, and it's *me*!"

Session four involves the issue of anger and how it relates to grief. Participants are taken through a guided fantasy that focuses on a memory of being scolded and are instructed to experience the feelings of the child within. In the fantasy, participants find a way to comfort the child. The discussion that follows focuses on two kinds of learning. First, participants find out that the experience of being scared is a shared experience and is a natural feeling under those circumstances. Second, the exercise teaches them that they can take care of themselves when they are afraid. For the female ACOAs who are in alcoholic/abusive relationships and are still frozen in their fear, this is a particularly important exercise. The recognition that they have needs and that they can take care of those needs is the beginning of their empowerment.

To begin session five, one of the leaders demonstrates a role play with a participant. The leader listens to the participant's inner child, acknowledging and accepting whatever feelings the child expresses. Participants then work in pairs, role playing an interaction between their own inner child and an adult. If at this time (or at any time throughout the workshop) the participants are blocked or confused about the child's response, the leaders can assist by asking questions such as "How old are you now?" "What is the child feeling? Anger? Fear? Sadness? Pain?" Another way to help participants past a block, such as identifying a need, is to instruct them to "Ask your child." The benefits of this exercise are twofold. In addition to enabling them to learn about the feelings and needs of their inner child, the role playing itself is experienced as nurturing. At the close, the participants are instructed to find or buy a gift for their inner child and bring it to the next session.

In session six, the participants are taken through a guided imagery where they give their children the gifts they have brought for them. When participants arrive at this session, they are typically very excited and childlike, and the exercise is experienced as very positive. An account of Janie-Rae Crowley's shopping for and finding the right toy, which appears at the end of this chapter, illustrates how meaningful the exercise is to most participants. After discussion, one of the leaders reads *The Velveteen Rabbit* (Williams, 1983), a story of a child's love for a little stuffed toy.

Session seven is a play session. The participants are provided with a variety of toys, including coloring books, marbles, bubbles, and so on. They choose the toy they wish to play with and whom they wish to play with or whether they wish to play alone. The play session is followed by a discussion. What emerges in the discussion is that ACOAs are often afraid to play, because they feel that they need to be perfect or they fear judgment or rejection from others. If they rediscover the pain of isolation, which often happens, this pain is now expressed within the safety of the group. A discussion of gender-role stereotypes and their influence on behavior may also take place in this session.

In the final session, there is discussion of the changes that have occurred for the participants and of the impact of the overall group experience on parenting. In addition, participants express their feelings about the group coming to an end. This is particularly important, because it is often very hard for ACOAs to say goodbye, given their profound experience of abandonment. The group concludes with each group member saying something loving and nurturing to each other group member and to each group member's inner child.

One note of caution to people who may wish to offer a group experience like the one described above. There will be many ACOAs who have experienced physical and sexual abuse as well as psychological abuse. Memories of this abuse may be uncovered in the guided fantasies. If incidents of sexual or physical abuse are uncovered, participants will need to be referred for individual therapy. It is important to tell participants that they can go as slowly as they need and to take as long as they need to develop trust and a feeling of safety in the group.

The reaction of the participants to the parenting group has been extremely positive. Parents who did not know what it felt like to have been nurtured as children welcome the experience of getting in touch with repressed childhood feelings. The leaders have learned that it is not necessary to draw conclusions for these parents about how this experience could benefit their own parenting. Time and again, as memories of childhood pain are shared with others and tears are released, parents are able to understand, in depth, that the needs of their children are similar to their own: to be heard, to be accepted, and to be loved. One woman realized that her son was afraid of her in the same way that she had been afraid of her own erratic alcoholic mother. She decided to remove him from a behavior modification program and find counseling where they could both be helped to deal with their feelings. Both men and women seem to derive benefit from this approach. One pleasant discovery made by male participants is their need for nurturing from other men. They also learn to nurture themselves. The men's learning has important implications for the women in their lives, who typically carry the burden of being the primary care givers. Often, the most profound learning for the women in the workshop is their becoming aware of the necessity of caring for themselves and not just for others.

The last word should, of course, belong to the parents themselves. The description that follows was written by Janie-Rae Crowley, a participant in a parenting group held in Edmonton in March 1988. The coleader referred to is Anne Cox.

Group Participant's Voice: Janie-Rae Crowley

I am an adult child of an alcoholic (ACOA). What does that mean? What significance does it hold for me today? When I decided to explore those questions, I had no idea what I would find. To borrow a cliche, I found out I was one "sick puppy." Over several months, I voraciously studied the disease of alcoholism and its dynamics on the family. I allowed my mind to open, and by doing so I learned about myself. The last few months I had spent in therapy work with a psychologist who was assisting me in grieving the loss of my alcoholic father. I joined a twelve-step self-help group of ACOAs and I took a seven-week course on the subject as well. The cyclic pattern of generational alcoholism and its effects on the family intrigued me. However, I felt fear for my own children, and I felt a powerful need to break the cycle. Recognizing this need in myself encouraged me to become vulnerable and seek help. All my life I had felt I could handle all my problems alone. Being in a helping profession, I had envisioned myself as the helper, not the "help me."

I was learning about the importance of spirituality in one's health and growth as a person. A spirituality retreat was sponsored by my ACOA group and I attended, anxious to learn more about recovery. My own personal growth seemed to be taking off, but I still felt anxiety, guilt, shame, overresponsibility, and confusion in regard to being a parent. My self-esteem and confidence were low. I wanted to "be there" emotionally for my children, supporting and loving them.

Recently I had changed to a new twelve-step ACOA group, where I heard a woman share with us. I was quite moved by her understanding, frankness and sensitivity toward herself. At the end of the meeting, she announced she was giving a six-week course on parenting for ACOAs. Her background professionally qualified her to be very knowledgeable, and her own personal experience as an ACOA helped me decide she could help me. Delighted with the opportunity to address some of my parenting concerns, I phoned her to arrange a meeting to discuss the course. In the interview, I was excited to learn that the approach she and the cocounselor would use was that of learning to get in touch with and beginning to nurture the child within. She explained that as ACOAs, some of our needs were not met in childhood, and now as adults we struggled with day-to-day life because the child within was stifled and needed help. It seemed challenging to me that if I could learn to find this child and learn to nurture her, I would become a healthier person and a better parent to my children. I was willing to try.

Both counselors presented in a very relaxed, gentle, and trustworthy manner. They openly shared their own difficulties with the hurts of the past. I could identify with them. I felt their kindness and genuine concern for me as a person. Feeling comforted, acknowledged, believed, and accepted, the course became a reprieve from the hassles of daily life. I began to share more of myself with others in the group, testing the water first, but then, feeling fairly safe, I could proceed.

Our homework after the fifth session was to acquire a gift for our inner child to present to her at the next session. The gift was to symbolize the beginning of a relationship with this child by recognizing her needs in a small way.

Driving home that night, I was excited with this project. My thoughts jumped with ideas of gifts my little girl might enjoy. I tried to jog my memory to see if I could remember something she had wanted but not received. Nothing came to mind. The likes and dislikes of my three-year-old daughter came to mind, but they did not offer any inspiration. Nothing emerged, but I had a concept of shopping for this little girl. Something in my conscience tried to convince me that spending money on this idea of an inner child might be silly, flagrant, and wasteful. However, another part of me wanted the experience of doing exactly what I might judge as "off the wall" and immature. Again my thoughts returned to what I should buy, and I felt strongly that it should have significance for me. My thoughts roamed through the past of dolls, cutouts, games, and dressing up. All of a sudden, I remembered the teddy bear I had lost when I had my tonsils out at four years of age. Recently I had been visiting in the same hospital where my surgery was done many years ago. Nostalgically and painfully, I recalled this traumatic time. During my week-long hospitalization and separation from my parents, my favorite toy—my teddy—had been lost. Reflectively, I saw myself in front of a huge white cupboard, crying. Beside me was an angry and impatient night nurse. She opened the cupboard to reveal what seemed like hundreds of stuffed animals and toys. However, my teddy wasn't there. She told me to take something else and get back to bed. There could be no replacement—my friend was gone. I could feel the anguish of that moment, the sadness and fear, confusion and anger that nobody seemed to understand or care about. I shuddered, and my thoughts returned to the present. That was it! I would buy her a new bear!

Delighted by the inspiration, I was also puzzled, because I couldn't remember what the bear looked like. A conversation with my mother did not give any clues, as she couldn't remember any bear at all. As I set off to shop, I thought somehow that my instincts would guide me.

I held, squeezed, rubbed, and fondled many bears that day.

All seemed to fail in some way, too big, too small, too cute, too hard—just not right. Feeling disappointed, defeated, and lost in my mission, I asked for help in the form of prayer. Within minutes, I felt the urge to enter a store with a very small supply of children's toys. Away in the back corner, staring right at me, was the perfect bear. He was all alone on the shelf, sporting a bright blue ribbon around his neck embossed with little white paw prints and the printing "Sick Kids Bear." I took him off the shelf. His little tan body was supersoft and huggable. His face was so kind. He won my heart immediately. Then I discovered an opening on his back for adaptation to a puppet and a little embroidered bandaid on his bottom. As a child, I'd never had a puppet, and being a nurse, the bandaid endeared him to me even more. As I took him to the counter, the clerk explained that with the purchase of this bear a donation would automatically be sent to the Toronto Sick Kids Hospital. It seemed all my needs were being met magically by this little bear.

I anticipated presenting this unique and wonderful gift to my little girl. The whole experience had been a real adventure for me, filled with fun and excitement. My little girl was absolutely delighted, and I feel she probably had a great deal to do with helping me find her bear.

The course progressed, and I tried through meditation to reach and listen to her. My own children became my teachers. One day, with my nerves a little frayed, I was exasperated by my failing attempts to terminate my daughter's temper tantrum. She was screaming: red faced, high pitched, with full velocity. A surge rose inside me; I opened my mouth and screamed with great intensity. No words; just noise. My daughter stopped and stared at me in wonderment, my son started to laugh and said, "Gee Mom, you're funny." I laughed too. The release of my own feelings of exasperation was astounding. As I reported my experiences to the group, I felt their support, and I learned from their experiences as well. We had moments of childlike unconditional love as we sensed each other's inner child. In going back into my past, I found a hurt and misunderstood little girl inside, but, at the same time, she was quite fascinating and lovable. She is beginning to tell me what she needs, and I am beginning to listen and answer those needs.

I was sad when the course ended, but, as an ACOA, I have

trouble saying good-bye. We were gentle with each other in our departure. Since the course, I parent my children differently. I know they own their own feelings, and I allow them to express them freely. I don't try to control them anymore. In trying to remember how it feels to be a little child, I attempt to understand where they are coming from.

When they communicate, I try to listen well. We have much to share and learn from each other. I take every opportunity I can to give positive messages both to them and to my little child inside. I am getting better at giving and accepting love, and in so doing I'm experiencing more joy and wonderment in being a parent. I'm not an expert parent, but every expert began as a student. I'm grateful to Cathy and Anne and the members of my parenting group for introducing me to another avenue for growth.

I shared this story with my six-year-old son Sean, who immediately drew a picture of his mom in the store with the teddy.

References

Ackerman, R. J. *Children of Alcoholics: A Guidebook for Educators, Therapists and Parents.* Holmes Beach, Fla.: Learning Publications, 1978.

Black, C. *It Will Never Happen to Me!* Denver, Colo.: M.A.C., 1981.

Bowlby, J. *Attachment and Loss. Vol. 3: Loss, Sadness and Depression.* New York: Basic Books, 1980.

Hereford, C. F. *Changing Parental Attitudes Through Group Discussion.* Austin: University of Texas Press, 1963.

Liepman, M., Taylor White, W., and Nirenberg, T. D. "Children in Alcoholic Families." In D. C. Lewis and C. N. Williams (eds.), *Providing Care for Children of Alcoholics.* Pompano Beach, Fla.: Health Communications, 1986.

Martin, B. "Parent-Child Relations." In F. D. Horowitz (ed.), *Review of Child Development Research.* Chicago: University of Chicago Press, 1975.

Middleton, J. L. "Adult Children of Alcoholics Become Parents: A Pioneering Effort." *Focus on the Family and Chemical Dependency,* Jan.–Feb. 1985, pp. 9, 37.

Middleton-Moz, J., and Dwinell, L. *After the Tears: Reclaiming the*

Personal Losses of Childhood. Pompano Beach, Fla.: Health Communications, 1986.

Perrin, T. W. "Issues for Children of Alcoholics: Parenting." *Alcoholism/The National Magazine,* 1984, *5* (2), p. 23.

Rummer, C. A. "Trust in the Alcoholic Family." *Focus on the Family and Chemical Dependency,* Nov.-Dec. 1985, pp. 27, 30.

Treadway, D. C. "It'll Never Happen to My Kids! Family Therapy with the ACOA Parent." *Focus on the Family and Chemical Dependency,* Jan.-Feb. 1986, pp. 10-11, 30-31.

Whitfield, C. *Healing the Child Within.* Pompano Beach, Fla.: Health Communications, 1987.

Williams, M. *The Velveteen Rabbit.* New York: Random House, 1983.

Wilson, C., and Orford, J. "Children of Alcoholics: Report of a Preliminary Study and Comments on the Literature." *Quarterly Journal of the Studies on Alcohol,* 1978, *39,* pp. 121-142.

5

Repairing Personal Boundaries: Group Therapy with Survivors of Sexual Abuse

Maureen McEvoy
Client: Leah Minuk

As increasing numbers of adult women who were sexually assaulted as children claim their right to heal childhood wounds, a variety of support groups have been formed to provide a healing environment. Although literature reviews support the efficacy of such groups, little information has been provided on detailed aspects of group structure and process. This chapter describes a model for group work with incest and child sexual abuse survivors that I first developed in 1980 by adapting some of the ideas presented by Hogie Wyckoff (1977) in her book *Solving Women's Problems.* In 1984, Support, Education and Prevention of Sexual Abuse of Children (SEPSA) adopted this model for its group work. Since then, the SEPSA program has been enriched by both facilitators and members.

The SEPSA model has numerous positive points; I focus here on its ability to foster and repair the personal boundaries of group

Note: The author thanks Shirley Turcotte, Peta Hamersley, and Janet Olson for their expertise and support.

members. Thus, after discussing the value of groups, I discuss the importance of personal boundaries, screening interviews, the general group structure, and the particular aspects of group work that relate to establishing boundaries, including examples of techniques and exercises.

The Value of Groups

Incest is about secrecy. Carrying such a secret inevitably breeds a sense of isolation, of being freakishly different, of being unspeakably dirty and shameful. In individual therapy, the therapist must struggle to convince the client that she is not alone and that incest and child abuse occur frequently, if not in epidemic proportions. In my individual work, I have shown videos and lent books written by survivors in order to make this point.

A group automatically breaks the isolation experienced by incest survivors. Sometimes I think the most healing part of group work can be the first five minutes, as a woman walks into the room, sees other women, and realizes that they, too, are survivors, and yet they look absolutely "normal." In the group, members experience emotional support, develop new friendships, try out new skills, and laugh and cry their way to health.

Not everyone benefits from group work. A woman who has only recently remembered or begun talking about her abuse may benefit more from the intensive care of one-to-one therapy, where she does not run the risk of being overwhelmed or of absorbing the collective pain of group members. Once she has identified her own issues, she may profit from the group interaction. Concurrent individual therapy that is philosophically compatible with the group approach is sometimes encouraged. If this is the case, I ask permission to consult with the therapist.

The Importance of Personal Boundaries

Most of us are familiar with the concept of personal physical space, that invisible demarcation that surrounds us and is tampered with every time we get on a bus during rush hour. If we can expand that sphere to include emotional and psychological space, we come closer to defining personal boundaries. The term *boundary* is used to describe the flow of information, feelings, and physical contact between two or more people. In her workbook for survivors, *Incest, Years After: Learning to Cope Successfully,* Mary Ann Donaldson (1987) has used the metaphor of fences to illustrate personal boundaries. Some people, she says, have high brick fences around them that keep them isolated. Others have low chain link fences, completely permeable and unable to guarantee privacy. Still a third group has a medium-height picket fence with a gate at the appropriate level.

All of us need personal boundaries. They give us a sense of safety, a means of regulating our interaction with others. More importantly, they tell us who we are and what our rights and responsibilities as persons are. Boundaries tell us we are unique individuals, entitled to needs and to having those needs met. Boundaries tell us we're worthy.

If a child communicates, verbally and nonverbally, that she does not want to be sexually touched and an adult ignores those messages, the child learns that what she wants doesn't matter. Gradually, she comes to believe that her needs should be secondary to others' needs, and finally she completely loses sight of her own needs. All forms of child sexual abuse, including incest, involve a repeated invasion and violation of the victim's personal boundaries, resulting in a blurred sense of self and loss of personal power. Consequently, most survivors would readily identify with the low chain link fence.

In professional development workshops, I often ask nonsurvivors to think of personal experiences in order to catch the merest glimpse of what repeated boundary invasion might be like. Common examples offered include someone opening your mail, rooting through your wallet or purse, reading your diary, pawing over your underwear, or robbing your home. One woman said that she felt violated every time her former husband arrived unannounced and helped himself to her refrigerator contents. Sometimes I bring a big ball of string and ask everyone to lay out their personal perimeter and then to experiment with overlapping others' boundaries and being encroached upon. This simple exercise graphically illustrates violations of boundaries.

It is important to remember that the issue of personal boundaries is a sex-loaded question, for women traditionally have less sense of boundary than men. It is "normal" for women to be constantly patted, pinched, and chucked, let alone punched, shoved, and kicked. The rooms that women claim as their own, such as the kitchen, are ones that anyone can enter at any time. One of the goals of SEPSA is to repair personal boundaries. Therefore, the group itself must set boundaries, from the initial screening interview onward.

Screening Interviews

In our experience, the energy required to conduct screening interviews is compensated for by the assurance that those who attend are ready for group work. That SEPSA's dropout rate is extremely low confirms this. Each prospective member is interviewed for an hour. Although they are sometimes considered difficult to arrange and time consuming, screening interviews offer many benefits, particularly when the interview is held where the group will meet. Members have an opportunity to locate and assess the environment prior to the first session, which decreases a little of the initial nervousness. Members can meet a facilitator on a one-to-one basis and feel that they know at least one person on the first night. I encourage them to ask questions and express hopes and goals, and I give them information to help them decide whether this group will meet their needs. The prospective member can discuss her personal goals and develop a contract to work toward, another step in establishing personal boundaries. As facilitator, I become aware of individual issues and goals and can meld them with the group goals and activities. I can also screen out anyone who would not benefit from a group at this time and make the appropriate referral for that person.

At the beginning of the hour-long screening interview, the prospective member is informed that the group will run for twelve weeks. She is then given a four-page handout covering group agreements, the general format, and possible educational themes (see Exhibit 5.1). Because potential participants are likely to be very nervous and unable to remember details, the handout will help

Exhibit 5.1. SEPSA Group Agreements, Routines, and Educational Topics.

Sexual Abuse Survivors Group Agreements

1. The group will have a maximum of eight members and will meet once a week for two and a half hours.
2. Members are expected to commit themselves to come to the group for a minimum of five weeks.
3. The group will run for twelve weeks. Members will have an option to contract for an extension or to create a self-help group.
4. To avoid complications, group members are asked not to have sexual relations with anyone involved in the group.
5. All members are asked to share their names and telephone numbers. Members are encouraged to call each other for support between meetings.
6. If any member has an individual session with a facilitator, she will be asked to provide a summary of that session at the next meeting.
7. All information about the people in the group and their experiences is confidential and not to be discussed outside the group.
8. Every member of the group has a contract. A contract is a brief statement of the change that you want in your life as a result of working in the group and acts as a goal for you to work toward.
9. Group members who are drugged, drunk, or stoned during a meeting do not attempt to participate in problem solving but can ask for support and nurturing.
10. Members agree to give up the option to kill themselves while they are in the group.
11. The group functions cooperatively. To this end, you will be urged to follow some important guidelines: no lies; no power plays; no rescues; checking out "fears"; and expressing concerns and resentments. If you are uncertain of the meanings of some of these terms or of your ability to fulfill them, don't worry, just bring your questions and concerns to the first group meeting.
12. The suggested group fee is $180, or $15 per session. However, a sliding fee scale is available. We will also consider an exchange or barter in lieu of fees.

Group Routines

1. A "round" or "check-in" where every member says how she is feeling and whether she would like to take time later in the meeting to problem solve.
2. Sharing any fears, concerns, or resentments that members may have from previous sessions.
3. Discussion of administrative details.
4. Problem solving. Women who have asked for time to work on a specific problem do so during this period. If a woman asks for fifteen minutes, she receives fifteen minutes unless the group agrees to extend her time. If the total number of minutes requested exceeds the available time, the

Exhibit 5.1. SEPSA Group Agreements, Routines, and Educational Topics, Cont'd.

women will negotiate for what they need. (The group decides whether problem solving or educational time takes place first. If the group agrees, the educational time may be postponed.)

5. Break (ten minutes).
6. Education or exploring common themes, through either a minilecture, group discussion, or exercise.
7. Strokes and appreciations.
8. Closing round.

Possible Educationals for SEPSA Group

An educational is simply a period of time set aside to explore an issue of interest to members of the group. It is an opportunity to learn and to explore common feelings and experiences. Below is a list of possible topics. Feel free to add others we may have missed. The cofacilitators believe that the first two topics are essential. We'd like you to tell us which of the others you are most interested in. We ask you to number your top ten priorities and then bring the list to the first meeting. From there we will draw up a tentative schedule to be presented for group approval.

—— Tools of communication—problem solving, sharing concerns, fears, appreciations, and so on
—— Child sexual abuse and incest—an overview of current knowledge
—— Socialization of men and women
—— Advertising/pornography
—— Bad experiences while seeking counseling or help
—— Mistrust
—— Sexuality (knowing our bodies)
—— Sexual problems
—— Worries about being a mother
—— Intimate relationships
—— Feelings of guilt, shame, depression, isolation
—— Feelings toward the offender
—— Feelings toward nonoffending parent, siblings
—— Self-abuse (for example, cutting yourself)
—— Support networks
—— Self-help groups
—— Feeling sexual pleasure at time of abuse
—— Flashbacks
—— Jealousy, resentment of nonvictims and survivors
—— Blocking memories
—— Being hit or battered in an intimate relationship
—— Privilege and oppression (exploring our differences in terms of class, race, sex, age, income, and other factors)
—— Sense of losing time, not being able to account for time
—— Bargains we made
—— Alcohol and drug abuse

Exhibit 5.1. SEPSA Group Agreements, Routines, and Educational Topics, Cont'd.

____ Being blamed for things you honestly can't remember
____ Eating too much or too little, using laxatives, and so on
____ Splitting or out-of-body experiences at the time of the abuse
____ Severe headaches followed by vivid dreams, visions
____ Nightmares
____ Seeing shadows
____ Being raped as an adult
____ Memories or worries about hurting or abusing others
____ Other topics we've missed: ____________________

____

____

them to remember what was discussed. I go over each group guideline, since particular ones can open doors for further clarification. For example, discussing the guideline of no sexual contact between group members gives me an opportunity to say that many survivors have been taught to interact with or respond to the world in a sexual way. It also assesses the woman's level of homophobia. Similarly, guidelines about no alcohol encourage discussion about past alcohol and drug abuse, current sobriety, and so on. I can inquire about previous depressions, hospitalizations, suicide attempts, and counseling experiences, individual or group. Discussing suicide allows me to explain that group work may intensify feelings and to initiate the exploration of options for handling those feelings.

The list of possible educational themes is reviewed in order to identify the person's major issues. Going over the list also serves to reinforce how common these issues are for survivors. For example, some people react strongly to the issue of feeling pleasure at the time of the abuse. "Why is that there?" they fire. I reply that feeling pleasure is very common but is often kept as a secret within the larger incest secret; that our bodies are designed to give pleasure, but in the context of abuse, this is experienced as our bodies betraying us or as proof that we asked for it.

In addition, I ask a potential member whom she can call at 2 A.M. if a crisis erupts. Usually, feelings are intensified long before the group trust is at a level that permits phone calls at 2 A.M., and, in any case, group support cannot substitute for ongoing, daily support. If a woman's personal support system is weak, my cofacilitator and I will need to be more available to her.

Next I ask about disclosure—to whom and when has she disclosed her abuse. It is not necessary for participation in the group that a member has disclosed or confronted her immediate family. However, if she hasn't yet spoken of her experiences to anyone, she may find group work very intimidating and might benefit more from working individually with a therapist, where she will feel safer. I will also want to know whether she is clear about the legacies—patterns of behavior, thoughts, and feelings—of her abuse.

Throughout the hour, I assess the woman's overall verbal skills and ease with the subject of incest. I want to know about her self-awareness, her strengths and tender spots, and her sense of her own personal boundaries. A woman who is not clear about what she hopes to get out of the group runs the risk of absorbing the other members' stories and pain and taking on the responsibility to care for others at her own expense. In this way, she recreates her own victimization.

If the prospective member and I agree that group work is appropriate for her, she proceeds to develop a contract that states her major goal for being in the group. This contract is customarily a single sentence that states: "In this group I want to. . . ." She is encouraged to develop a specific goal that realistically reflects the constraints of the time limits. For example, she might say that she wants to learn some of the effects her abuse has had, to develop self-help tools, or to begin to nurture and prize her body.

The SEPSA Group Model

In general, SEPSA groups are time-limited, ranging from twelve to twenty weeks, and are offered at two levels. First-level groups are highly structured to allow time for individuals to work on common issues and to gain information. A variety of exercises and approaches, informed by a feminist analysis, are used. Second-level groups, which are more flexible to allow for more individual problem solving, will not be discussed here.

Each group has two facilitators: one who has survived child

sexual abuse and one who has not experienced child sexual abuse but who has good group facilitation skills. The survivor facilitator assists group members to identify common themes and experiences and models one way of healing. The nonsurvivor facilitator ensures group safety and assists in the identification of issues that all women face in a patriarchal society. Most survivors have developed hypersensitivity to their environment and the people in it. For many, the experience of their abuse has been like a menacing hand reaching for them out of nowhere. Consequently, their guard is up. The purpose of establishing a structured format in the weekly meetings is to provide enough consistency and predictability that members may be able to lower their guard and thus derive full benefit from the activities.

A typical group meeting begins (each week after the first week) with an opening round or check-in, wherein each member takes a minute or two to describe how she is feeling that day and to relate any major events that occurred during the week. This round is intended to be a check-in activity only, so individual attention is postponed until all members have spoken. Members can at this time ask for individual time later in the meeting to discuss specific issues in their life, such as memories of their sexual abuse, relationships, work, or other pressing issues.

Immediately following the opening round, the facilitator asks whether there is any leftover business from previous sessions. This gives members an opportunity to clear up any misunderstandings, hurt or angry feelings, fears, or concerns that may have arisen from the previous session. It also provides a safe environment to practice good communication skills. Facilitators inform group members that it is unusual for perfect communication to take place in any group dealing with painful material. If nothing of this kind has been raised by about the fourth week, the facilitators may wish to make a joking comment along the lines of "I can't believe we're all doing such a good job here that no one leaves with any questions or concerns." Such a comment again gives permission to raise personal issues and endorses the belief that members can and will sort out any tensions that may occur. Obviously, if the facilitators are aware of an issue that is not being addressed, they may raise it.

Group members then decide whether problem solving or education comes next. When problem solving is done, women who have asked for time to work on a specific problem do so during this period. If the total number of minutes requested exceeds the available time, the women negotiate for what they need. Every group is different. Some groups like to focus on individual problem solving, while others prefer structured activities provided by the education component of group work. When a woman asks for time, that time is hers to do with as she likes. Not only may she address any issue she wishes, she is also free to choose how this happens. She may just talk, or she may request feedback and suggestions. She may ask to be guided through a Gestalt, drawing, or movement exercise, or she may prefer focusing or imagery. What is important here is that the woman must decide what she wants and then ask for it. As members grow in confidence, they also grow in creativity. Some members have brought in music, poetry, art, and performance rituals to use during their time.

Education, or exploring common themes, is accomplished through either a minilecture, group discussion, or exercise. The educational theme for the week is decided by group members. After the members have chosen their top ten priorities from the list of topics presented in Exhibit 5.1, the facilitators draw up a tentative schedule and present it to the group for changes and approval. Members have the option of changing, postponing, or deleting topics according to their needs. The facilitators also develop a tentative list of activities and exercises to accompany the educational themes. Exercises may be drawn from a variety of disciplines: imagery, drawing, writing, role plays, psychodrama. As facilitators, we always have activities planned that we are prepared to postpone or discard according to the group's wishes.

The next stage of the group work involves giving appreciations or strokes to other group members. Appreciations usually begin at a surface level with comments such as "I like your earrings" and progress to more meaningful ones, such as "Thank you for sharing that about your family. That took guts, and it helped me understand my family better." Frequently, members resist appreciations because they have been taught that it's rude or boastful to sincerely accept compliments or because they have little self-esteem. When this happens, my cofacilitator and I introduce the issue of appreciations by a brief role play, where one compliments the other on an item of clothing and the other responds "This old rag? It's nothing special." This role play provides a springboard for discussion. Appreciations may be given to individuals or to the entire group, although no one is required to do so. The only "rule" is that a member must say "Thank you" when given one. Halfway through the sessions, members are required to respond, "Thank you, I agree." Among howls of protest and laughter, the facilitators deliberately give each member an individual appreciation. Our follow-up questionnaire indicates that this simple activity is very powerful and stays with members long after the group ends.

The session ends with a closing round, with each member making a simple statement such as "I feel good" or "I feel tired." If a member tries to bring up an issue at the end of the session, the facilitator might gently but firmly state, "We're at the end of today's session. If you like, we can begin with you next week, or you can call one of us during the week to prepare and discuss what you'd like to say." It may seem cruel to shut down a member; it certainly is difficult. Nevertheless, to rescue her communicates that victim behavior is acceptable and undermines the group's strategy. It also assumes that the time of the other members and facilitators is not as important as the individual member's needs. According to group agreements, a group boundary of time is established by beginning and ending meetings promptly. To extend the group without explicit permission of all group members is to violate that boundary. Obviously, if a member is in severe distress, the group might readily agree to continue for another fifteen minutes, or the member might speak with a facilitator immediately after the group session ends. However, this is an emergency response and must be checked if it begins to occur regularly.

Exercises for Encouraging Boundaries

A variety of opportunities present themselves in group work to foster boundaries. On the first night, for example, members are invited to write their names and telephone numbers on a sheet that will be distributed. Each member is asked to consider the degree to which she would like to be available. Does she want to put her work number down? What kind of calls can she accept at work? Will she accept calls at home or work for purposes of just chatting, or does she prefer only calls related to the group? What times are not good for her to receive calls? Is she in bed by 10 P.M. and up at 6:30 A.M. or awake until midnight and asleep until 9 A.M.? In other words, we hope to stimulate the building of medium picket fences with appropriate gates.

I often tell group members that it was difficult for me to establish a personal code about telephone calls. (I accept emergency calls twenty-four hours a day and calls about group concerns during the day and early evening. Social calls are not encouraged.) I tell them that at first I believed that I should be continually available for all calls but found that too draining. Then I felt mean-spirited about setting limits. Now, however, I feel comfortable and secure. Consequently, I do not resent crisis calls at whatever times of the day. Setting my own limits around phone calls serves as a model to group members for the establishing of personal boundaries.

Another effective way to encourage the building of personal boundaries is to inquire about what members plan to do with their journals and drawings produced during the course of the group sessions. As these articles reveal personal information, they are considered extensions of the person. If the materials are going to be saved, group members are encouraged to discover a safe and private place to store them.

There are a number of exercises that promote the establishment of personal boundaries. Any drawing exercise in which the body is represented or outlined creates and reinforces the idea of a boundary. In one art exercise, the members are divided into pairs and asked to outline their partners' bodies on a large sheet of paper. As one partner lies down on the paper, some negotiation takes place as to how closely the other person should draw, particularly around the breasts and genitals. The second part of the exercise is a guided imagery that may involve a regression of the member's age from adult to infancy, recollection of body memories, attention to current injuries and tender spots, or whatever theme the facilitator adopts. After the imagery exercise, members are instructed to fill in their outlines with color, shapes, and symbols that are appropriate for them.

Other drawing exercises include depicting the inner and outer parts of a person and portraying the personality traits and characteristics that constitute the unique person. Inevitably, these exercises stimulate the conceptualization of a personal border. In another imagery exercise, members are invited to develop metaphors for personal boundaries. In one person's metaphor for the group, every member was in her own inner tube, connected by strong strands of rope. There are a number of writing exercises, too, that help to establish boundaries. Ones that develop bottom lines, such as "five things I deserve in a relationship," are often very effective.

We have adapted an exercise that Susan Forward (1986) describes in her book *Men Who Hate Women and the Women Who Love Them*. Members are asked to write a separate address label for each negative name they have been called and to paste the labels on a sheet under the heading "labels people have stuck on me." On a second sheet, headed "what I really am," they label all their positive qualities. Their challenge is to come up with as many, if not more, positive labels as negative labels. In the second part of the exercise, members visualize themselves as a castle, surrounded by a magical wall constructed of the positive labels. Then the castle is imagined to be under siege as the negative labels become arrows, slinging out of the blue. However, rather than piercing, the arrows are rendered impotent by the protective wall. In order to accommodate the various problems that group members experience in defending their castles with their protective walls, we have found it important to build in suggestions that the wall is able to transform itself and become whatever is necessary to stop the arrows. In the debriefing, we salute creative adaptations and acknowledge our inner knowing. Then we suggest that members repeat the imagery at home.

"Ask for 100 Percent of What You Want"

SEPSA facilitators utter this phrase many, many times during the course of a group. We have found the process of internally clarifying what is desired and then asking for 100 percent of it to be an extremely effective exercise to reestablish boundaries. Usually we use the phrase to encourage members to ask for individual problem-solving time, but we may also use it in any situation in which a group member needs to assert her wishes. Group members frequently underestimate the amount of time they require and ask for only five minutes when fifteen minutes would be more realistic. Early in the group process, facilitators matter of factly explain that five minutes probably isn't enough and suggest that members ask for fifteen minutes and not worry if they don't use it all. Typically, as the group progresses, members become more comfortable with stating their needs and more confident about gaining group support, and they begin to ask for twenty minutes or more.

No group member is forced to take time for herself, although facilitators may encourage members to do so. For example, if a woman who has not previously taken time begins to relate several issues during her check-in, a facilitator may say, "Sounds like you have a lot going on. Would you like some time to discuss it?" Or, if there is a shy member who needs encouragement, a facilitator may ask, before problem solving begins, "Would anyone else like time?" and makes eye contact with the shy woman. Sometimes a group member will comment, usually at the end of an exercise, "I should take some time next week to work on that." The facilitator can make note of this comment and indicate that she will remind the woman of her request at the next session. Of course, the member still has the option to refuse the time or to work on something else. The procedure of noting and following through with a request for time does, however, reinforce an individual's rights within the group.

An interesting situation develops when more time is requested by members than is available—if, for example, an hour is available but five members have requested fifteen minutes each. Members must now negotiate among themselves to decide how the hour will be used. Awkwardness reigns the first time negotiation is required, and members tend to flounder and look to the facilitator to decide whose needs will be met. As facilitators, we turn the control of this decision-making process back to the group members and guide them only by outlining the various options available (everyone take five minutes less, no cigarette break, no exercise, and so on). Often, one member will offer to forgo her time. We discourage this, gently explaining to the member that her needs are as important as everyone else's and that she does not need to rescue anyone. Learning not to sacrifice oneself is an enormous step toward recovery and toward setting limits; negotiating and compromising are life skills that are useful in many other situations.

Speaking for Ourselves: Defining the "Me" Behind the Boundary

For most of us, having the undivided attention of everyone in a room is a rare occurrence and is often associated with an embarrassing or punishing past experience. Group members bring these associations with them. In addition, few of us were ever taught listening skills, so when someone is speaking we only half listen and begin forming our reply. In the group, we use an exercise, "If I thought you wouldn't judge me . . . ," to teach group members the roles of speaker and listener. Members are divided into pairs. Partner *A* speaks for two minutes, completing the sentence "If I thought you wouldn't judge me, I'd tell you. . . ." Partner *B* listens. After two minutes, the partners switch roles. Feedback is shared first among the pairs and then in the larger group.

This exercise illustrates a number of points about group process. It mimics a woman's experience in the group. The spotlight is on her; she is free to unburden or censor herself, and she often finds herself seeking some type of feedback, if only eye contact, in order to continue. Listeners find it difficult to remain quiet, wishing to give reassurance and, in some instances, similar personal testimony. Most importantly, the exercise illustrates the seductive nature of groups. The speaker habitually begins with innocuous examples. "If I thought you wouldn't judge me, I'd tell you that when the alarm goes off I usually hit it and roll over," "that I feel stupid doing this exercise," "that I was really afraid to come to group tonight," and so on. Some partners find themselves carried on a stream of words that lead to personal exposure.

Group work, especially if it is in a safe, warm environment, encourages members to reveal painful memories, thoughts, and feelings. Sometimes, however, the member feels that she has unveiled too much, too soon. Rather than feeling safe and supported, she feels exposed and vulnerable and fears that she has been negatively judged. Therefore, group members need to know that they are in control of how much or how little they say. At the beginning of every exercise, facilitators explain that members must decide how much they will tell. During the postexercise debriefing, this principle is reinforced.

SEPSA facilitators also try to prevent premature self-disclosure by adopting a very structured format for the first two sessions while members are experiencing the first blush of euphoria at discovering a safe group. I distrust instant bonding—that early feeling of finding a soul mate—because it is not based on shared experiences and cautiously built trust. Thus, the first evening is largely spent in housekeeping and getting acquainted. The second session consists of a discussion of myths and realities of incest dynamics and the "If I thought you wouldn't judge me . . ." exercise. The first opportunity for members to take time and thereby risk overdisclosure is the third session, and, by then, the euphoria has diminished enough so that members are better able to assess the safety level of the group.

It is taken for granted that all members have suffered. We believe that the abuse occurred; members are not required to divulge details of proof. If they believe that it is important to give details, they will. Our objective is that they connect those painful experiences with their current mode of interacting with others. Another, related objective is to celebrate their survival. Sometimes the only coping mechanisms that were available to incest survivors—alcohol, drugs, slashing themselves, prostitution—are an additional source of guilt. We encourage group members to appraise their coping skills, keep the useful ones, and develop new skills as needed.

Timing is everything in healing the child that resides within every adult who has survived child sexual assault. Survival often depended on the ability to forget, block, and regress. I believe that people remember, even in a hypnotic trance, only what they are ready to remember, when they are ready to remember it. Thus, it is neither useful nor respectful and, in fact, is potentially harmful to push group members to recover memories.

A major ingredient in recovery and reparation of self-esteem is the member's knowledge that she healed herself. She must be encouraged to credit herself and recognize that the facilitators are merely witnesses to her journey. Therefore, it is critical that facilitators do not begin predicting or expecting future behavior. The member must be allowed to find her own voice and her own path, thereby finding her own boundaries. It is the restoration of personal boundaries that creates a clear sense of self and restores personal power.

Client's Voice: Leah Minuk

I called up SEPSA because something inside of me wanted out, wanted to be healed. A long time ago I had tried to work on this, but how could I? I went to two therapists. One I just couldn't tell anything to. I mentioned my first abuse to the other, and she asked me what he'd done to me. I only felt embarrassed. It came clear that there was no one and nowhere that was safe. Who could possibly understand? There were just too many painful secrets.

Then I heard of SEPSA and the group work done there. I called and was greeted by a calm, kind, and understanding voice. I heard respect and gentleness in that voice.

I went to the first group meeting terrified. Terrified to share and terrified not to. If I failed here, where else could I possibly go? This was the last stop, the last chance. Would they think I was a whiner, full of self-pity? I mean, my experiences weren't *that* bad, were they? How could they possibly have time for *my* pain? How could they possibly care? The facilitator said, "It's okay, you belong here." Huh!

Then the first night is reality and the group comes together. Eight women sit together in a cozy room, checking each other out. Some are scared, some angry, most not trusting, and all nervous. We do an exercise, we share a bit, we discuss rules, expectations, purposes, and goals. We work.

When I leave that night, I have something I have never had before—safety. Total and complete. I have a place and people I can *trust*. I can say anything, I can be anything, and I will not be judged.

As the sessions went on, the safety and love and caring just got truer and truer. We criticized some, we shouted a lot, and we took whole chunks of time just for us! I took time *just for me!* We grew and we grew and we grew.

At the end I realized that I had barely scratched the surface of my pain, and yet I'd gone over one huge hurdle. The secrets were out, and I could now move on.

I will continue exploring and learning and healing; possibly in another group, definitely in individual therapy. I have to face my "demons" and do my healing—no one can do it for me. I am ultimately responsible for getting what I want. These are all things that got through in the group. Most of all, though, I learned that I *can* reach out, I *can* ask for help, someone *will* be there. Knowing this makes trust a possibility and maybe even a reality.

References

Donaldson, M. A. *Incest, Years After: Learning to Cope Successfully.* Fargo, N.D.: Village Family Service Center, 1987.

Forward, S. *Men Who Hate Women and The Women Who Love Them.* New York: Bantam Books, 1986.

Wyckoff, H. *Solving Women's Problems.* New York: Grove Press, 1977.

PART TWO

SENSING OUR OWN REALITY

6

More Than Meets the Eye: Using Ordinary Snapshots as Tools for Therapy

Judy Weiser
Workshop Participant: Jenny Nash

We see things not as they are, but as *we* are.
—*Source Unknown*

An often-quoted anecdote tells about a group of blind people trying to describe an elephant solely through touch (and probably smell also, though this is never mentioned!). Each can only extrapolate from his or her small radius of reach what the entire elephant must really be like. This illustration demonstrates what we all know instinctively but rarely stop to consider: that how people organize meaning from things around them has a lot to do with who they are and where they come from (often quite literally). It isn't just beauty that is "in the eye of the beholder"; in some ways, everything we call reality is. If we pay attention to something, it is because we have noticed that it is there and, therefore, has some kind of meaning for us. If we haven't noticed it, it really hasn't made enough difference to stand out and thus doesn't really matter. In some ways, it doesn't exist for us at all.

We usually notice those things that stand out from the general amorphous background, the things that, for various reasons, we give meaning to. Thus, we take the vast uncharted territory of our experience of the world around us and, through our perceptions, cognitively map it into symbols of meaningful understanding. These symbols give us some power to manipulate the parts and to communicate internally and to others about what we have found. Our most personal internal symbols may be known quite well to us, yet they are usually rather difficult to express in words.

The only way that humans can take in information is through our five senses (sight, sound, touch, taste, and smell). Since it is estimated that about 80 percent of this sensory stimuli data enters through the eyes, sight is obviously extremely influential in guiding us in our attempts to understand what we encounter. When we experience (or try to remember or predict) any given moment in time, it is important to recognize that there will be a predominantly visual component inexorably bonded to each slice of time that we are examining.

We talk to each other in written and spoken words, but we sometimes don't stop to realize that these are just *attempted representations* of what is really stored inside us. Most of us think, feel, and recall memories not so much in direct words as in iconic imagery or thought pictures (sometimes accompanied by auditory, kinesthetic, or other cues). Therefore, we can see how communications and the personal meaning we give to our experiences would be processed predominantly by visual codes and concepts. Thus, when attempting spoken or written representation of our inner ideas and feelings, we use a complex *visual literacy* as our cognitive language. In fact, English idioms often unconsciously reflect this: we say things such as "I see!", "See what I mean?", "Get the picture?" and so on when we want to make sure that we understand or are understood.

None of us has little words running around in our bodies or heads; instead, neurochemical and electrical impulses fire, combine, and convey thoughts and feelings nonverbally. And when we are in dialogue with our inner selves, words are not particularly useful or necessary. They simply translate what is inside us as we try to share this inner experience with others or, in listening to others, match our understanding of their words to their inner thoughts and feelings. True communication occurs only when the two parties can agree that their perceptions have been shared in concentric meaning, not just when words have been exchanged.

Each of us has unique perceptual "filters" that are constructed of what we have learned personally, familially, and culturally, through past experiences and teachings. We are sometimes further influenced by what we expect or have been taught to look for. Thus, in some ways we contribute to the meaning of any stimulus by what we ourselves have brought to that moment of perception. Meaning doesn't really exist "out there" apart from us, but rather it exists within the relationship between the object-stimulus and the person-perceiver—either one just on its own without the other wouldn't have the same meaning.

Communication and Its Problems: The Why and How of Therapy

If reality and meaning are so personally constructed and perceived, it should be no surprise that everyone sees the same thing a bit differently. Just because we see the world a certain way doesn't mean that everyone else around us will automatically be in agreement with us. But that's exactly where so many of our problems erupt, where people are so locked in to one way of thinking that there's little room for divergent opinions. Emotional communication is blocked when one person fails to grasp the feelings behind another person's words. Whether one is dealing with physical or emotional problems, improvement cannot happen without people becoming more aware of how they uniquely perceive and construct meaning. They fail to understand how their particular way of handling emotions may not be clear to or shared by others. Further, their communications may not be taken the way they intend. If this were understood, there would be more appreciation of and tolerance for individual differences and less animosity toward and fear of others who aren't like ourselves.

In the various mental health fields, where counselors and therapists spend their time trying to help people with problems, words are often not enough to give people "a better picture" of what is meant. Clearly, "people helpers" need to use more visual and other-than-verbal techniques along with their usual verbal interactions with their clients. "Expressive" or "Arts" therapies are based on these assumptions, and PhotoTherapy is no exception. Viewing photos usually results in some sort of reaction, even if it's only that we find an image incomprehensible or simply boring. Feelings are stirred, memories recalled, subject content reflected on, as we are brought into contact with information stored nonverbally inside ourselves. Ordinary snapshots that people take and react to can be conceptualized as metaphorical markers indicating meaningful experiences and emotions. They act as "footprints" showing where we have been, emotionally as well as physically, and where we might be heading (sometimes without even knowing it yet).

Adult Healing, Childhood Pain

I have found that when people begin therapy, they may be feeling hurt, confused, and so on when we first meet, but that often these feelings come from deep inside, places where it is difficult for words to go. Problems explained as happening currently often turn out to be rooted in scripts or memories tied to long-ago causes or associations. Such memories from our pasts we find hard to fully describe verbally (if indeed they can be consciously remembered at all). Because each moment of time we've encountered has been stored as an overall all-at-once blend of sights, sounds, feelings, words heard, smells, and so forth, it is hard to focus on one facet without being affected by all the others that were tied to it.

Each event that has had intense meaning for us (positive or negative) is stored as initially experienced through our senses, and that meaning is integrally embedded within the memory as it happened then. When a person has experienced severe trauma in early life (sexual or physical abuse, unexplained abandonment, death, and so on), especially if this has happened at a young age when one's life rarely contacts anything outside the immediate family and home, those experiences will have been stored in the brain (and heart) as feelings and experiences unstructured by word interpretations. And if the time was very early, before the child has good functional understanding of speech, there is no verbal coding or symbolizing of the experience available.

At the time of such an event, such feelings leave the child unable to make rational sense of what has happened (especially if everyone is pretending that nothing happened, nothing is different, or if the child tries to verbalize the pain and finds it ignored or denied or diminished). Unable to get support even that the event did actually occur or that it was awful and wrong, children may begin to doubt the ability of their own memory to dependably document "truth." Similarly, they may begin to internalize responsibility for the terrible events. They have perceptions such as "It must have been my fault; why else would this happen?" "Nobody else has such terrible things happen to them—I've never heard about it." "If I tell, no one will believe me." (Or "When I did tell, I got hurt worse with the violence and punishment and consequences than if I'd just kept my mouth shut.")

Victims usually find it safer to share their pain with no one and often end up feeling powerless. They sometimes learn to protect themselves by managing to distance mind from body as a natural defense. This may be difficult to reverse later in life. Survivors often mention feeling unalive or unreal and find it hard to let go with any spontaneous feelings (or even to recognize they they could have any). Later on in life, as teens or adults, when looking back at these memories, they usually experience some guilt around "Why didn't I stop it?" "Why did this happen only to me?" "Why didn't somebody do something?" These unanswered questions mirror internal guilt, shame, self-blame, feelings that there must have been something wrong with them for this to have happened. Unable to trust their most intense feelings, having their true memories essentially voided by the nonbelief of others, finding the guilty party long unpunished (and probably unrepentant), survivors usually have no relief for the nonvalidated pain. In relationships, they often fear vulnerability and usually find it very difficult to risk full emotional expression (as there's been a lifetime experience of not knowing which feelings will produce which results.)

In therapy, such problems can take a long time surfacing, often contained within masks of "I can't have a comfortable sexual relationship" or "I never get angry, because when I do finally blow up, it all just explodes terribly, and I get very scared about losing control" or "I really don't know how to know what I feel; I don't think I really do feel anything really deeply." The actual past experiences that are precipitating such statements have usually long ago been put away (either consciously, without ever being finished, or, more usually, unconsciously, with vague gnawing feelings that have no clear identity).

There is usually a child still hurting in most adult therapy clients I've treated. This "adult child" has been severely victimized in one way or another, and the memories, pain, and lack of understanding about the event, as well as resulting feelings of worthlessness, taintedness, guilt, and so on, all contribute to blocking the adult from a freely expressive, self-respecting life. More importantly, the lack of being validated and respected as a person who did have such terrible things happen and who did have to live for years in undeserved confusion, shame, and hurt has usually never been dealt with to any completion of purging the guilt, blaming the abuser instead of the victim, or accepting the child's powerlessness to have ever been able to stop the abuse on his or her own.

We adults "see" our memories of events that happened at an early age through the filter of *being* that age: backyards that we remember as endless turn out to have been of ordinary size; pet dogs that appeared giant and massive turn out to have been just ordinary spaniels; kindergarten classrooms that loomed huge with many roomy desks turn out to have been just of ordinary size (and the desks tiny!) when we return as adults to view them all once again. The same thing happens with emotional memories; moments and feelings are remembered as if it were the child still encountering them firsthand (because they were initially coded into our minds through the filters of who we were then).

Therefore, to heal adult clients, therapists must somehow try to reconnect them with their inner child, helping those earlier memories to be processed with the intelligence and perspective of the adult who now looks back to understand that the child was truly powerless and honestly unable to comprehend or act in self-protection and to enable the feelings from the past to be reexperienced as much as needed for their validation and relief. Really forgetting is not only impossible but unnecessary, and needing to forgive the abuser is a hotly debated issue (and usually equally truly impossible); however, forgiving one's own inner child for not having done more than was humanly possible at that age is an absolutely essential step in the process of healing and growth. If no one else was available then to bear witness, at least the adult self can provide that substitute role in grounding memories so that they do not control one's life in their unendedness.

For people to reexperience the past unfiltered, they must be able to get back as close as possible to the moment as it was originally encountered. Memories are often decorated with details we've added later in our filtering them through the years of change. Similarly, we often conveniently forget (or lose to our conscious recall) those components that were irrelevant or painful at the time—but those "disappeared" facts are sometimes the very ones needed to regain the perspective for improved comprehension of the events that they document.

Photographs are the natural language for bridging these years; they record what was actually in front of the camera at the time, and in being reviewed, they bring along accompanying feelings and thoughts that were inseparably coded into them as frozen in time. In reencountering a family photo, for example, we not only see the portrait grouping but very possibly get a memory of a smell, a feeling of how it felt to be posed that day that way, a blend of remembering that encompasses not only the people in the image but perhaps how one felt about them at that time. Places are viewed not only as the setting but also perhaps as cues for what was going on in them then. Family members are viewed simultaneously as they appeared in the image and as one remembers they "really were" that day when not trying to pose. Thus, adults can get back in touch with how it felt to be there that day, to be the child in that family, to have to stand next to siblings or parents who had "double identities," who were basically living lies. The paradox between truth as unexpressed and image as presented can be reexperienced through talking about the photo and exploring the various dimensions simultaneously bonded to it.

Sometimes reliving one's life through albums and photographs can reawaken "lost" facts; better yet, this can sometimes bring to consciousness information or feelings that have been lost within oneself. One woman reflected on a family portrait taken when she was seven. Commenting on a seemingly innocent grouping of people that had left her seated father's shoulder visually covering the lower part of her face as she stood behind him, she wryly reflected, "That picture really says it all, though I've never noticed until today. He was always smothering my mouth, my voice, pushing himself sexually into every hole my body had, choking me, keeping me from screaming, keeping me from telling later what had happened by threatening me with terrible consequences if I told. Both literally and figuratively, I couldn't talk, wasn't allowed a mouth, never got to open it, probably never even to cry. My voice when I spoke was very small." If she'd been "given" a mouth? "At that age, a hundred mouths wouldn't have been enough—I wouldn't have known what words to risk." Is there anything she would want to tell the little girl in that photo? Bursting into tears, she sobbed, "It's okay, Honey, you'll survive and he won't. You'll make it, I promise. You're doing the very best you can do under the circumstances, and somebody ought to make sure to tell you that, so that you won't hate yourself later."

This kind of healing cannot be given to the client; it must come from within. Healing like this frequently occurs naturally when given enough time in a safe environment, when there's the opportunity to examine one's life while still retaining some control over the intensity and depth one gets into. Photographs are a less threatening, more natural way for people to do this; if no family photos can be found, one can just as easily work with remembered, imagined, or remade ones.

Snapshots, Cameras, and People

Oliver Wendell Holmes called photos "mirrors with memory." These reflections from inside our minds and hearts can be very powerful tools in the hands of someone using them properly to explore what people know and, more importantly, *how* they know what they know (their values, beliefs, reasons, traditions, and expectations). When a therapist uses ordinary snapshots as catalysts, the client's long-buried and well-defended emotions and memories often surface less guardedly, sneaking in sideways without words to protect them. These techniques have been used successfully not only in traditional psychotherapy but also with the communicatively disabled, the culturally disadvantaged, the hyperverbal (overly defended), and the physically and mentally disabled, and in educational settings with people who have no identified problems but who are interested in personal growth. PhotoTherapy can provide alternative ways to communicate, complementing or even bypassing the verbal channels, allowing people to show, rather than just tell. Indeed, people in general (neighbors, friends, relatives) who want to share more intensely can use the same tools to increase their understanding and appreciation of each other's differences and uniqueness.

Using images in therapy is not new. In the past, therapists have approached the challenge of learning more about the inner lives of their clients by utilizing various "projective" techniques. They have shown a stimulus image and asked their clients to comment out loud about the image, indicating any associated thoughts, feelings, and memories. It was believed that these more spontaneous revelations provided insight (in-sight) into areas that might not be uncovered by direct questions or verbal inquiry. Clients have been asked, for example, to look at blobs of ink on paper (the Rorschach ink-blot test) or simple sketches (the Thematic Apperception Test) and give responses. In some cases, answers were simply listened to within the larger contexts of overall therapeutic dialogue; in others, interpretation manuals were consulted to find out how to understand and evaluate the response "properly." In comparisons of the responses from one's client with those given by a standardized "norm" group, measurements were supposed to suggest areas of difficulty or provide diagnostic criteria. The problem in using these standardized tests, however, is that if a client happens to be from a different population, culture, class, or sex from the test's designers, comparison to their standardized norms can often be very inappropriate and lead to distorted conclusions (Weiser, 1986).

In my experience, very effective work in projective imagery can be done using simple cameras and ordinary snapshots to provide those stimuli. Unlike the standardized images, this method is more flexible, open-ended, and ethical. It doesn't matter whether the image is taken by the counselor or the client or pulled from the pages of a magazine or calendar. As long as it visually depicts a slice of frozen time, it can serve the therapeutic purpose extremely well.

For the purposes of PhotoTherapy, I wish to be very clear that the tool we are using is photography as communication, not photography as art. (Esthetics is not the issue, and in fact these techniques work equally well with people who have never used a camera before.) PhotoTherapy uses photography actively, as a verb; as communication, as process in addition to just product-art form, noun alone. Thus, the actual snapshots are equally as effective if they are tattered, folded, stained, or even torn. Projective work can be done with photos taken by the client, provided by the therapist, taken during the counseling session, or gathered from other sources (for example, snapshots belonging to other people, family albums, postcards, pages from old magazines, driver's licenses). Therapy can also be facilitated by the use of photolike scenes, that are only imagined or remembered.

An advantage to using photography is that it is relatively nonthreatening because it is so familiar. Most people have seen snapshots and understand that they represent the "reality" that was in front of the camera at the moment of picture taking. In viewing photos, they unconsciously make the cognitive leap to being there at the moment the camera documented the scene. Further, most people keep those snapshots that have the most intense personal meaning for them—memories of people, places, or times that have strong feelings (usually positive ones) associated with them. People rarely photograph things that don't matter to them. Snapshots that "don't matter" are rarely taken, kept, or given.

People taking pictures usually have a goal in mind. When viewing their creation later, they have a strong idea (though not always conscious) of what they were hoping to capture on film. If the photo pleases them, it does so because they got what they wanted (or better than they expected), and if it does not, they can usually be encouraged to bring to conscious awareness that missing facet that should have been there but wasn't. If asked what would have to change to make the snapshot what they had originally hoped for or expected, they usually can provide answers describing the visual message (and accompanying meaning) that was lacking. It may be hard to describe these things in words, but as many people have expressed, "I'll know it when I see it!"

Although photograph taking and keeping are practically

universal activities, cultural and societal traditions, including sex-role stereotypes, have affected these behaviors over the past century. Males (usually fathers) traditionally have been the family photographers, whereas females (usually mothers) have most often been the family's recorders: making the selections for the album, keeping the album history current, choreographing how the family is publicly presented over time. The behavior of how to be (or how one should be) for the camera most often was directed by the male standards in effect at the time, the "gaze" of the camera most frequently being focused by male attention, values, expectations, and preferences (and, for the most part, pointed at women). This has spilled over into advertising and all other visual media; it has also influenced family documentation of who is important and why, how one must look in order to be part of the accepted family (at least in terms of portraits), and a host of other factors determining how women have been allowed to be seen over the hundred-plus years since the invention of photography (which itself was influenced by earlier centuries of what was allowed into the teaching and expectations of "art").

Gender stereotyping and values dominance are a pervasive component of the photography that is seen today as art; certainly these factors have also long carried over into everyone's ordinary snapshot taking, making, viewing, keeping, and especially posing behavior of women (and men, too, but to a much lesser degree). Evaluating one's own self-image in a photograph cannot help but run into one's expectations of how one "ought to" be looking. In a society where women's role has long been devalued, diminished, and to varying degrees oppressed, it would come as no surprise to find these "scripts" incorporated into the photos that women have learned to make (and expect) of themselves and their loved ones. Even in making choices as to which images are "better" than others, people run into guidelines unconsciously created by sex, class, cultural, and other stereotyping prejudices.

Many authors have focused specifically on these factors that cannot help but influence people's real-life behavior, attitudes, and feelings as they mimic what they have been taught to believe by both history and the media. A whole field of study has been developing over the past few decades to bring to light the unconscious influence and the subsequent damage to women's self-esteem and empowerment that such attitudes can inadvertently bring about (for further reading on this topic, see, for example, Belloff, 1985; Berger, 1972; Braden, 1983; Gassan, 1986; Grover, 1988; Hirsch, 1981; Martin and Spence, 1985; Musello, 1980; Sontag, 1977; Spence, 1978, 1983, 1984, 1986a, 1986b; Roskill and Carrier, 1983).

PhotoTherapy Techniques

The field of PhotoTherapy makes use of several different components of the person-camera-photo interface. The "projective" application conceptually underlies all the others, as any image that one visually encounters automatically involves "projecting" on it in the immediate process of perceiving it, just as all photos are in some ways self-portraits. Anyone who has ever looked at a photo and felt some gut-level response arising from what he or she is seeing is one of the "inventors" of this technique. Anyone who has ever gone to a photo exhibit and wondered what was supposed to be so great about the display that they found terribly boring is him- or herself demonstrating how selective perception works.

If we look at a group of several photos and are asked to comment about some in relation to others, it is possible to learn how we judge, evaluate, and prioritize one thing, person, place, or event in relation to others. How things are similar or different, how we know what we know, what would have to change for our perception of that photo to be different are clues to our underlying value system and our unique personality. When viewed within a therapeutic context, such details will be rich in information about personal data that is difficult for words alone to reveal. As a result, they can help people to get their lives "in better focus."

PhotoTherapeutic techniques can be useful with almost any client group of any age in any culture (Weiser, 1988a; Ziller and Smith, 1977; Ziller and Lewis, 1981; Ziller, Rorer, Combs, and Lewis 1983) or setting (Combs and Ziller, 1971; Krauss, 1983; Weiser, 1988b; Zwick, 1981), in direct psychotherapy and counseling (Cornelison and Arsenian, 1960; Gosciewski, 1975; Hunsberger, 1984; Wikler, 1977; Wolf, 1976, 1982, 1983), in rehabilitation (Phillips, 1986; Mann, 1983; Zabar, 1987), in education (Ammerman and Fryrear, 1975; Hogan, 1981a, 1981b; Nath, 1981, 1984; Weaver, 1983), and even in preventive work (Williams and Williams, 1981; Zwick, 1978).

Most creative and effective practitioners use PhotoTherapy techniques in various combinations because they really are an integrally related system. Like so many holistic approaches, these techniques suffer somewhat from having to be analyzed in a disjointed or linear manner. Nonetheless, what follows is a brief description of some of the techniques that therapists can be trained to use.

Projectives. Viewing photos usually results in some sort of response: feelings appear, memories are recalled, thoughts are associated. We can place ourselves in the photo to explore alternative possibilities, consider options in the role of photographer, project emotions and "scripts" onto the image coming from our own life, and create themes, stories, or larger contexts. While traditional projective techniques tend to require a passive viewing procedure, there are several active applications of photo projectives, such as phototaking and photo-gathering assignments, which can even include using cameras without film. It is the process of interacting with the snapshots as much as the image content itself that is of importance in PhotoTherapy applications. The information and emotions revealed almost as by-products, as contexts, for the photographic investigations are what prove so valuable. Nonjudgmentally listening, observing, and questioning in response to photographic imagery stimuli in the lives of those we help are tools of vast potential. What the client sees as relevant or selects for responding to usually tells us more about that person than the subject content of the stimulus image itself. Even abstract or blurry images can be used because they may evoke gut-level feelings and responses even though the person may not be able to explain them verbally (Walker, 1983).

Historical/Album/Biographical Photos. Clients with long-buried and well-defended emotions may respond less guardedly to a visual stimulus. Thus, photos can be used to reconnect them with strong memories and feelings around past events, people, places, and times, because we view them as if they were happening right now. Family photos, home movies, and videos offer proof of existence over time, documenting permanence and change, continuity, roots, traditions, values, and degree of freedom for the individual within it all. These snapshots can give insights to the full system of several generations, to relationships, and to networks. Clients see themselves and their contexts and thus are better able to appreciate existing situations and feelings and even, perhaps, recognize the source of many expectations.

Photos Taken by the Client. The photos we take and the decision process we go through in taking them—our desired outcomes and reasons for a particular choice—can indicate what is important in our values and beliefs. If they don't work out as expected, asking what went wrong and what it would take for them to become successful can be equally revealing. A careful probing of the chosen moments recorded in photos can reveal themes and interests, personal metaphors, and symbols that the client was possibly unaware of at the time of shooting. Specific assignments can be given to explore particular areas of concern, while more open-ended, creative projects can yield further insights.

Photos of the Client Taken by Others. How other people see us gives us an idea of how we present ourselves to the world; in dialogue with others (or with their photos of us), we gain valuable clues to the identity we convey. This is often a safe channel for interpersonal feedback, as different interpretations of the same photo can be compared. In realizing that different people photograph the "real" us differently, we come to appreciate the flexibility of our identity and our possibilities, as well as to recognize the limitations of labeling ourselves and others.

Self-Portraits. The issues of self-image, self-esteem, self-acceptance, and self-confidence lie at the core of most therapeutic work. Self-portraits provide a powerful way to gain access to these concepts, and thus people often find them the most threatening and risky kinds of photos to encounter. If carefully guided during their most vulnerable moments, clients can explore, confront, and engage in dialogue with themselves (using still photo self-portraits or video therapy self-confrontation) and document for themselves any changes that are occurring.

Video. Videotape techniques greatly enhance client ability to mediate and document the growth and change process through immediate, delayed, and long-range replay applications. Video provides numerous opportunities for self-discovery, confrontation, direct access to emotions and affect, nonverbal messages, study of family or group structure, and interaction otherwise unavailable in direct verbal-only sessions. As clients find viewing themselves live in motion an unarguable documentation of how they communicate and present themselves, they may speed the therapy process by assuming more responsibility for their own actions.

The following section provides an in-depth discussion of the use of the projective technique in PhotoTherapy. As this chapter is concerned primarily with the use of photos as projectives, other PhotoTherapy techniques are not discussed in full detail. The references at the end of this chapter list many useful readings. In addition, the PhotoTherapy Centre offers training and workshops in the use of PhotoTherapy techniques and maintains a file of more than 200 articles, books, and other reference literature documenting projects and studies using photos as therapeutic tools. For further information or to order the Centre's twenty-three-page reference bibliography, readers may contact the author at the PhotoTherapy Centre, 1107 Homer Street, Suite 304, Vancouver, B.C., Canada, V6B 2Y1, phone 604/689-9709.

How to Use Snapshots as Projectives

There is no single "right" way to take or interpret any given photograph; each person's interpretation is extremely idiosyncratic. Similarly, there is no single right way to do PhotoTherapy; each technique is flexible and can be interwoven with others to tailor the approach for the particular therapeutic goal being worked on. Depending on the desired outcome (for example, increased self-awareness, improved self-esteem, individuality and differentiation, personal insight, improved communication with others, reduction of prejudice), techniques such as photo projectives can be molded to fit the need and assignments designed to guide the direction of growth desired.

Responses to viewing photos do not necessarily have to be verbal, immediate, or even consistent from one encounter to another with the same image. Therapists doing projective work are not looking for *the* answer, some specific missing link that they are trying to get the client to discover. Rather, they use the photo as an initial tool for making contact and gaining rapport with clients through dialogue that initially concentrates on the symbols in the image and then moves its focus to the client (Krauss, 1983). During this process, clients often supply additional information and will also "correct" therapists' mistakes in analysis or interpretation. As a result of this process, clients can have more awareness and a better understanding of their personal symbols (Krauss, 1981).

Photo-Projective techniques can be an excellent way to demonstrate that we all see the same thing differently, that there is no "right" and "wrong" existing a priori out there independent of our perceptions of it:

> A couple viewed a collection of photos on my office wall, and the wife was particularly drawn to a "cute" photo I took of a young girl hugging a cat. (See Photo 1.)
>
> *She:* That's so sweet, such a loving hug, it's all homey and warm and comfortable. They look so happy together.
>
> *He:* My God she's smothering that poor animal—How can you call that 'love'; it's pure suffocation! If she'd let go, that cat would dash away immediately, and if she kept grabbing it like that every time it came near, it would never stay close. The only way it would stick around would be if she relaxed her grip and waited for it to approach her!
>
> When probed further, the couple was able to see how, through their projections onto the photo, they

Photo 1.

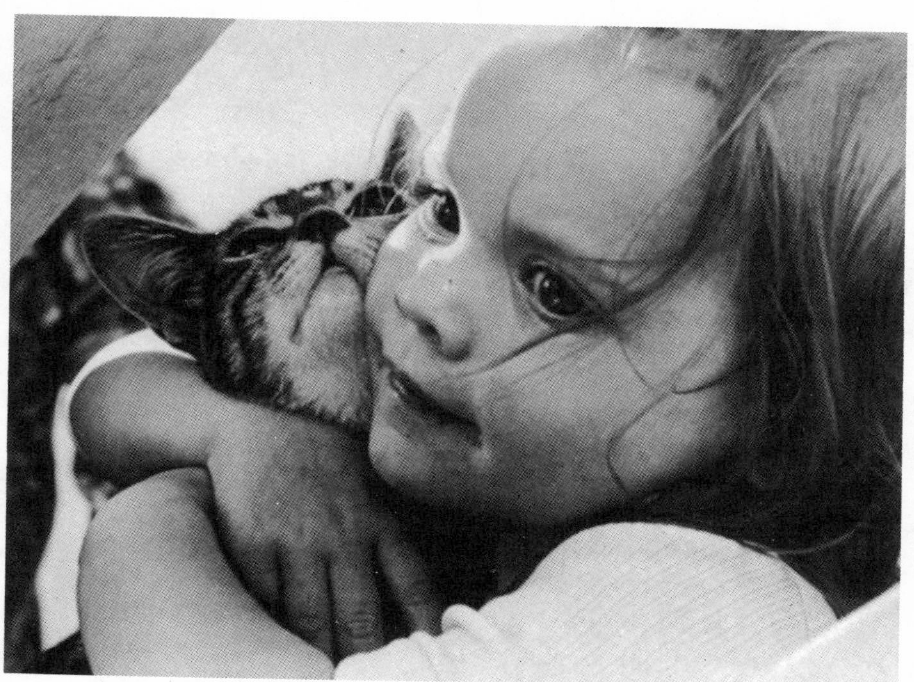

had actually been expressing some of their relationship difficulties: the wife was from a very traditional home-centered and religious family, and doted on her husband, actually following him from room to room when he returned home from work at night. She was jealous of any outside interests he might have, not comprehending that his need for time to himself was not meant to be hurtful to her, but rather would renew him for more mature communication if she would only "loosen her grip a bit" and give him "breathing room."

A mother and her adult daughter, upon viewing another photo of mine of a woman leaning on a fence holding a watering hose (see Photo 2), came face-to-face (somewhat literally) with their differing perceptions of sex roles and work attitudes (and generations) when discussing how the woman in the photo "was feeling":

Mom: She's so relaxed and dreamy; the kids are in school, her husband's at work, her chores are done, and she's got time to herself while she waits for them all to come home.

Daughter: What a terribly bored person she is! Look at her posture and her slouch. She's smoking and probably strung out on tranquilizers! An empty aimless existence, doing nothing and expecting nothing; just the same routine day in and day out—no wonder she's so depressed!

[Weiser, 1988b, pp. 260–261; reprinted with permission of Hogrefe Publishers.]

In applications such as those described above, therapists are not particularly concerned with "correctness" of answers given to questions probing selected images but are rather concerned with the myriad additional clues to clients' nonverbal evaluating and judging systems that come through "sideways" during the dialogue, while clients think they are discussing the photo itself. Projective work is most effective when the therapist is simply listening carefully for what goes by in apparently ordinary conversations about snapshots, using the photos to focus the subject matter under discussion. The therapist waits without any fixed agenda to hear (and then make use of) material that appears as unconscious by-products to these discussions. In the first example above, I proceeded to explore the husband's response to his wife's comments, probing to see whether she felt validated and needed in their relationship. I asked her to visualize her animal symbol for him and share that discussion with him for further feedback. In the second example, the women were encouraged to further compare and contrast their real with

Photo 2.

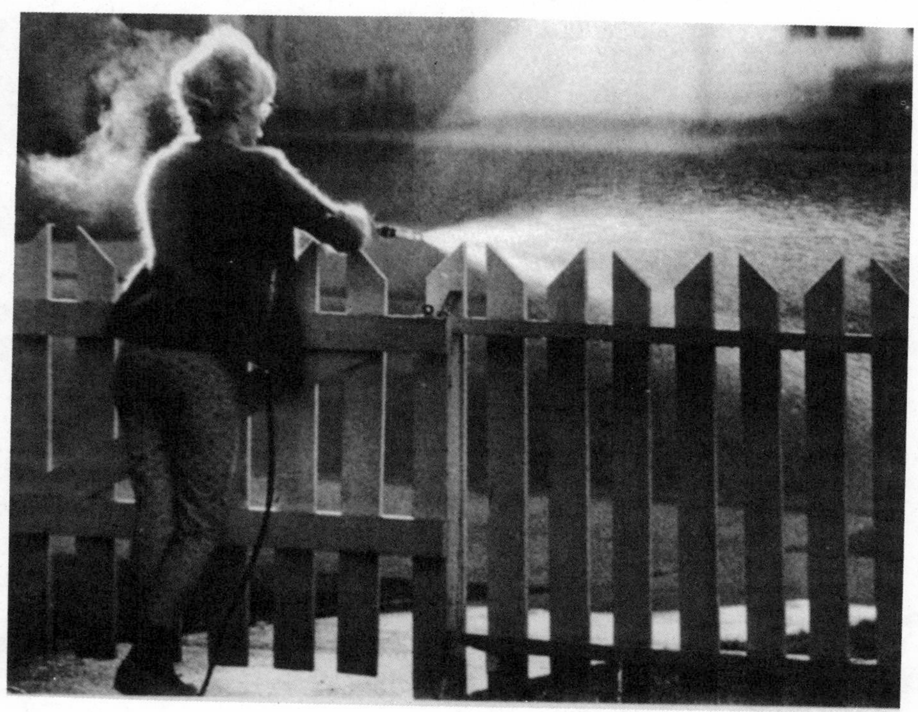

their ideal lives, noting differences but recognizing where these came from in their backgrounds and respecting them for what they represented.

One interesting technique is to show a collection of several photos of various people and ask clients questions relevant to the particular focus of the therapy, such as "Which of these people do you think is a/an ______ ?" (choosing categories that are appropriate to the specific therapeutic inquiry, such as artist, teacher, homosexual, cancer patient, dyslexic, farmer, and so on). The actual answer is secondary to the information and emotions that emerge as people explain *how* they knew their answer. Thus, the immediately accompanying question to all these exploratory "guessing games" should be some version of "Why?" Questions such as "Which of these people do you suppose is sad (divorced, deaf, and so on)? What in the image do you think gave you those clues?" explore how the person uses visual cues to create meaning and code differences. This technique can also be used to explore nonverbally stored prejudices with photos of people of different ethnic backgrounds, classes, sexual orientations, ages, and so forth. The therapist might ask, "Which one do you think is a recent immigrant?" "Which are on welfare?" "Which is a bank manager (or former prisoner, or very rich, and so on)?" and then explore how these answers were arrived at and what would have to change visually in the images for the response to be a different one.

These judgment exercises can be used on a more emotional level with questions such as "Which person seems to you to be content with their life?" "Which would you like to meet?" "Which would you be afraid to have as a next-door neighbor?" "Which do you think could be having the same kinds of problems you are experiencing?" "If you could go somewhere with any of these people, who would you pick, where would you go, and what would the conversations and feelings be like?" There is no set list of questions; rather, the therapist begins in a general manner and then focuses on areas that seem more worth examining, moving from the relative safety of generalities into the more vulnerable and risky specifics. The therapeutic interest lies not just in the direct answers given but also in the explanations for why each answer was as it was. Unconscious attitudes, biases, and expectations may be revealed.

It is sometimes helpful for therapists to provide their own contrasting perceptions, not to claim "truth" or overpower the clients' right to have their own interpretation but rather to share how differently two people might perceive the same clue or detail whose initial meaning for them could be so different: "You know, if I were that woman, I'd be holding my head like that to indicate disapproval, not shyness; I wonder how it is that you and I see the message her pose suggests so differently—let's talk about this for a while."

In seeing that a given snapshot is interpreted so differently by people they thought they knew quite well (a spouse, a friend, a sibling), clients are freed to appreciate and explore these differences. Photo projectives are a tangible way for clients to realize for themselves (rather than being told) that their position is not necessarily the only way to look at things, that others' perceptions and feelings are just as valid, that in real life there is not necessarily just one right answer to be found. Once one recognizes such differences and differentness as acceptable and natural, they can become less threatening; in family work particularly, this can be a major step toward differentiation from one's own family of origin and toward more maturity and independence.

Obviously, if a client is verbally fluent in fully expressing memories and emotions, photo-projective work may not be necessary. However, when the client is not verbally fluent, or when direct verbal work seems too threatening, the therapist can bring in photos for the client to discuss. Alternatively, the client could be given an assignment to go out and photograph (or find from magazines) images along a particular theme ("Bring in photos of people who look tired," "Go take pictures of things that make you angry," "Find and photograph four objects that you believe symbolize you," and so on). The photo can be a supportive ally in serving as a "proof" of what the client feels but may not yet be assertive enough to risk stating directly. The following is an example of how this can work.

> "You told me to bring in some pictures of women I could tell were divorced/single mothers," L. stated. "So here they are!" I scanned the twenty or so photos she'd torn from magazine pages and placed before me, and was struck by what seemed to me to be the dismal, severe, austere, empty and sad tone of all the images. None of the women pictured seemed to me to be happy, relaxed, or self-content.
>
> I asked her to pick one photo: "Please 'be' this woman, and tell me how you are feeling, what you are thinking, and what you might want," I requested. In "becoming" the pictured woman, she spoke of exhaustion, frustration, and depression—feelings she had not been able to "own" when earlier describing her life as a single mother. Previously she'd presented

> herself as competent, coping, and calmly accepting. Once she compared and explored the "real" perceptions with the "ideal" she was demanding of herself, she was able to accept herself as someone with faults and negative emotions, who was nonetheless worthy of knowing just "as is" rather than having to wait until she became perfect before she could risk trusting others.

What clients notice in a photo can give clues to their past as well as to their present feelings. Information that has been buried can surface unexpectedly (Krauss, 1980). Whereas words are often met with denial, photos frequently touch the pain at unexpected depths and demand cathartic release. For example, in portraits of children, people sometimes perceive the faces that they themselves remember making with their own abusive families. They identify a whole story of abuse and cover-up.

> One of my own photos of a young child solemnly peering out of a window has called forth many different kinds of responses ("She's wishing she was off at school with her older sisters"; "she's dreaming about being a princess"; "she's daydreaming, but can smell the cake in the oven almost ready"; and the like). One woman's casual comments, "She knows someone is watching her and doesn't want to show any expression on her face" tweaked my therapeutic curiosity, and as I asked further questions ("What kinds of feelings do you think she would show if she could? What would happen if she did?"; "Where are all the other members of her family? What would she want to say to them?"; "If she had a magic wand and could change anything in her life that she wanted to, what do you think she would do?"), she began to relate previously undisclosed details about her childhood that she hadn't told anyone in a long time, about her father's physical and sexual abuse of her and his threats to kill her cat if she told anyone. This began her healing process.

Projective work is also possible with a group of several photographs—what one can do with a single snapshot can be exponentially increased with several. Simply giving a person a pile of fifty to a hundred photos (old magazine pictures, whatever) with instructions to "sort these into groups that 'go together' or 'fit' with each other" can produce nonverbal insight into how people order their world, how they separate out the categories that matter. From a similar pile, clients can be instructed to "choose *X* numbers of photos" (either open-ended without guidelines, or with particularly focused ones, such as "places you'd like to go to" or "photos that particularly catch your attention" or "people you'd like as friends") and then explore how (and why) they made their choices. Ideally, of course, these and all other PhotoTherapy exercises would be videotaped, so that people could explore not only their verbal reflections of choices made but also their nonverbal behavior in the actual process of thinking, pondering, and choosing.

Collections of photos can then be used to make collages or put into an order for storytelling. The images can thus be connected by the client into a theme or narrative. They can also be used so that the client "becomes" all or part of each image ("I am the photo; I would title myself ______ or like to say ______." "I am the tree; I feel ______." "I am the chair; I remember ______.") Each thought or feeling projected on the visual components is tried out for possible ownership on the self. Alternatively, one can select a few photos that collectively "stand for" a particular thought or feeling or that can be used to create a script.

Clients can speak to and with the snapshots, asking them questions and telling them important messages. Or they can respond to questions and comments that they imagine the photo would say if it could speak. They can also describe an imagined dialogue between two photos or provide titles or captions for each. Frames of the borders can be imaginarily pulled back to see what else might be "in" there. Therapists may invite clients to step into the image and walk around in it, looking back to the original photographer to imagine why the photo was taken in the first place or even to ask direct questions. Clients can predict what happened at the moment before or after the shutter was snapped, what other pictures that photographer took that day, where the people in the photo went after it was taken, and what they did then. The possibilities are endless!

The role for the therapist in all this is not only to seize the big nuggets of information and emotional responses that occur directly in the process but also to collect all the seemingly innocent little tidbits and by-products that can be processed at a later time. It is strongly stressed that therapists using these techniques cannot presume to interpret photos *for* clients; the input should come at all times from the client guided by the therapist's questions, with there being no "wrong" answers possible (though comparing each other's differing perceptions is certainly encouraged).

Similarly, a person's responses cannot, on their own, indicate any particular problem or illness—no analytical decisions can be made from singular responses; competent therapists trained in using these techniques are looking for patterns, response clusters, consistencies through time and often generations, unusual or symbolic content, and, most of all, emotional responses indicating inner feelings that may or may not be conscious. Thus, the therapist's primary role is to encourage and support the client's own personal discoveries, using various forms of photography as an active partner in the process. Although the art of photography can be appreciated for itself while PhotoTherapy is done, it is more "photography as a verb" that is important here.

Most of the examples in this chapter describe events that occurred during my private practice as a psychologist and art therapist. Since 1982, I have been giving introductory and advanced training workshops in PhotoTherapy techniques, in addition to maintaining a private therapy case load. However, since 1986 I have taken no new private clients, as I have become a PhotoTherapy trainer full-time, choosing to work at the metalevel of sharing these skills indirectly by teaching other therapists and counselors how to make use of them for the benefit of their own clients. Workshop participants are not clients per se but rather other mental health professionals learning through their own personal experience with the various PhotoTherapy techniques exactly how it *feels* to work with these tools (before putting their own clients through the experience). Sometimes the experiences are quite similar to what would take place in a therapeutic setting, yet they take place with people who were not required to have specific problems in order to learn. In fact, the workshop is clearly advertised as "not for personal therapy," so all personal occurrences are purely voluntary. One interaction between myself and a workshop student demonstrates the immediate intensity, power, and vast potential of photo-interactive dialogue (Weiser, 1988b, pp. 263–265).

A student, Jenny, was quite taken with a portrait of a woman. (See Photo 3.) Jenny stated that she felt a fondness for this woman, that the woman was probably an artist or a dancer and very talented. I asked her to imagine becoming that woman, and Jenny immediately smiled in pleasure at the thought. She assumed the pose, gazed into the distance, and told me that she was viewing a peaceful sunset. When I asked her what the woman would say if she could speak, Jenny replied, without a moment's hesitation, "When I think of you I feel love in my heart," looking rather surprised that these words had so spontaneously popped out. Because it was a workshop setting rather than client work, I could not probe further individually, but I suggested that, since we were videotaping, she consider reviewing the tape sometime if she'd like, and we could talk further.

Three years later, Jenny reappeared and asked whether she could watch the videotape from that workshop session. Something in her life was bothering her, she had a deep sadness that she couldn't get connected with consciously, and she thought that she had touched on it at the earlier workshop and wanted a "second glance." While she watched several sections of the tape, I was surprised to hear, from the viewing room, her talking out loud *to* the tape. When I could tactfully interrupt, I found that she had realized upon this re-viewing that in her mind the photo represented her mother, who had been an artist for many years. It was almost identical to an actual photo of her mother at age twenty-two, in much the same pose. Jenny had carried that photo for years, as she had been living a continent apart from her family.

Jenny's revelation was her discovery that her sadness was meaningful. The photo reminded her of the times when her mother had experienced schizophrenic breakdowns and wasn't in touch with reality. The unfocused gaze was one indicator of when she was not in touch, and this triggered Jenny's sadness. She explained, "As

Photo 3.

her daughter, this was very difficult to understand. When she was at her most creative and beautiful, like in that photo, it was the most scary for me. I guess my quick comment about 'love in my heart' wasn't what the woman in the photo would say, but rather what I wanted to somehow say to her, my mother, the love (and acceptance) in my own heart for her!"

At the time of the workshop, her elderly mother had recently experienced a major crisis and was planning to move in with Jenny. Jenny expressed ambivalence, anger, and apprehension about the idea. We also explored her "mother" gazing at the sunset as a possible metaphor for an ending, a closing, perhaps even her mother's impending death, or Jenny's loss of freedom from her mother's nearness, events they could not yet discuss out loud. But this understanding had not been consciously available at the time of Jenny's original interaction with that portrait and did not surface into awareness until three years later. Jenny's account of this experience is included at the end of this chapter.

Conclusion

Photos are only split-second recordings of time, a quick slice of reality frozen forever—we do not want to give them disproportionate power, only to make use of them as tools when they can help people better understand themselves and others. Every photo we respond to, take, pose for, or decide to keep, give away, or throw out is in some way a projection of and from ourselves, a self-portrait revealing something personal, meaningful, and even symbolic. As a visual language far beyond verbal limitations, ordinary snapshots are worth far more than the proverbial thousand words, if only we have the eyes with which to clearly listen. As a young client so eloquently expressed it when I told her that I still had the school photo of her that she had given me months before, "Good! If you still have my photo, then I'm still safe in your heart!"

Workshop Participant's Voice: Jenny Nash

I am looking at a table covered with many photographs. There are scenic views, cars, buildings, people of all kinds and colors. I am drawn to one photograph in particular. I pick it up and hold it in my hand. This is a beautiful young lady with long wavy fair hair. Judy looks over my shoulder: "What kind of person is she? Is she a student? What's she doing? Tell me about her. Does she work? Is she on welfare?"

I laugh at the idea that she could be on welfare and exclaim in surprise, "Oh, no, she is definitely not on welfare. She is an artist of some kind, possibly studying fine arts. She paints delicately and finely. I don't think she is working for money as an artist. She just loves to express herself through art."

Judy asks me, "What is she thinking about?" I say without hesitation, "She is thinking of the one she loves." Judy says, "If she could speak, what would she be saying?" I respond, "When I'm with you, I feel love in my heart." Judy asks me to pose like the woman in the photograph. I sit with my chin on my hand and gaze into the distance. I feel sad as I sit in this pose. Judy asks me what do I see; I reply that I am looking at a sunset. The sunset fills me with sadness, and I am reminded of endings. Judy is asking something; I am feeling afraid that I will burst into tears, and I am aware that I feel self-conscious with this group of strangers—for a while I had forgotten their existence. I am remembering a sunset now in Mexico, a beautiful orange ball sinking into the ocean, and I am with a man I love. This relationship ended many years ago, and I am wondering why I should think of it now. Judy asks me if I want to stop or go on with this exploration. I choose to stop.

I go home and look through many photo albums until I find a sunset photograph that I know I want to take back with me to the workshop the following day. I look at the sunset picture and remember all the trials and struggles of this old romance in Mexico. I know that love relationships, the complications of trying to understand a loved one and be understood in return, and endings, are very much on my mind right now, although at this point in the workshop I am not sure why.

The following day I am looking at the same lady again. Judy asks me how I know she is not on welfare. I say that the shiny glossy hair shows she washes it with good shampoo and conditioner each day. Judy asks me something about my own hair. I have a sudden flash of my mother recently asking me how often I wash my daughter's hair. I have this feeling of sadness again, and now I realize that my mother seems to be disapproving and critical of the way I am parenting my small daughter. I say out loud that I have lived in Canada for seventeen years away from my parents; I have encouraged my mother to come to Canada from England so she can be near her only daughter (and only grandchild). It seems terribly important to me that my mother approves of me and approves of the way I am parenting my daughter.

As I hear the seriousness of my own voice, I have to laugh. Why can't I relax around my mother and appreciate that of course she will have different viewpoints from me and of course she has every right to express them. I feel the laughter leave and feel the terrible hurt and pain inside me. I am crying and raging all at the same time now. My mother leaned on me as a child, told me all of her problems with her husband (my father), and I felt I would explode with all the woes that my mother suffered and dumped on me. Why didn't she tell her husband how she hated him; why me all the time? I am really sobbing now. I left England to be able to breathe, to be my own person, to not have my mother living her life through me, to be living her life only for her children—why couldn't she live her own life? Why can't she live her own life now? That's it, *that* is what bothers me. While my mother is checking on whether I bathe and wash my daughter often enough, and worries aloud about how can I possibly work and be a good mother at the same time, I am feeling that old familiar feeling of being lived through.

My mother finally divorced my father when she was sixty-nine years old after forty years of misery. I encouraged my mother to come to this country when she was seventy-two years old, and I am terribly afraid that our relationship will continue as it always was. I will continue to listen to stories about what an awful man my father is and was, and my mother will take a close interest in my life and I will feel smothered, unable to breathe, unable to be my own person. I want my mother to accept me as I am, that is, a mother who works, a mother who washes her child's hair twice a week, and so on. Why can't I accept my mother the way she is? A mother who worries about her daughter getting stretched too thin by being a working mother; a mother who wants her grandchild to look clean, well dressed, and to never forget to say please and thank you.

Ah, now, that *really* sticks in my craw; something here smacks of how horrible I felt at not being able to run, balance on curbs, get dirty, swim, ride a bike. How I looked to others seemed extremely important, but what about how I felt inside, Mum? I felt so lonely. We didn't mix with many people. I didn't seem to play with other children. I remember you telling me to pull my socks up, when I was just trying to be brave enough to speak to a little boy in my first year in school. Who cares whether my socks were up or down? Not me—I cared to try to connect to other children. Judy sums up some of what I've been rambling about, and I feel tired and empty.

Our assignment now is to take our camera outside and photograph anything we like. This workshop is at the university. I walk out into the campus grounds and photograph a couple in love. This couple are from my workshop. I follow the couple, taking five or six shots of them walking through flowers, stopping to look at a waterfall, and finally eating lunch in the cafeteria. I now take a park bench shot. The scene is peaceful—an empty bench sitting in nature, flowers in bloom, trees fluffy and green. I walk alone feeling content. I pick two violets and place one in each of my shoes, poking the stems through the lace holes. I smile at my feet.

Judy asks us to pose ourselves in any way that we'd like, an open-ended assignment with absolutely no rules of how we "should" behave for the camera. A photograph is taken with Polaroid instant film, so that we can see it and work with it immediately. I pose like the woman in the photograph. I am pleased with the photograph and label myself "The Philosopher."

The next exercise is to study the Polaroid picture and see if there is something we want others to know about us that doesn't show in this particular pose (actual assignment: "Photograph the 'you' you would be if you weren't being the 'you' you are now!"). Right away I know I want a picture of my feet since they are not showing in the first shot. I now pose my legs and feet, and particularly want the flowers on the shoes to show up. I am pleased with the second picture too and label myself "The Fool."

I am asked to make notes about each photograph. The *Phi-*

losopher is the worrier who worries about what others think—the one who wishes to please—the one who analyzes how to please—the one who is very alert—very present—wakes up with the sunrise. Now the *Fool,* however, is without a brain, spontaneous, spontaneous as a child—hasn't a care about what others think.

Judy asks me to hold up the two photographs facing each other, and have them speak to one another:

Philosopher: I am alert and tuned in to people. I understand them because I listen so attentively. I please many people. I am a good girl.

Fool: I don't want to be a good person. I want to have fun, dance, play, and laugh. I want space for myself. I love to be alone with the sunset.

Judy asks if it is safer to say I am a "Fool" rather than a "Dancer" (as the Fool appears in the photo to be dancing). I have to admit that I would love to be a dancer and do love to dance, but it would seem conceited to say I am a dancer, since in a traditional sense I am not. Yet when I change the words to "I am a dancer" instead of "I am a Fool," I experience this smile throughout my whole being, which finally is expressed on my face.

Judy asks, "Does your mother dance?" I say the times that stand out for me were my mother dancing in the living room and trying to kick up over the door knob. She would laugh and express joy as she danced, and she would appear worry-free for once. She only danced for her children, though. She certainly *didn't* dance for my father.

As I speak now about my mother, I can feel the love in me that I have for her. I realize in some ways how much we are alike. I think I have grown beyond my mother in that I have conquered many fears that my mother has not conquered, particularly fears of men. I find it hard to not push my mother toward exploring more of herself. Yet I realize that this was a courageous move for my mother, to risk coming to Canada. I need to relax around my mother and accept her just the way she is, without compromising who I am or twisting myself about to please her. I want my mother and myself to have a good relationship as the end of her days draws near. Sometimes I want to push our relationship to work more easily since I feel we are running out of time. However, I realize that if I can relax and not react to what seems like criticism from my mother, then I can help our relationship to be different from the way it was when I was young.

References

Ammerman, M. S., and Fryrear, J. L. "Photographic Self Enhancement of Children's Self-Esteem." *Psychology in the Schools,* 1975, *12* (3), pp. 319–325.

Belloff, H. *Camera Culture.* New York: Basil Blackwell, 1985.

Berger, J. *Ways of Seeing.* New York: Penguin Books, 1972.

Braden, S. *Committing Photography.* London: Pluto Press, 1983.

Combs, J. M., and Ziller, R. C. "Photographic Self-Concept of Counsellees." *Journal of Counselling Psychology,* 1977, *24* (5), pp. 452–455.

Cornelison, F. S., and Arsenian, J. "A Study of the Response of Psychotic Patients to Photographic Self-Image Experience." *Psychiatric Quarterly,* 1960, *34,* pp. 1–8.

Gassan, A. *Summary Report on Father-Daughter Incest Research Using Photographs and the Semantic Differential.* Athens, Ohio: A. Gassan, 1986.

Gosciewski, W. F. "Photo Counselling." *Personnel & Guidance Journal,* 1975, *53* (8), pp. 600–604.

Grover, J. Z. "Beyond the Family Album—The Autobiography of Jo Spence." *Afterimage,* Feb. 1988, pp. 8–10.

Hirsch, J. *Family Photographs: Content, Meaning, and Effect.* New York: Oxford University Press, 1981.

Hogan, P. "Photo Therapy in the Educational Setting." *Arts in Psychotherapy,* 1981a, *3* (4), pp. 193–199.

Hogan, P. "The Uses of Group Photo Therapy in the Classroom." *PhotoTherapy Quarterly,* 1981b, *2* (4), p. 13.

Hunsberger, P. "Uses of Instant-Print Photography in Psychotherapy." *Professional Psychology: Research and Practice,* 1984, *15* (6), pp. 884–890.

Krauss, D. A. "A Summary of Characteristics of Photographs

Which Make Them Useful in Counselling and Therapy." *Camera Lucida,* 1980, *1* (2), pp. 2–12.

Krauss, D. A. "Photography, Imaging, and Visually Referent Language in Therapy: Illuminating the Metaphor." *Camera Lucida,* 1981, *1* (5), pp. 58–63.

Krauss, D. A. "Reality, Photography, and Psychotherapy, and the Visual Metaphor: Some Underlying Assumptions of Phototherapy." In D. A. Krauss and J. L. Fryrear (eds.), *Phototherapy in Mental Health.* Springfield, Ill.: Thomas, 1983.

Mann, L. M. "An Album of Albums: Phototherapy with Schizophrenic Adults." Unpublished master's degree thesis, Lesley College Graduate School, 1983.

Martin, R., and Spence, J. "New Portraits for Old: The Use of the Camera in Therapy." *Feminist Review,* 1985, *19,* pp. 66–92.

Musello, C. "Studying the Home Mode: An Exploration of Family Photography and Visual Communication." *Studies in Visual Communication,* 1980, *6* (1), pp. 24–41.

Nath, J. "Phototherapy in the Education of the Mentally Handicapped Child." Unpublished master's degree thesis, Faculty of Education, University of British Columbia, 1981.

Nath, J. "The Use of Still Photography as Learning Assistance for the Language Handicapped in the Classroom." *Phototherapy,* 1984, *4* (1), pp. 15–17.

Phillips, D. "Photography's Use as a Metaphor of Self with Stabilized Schizophrenic Patients." *Arts in Psychotherapy,* 1986, *13* (1), pp. 9–16.

Roskill, M., and Carrier, D. *Truth and Falsehood in Visual Images.* Boston: University of Massachusetts Press, 1983.

Sontag, S. *On Photography.* New York: Farrar, Straus & Giroux, 1977.

Spence, J. "Facing Up to Myself." *Spare Rib,* 1978 (68), pp. 6–9.

Spence, J. "War Photos: The Home Front." Unpublished master's degree thesis, London Polytechnic, 1983.

Spence, J. "Public Images/Private Functions: Reflections on High Street Practice." *Ten-8/Face Values,* 1984 (13), pp. 7–17.

Spence, J. *Photo Therapy. Venue,* 1986a, *14* (101), pp. 48–49.

Spence, J. *Putting Myself in the Picture: A Political Personal and Photographic Autobiography.* London: Camden Press, 1986b.

Walker, J. "See and Tell." *Phototherapy Quarterly,* 1980, *2* (3), pp. 14–15.

Walker, J. "The Photograph as a Catalyst in Psychotherapy." In D. A. Krauss and J. L. Fryrear (eds.), *Phototherapy in Mental Health.* Springfield, Ill.: Thomas, 1983.

Weaver, P. L. "Photography: A Picture of Learning." *Phototherapy,* 1983, *3* (4), pp. 6–12.

Weiser, J. "PhotoTherapy: Photography as a Verb." *BC Photographer,* 1975, *2,* pp. 33–36.

Weiser, J. "Using Photographs in Therapy with People Who Are 'Different.'" In D. A. Krauss and J. L. Fryrear (eds.), *Phototherapy in Mental Health.* Springfield, Ill.: Thomas, 1983.

Weiser, J. "Training and Teaching of Photo and Video Therapy: Central Themes, Core Knowledge, and Important Considerations." *Phototherapy,* 1985, *4* (4), pp. 9–16.

Weiser, J. "Ethical Considerations in PhotoTherapy Training and Practice." *Phototherapy,* 1986, *5* (1), pp. 12–17.

Weiser, J. "PhotoTherapy: Using Snapshots and Photo-Interactions in Therapy with Youth." In C. Schaefer (ed.), *Innovative Interventions in Child and Adolescent Therapy.* New York: Wiley, 1988a.

Weiser, J. "'See What I Mean?'" Photography as Nonverbal Communication in Cross-Cultural Psychology." In F. Poyatos (ed.), *Cross-Cultural Perspectives in Nonverbal Communication.* Toronto: Hogrefe, 1988b.

Weiser, J. "What You See Is What You Get: Using Ordinary Snapshots as 'Projectives' in Counselling." In V. Scalingi (ed.), Special projects manual. Cambridge, Mass.: Polaroid Corporation, forthcoming.

Wikler, M. E. "Using Photographs in the Termination Phase." *Social Work,* 1977, *22* (4), pp. 318–319.

Williams, R. D., and Williams, R. C. M. "Photography as Bridge Between Institution and Community: A Preventive Intervention." *Phototherapy Quarterly,* 1981, *2* (4), pp. 8–12.

Wolf, R. "The Polaroid Technique: Spontaneous Dialogues from the Unconscious." *Art Psychotherapy,* 1976, *3* (3–4), pp. 197–201.

Wolf, R. "Instant Phototherapy: Some Theoretical and Clinical

Considerations for Its Use in Psychotherapy and in Special Education." *Phototherapy,* 1982, *3* (1), pp. 3–6.

Wolf, R. "Instant Phototherapy with Children and Adolescents." In D. A. Krauss and J. L. Fryrear (eds.), *Phototherapy in Mental Health.* Springfield, Ill.: Thomas, 1983.

Zabar, S. "Photo-Expressive Activities in the Health Care Environment." *Phototherapy,* 1987, *6* (1), pp. 2–6.

Ziller, R. C., and Lewis, D. "Orientation: Self, Social, and Environmental Percepts Through Auto-Photography." *Personality and Social Psychology Bulletin,* 1981, *7,* pp. 338–343.

Ziller, R. C., Rorer, B., Combs, J. M., and Lewis, D. "The Psychological Niche: The Auto-Photographic Study of Self-Environment Interaction." In D. A. Krauss and J. L. Fryrear (eds.), *Phototherapy in Mental Health.* Springfield, Ill.: Thomas, 1983.

Ziller, R. C., and Smith, D.E.A. "Phenomenological Utilization of Photographs." *Journal of Phenomenological Psychology,* 1977, *7* (2), pp. 172–185.

Zwick, D. S. "Photography as a Tool Toward Increased Awareness of the Aging Self." *Art Psychotherapy,* 1978, *5,* pp. 135–141.

Zwick, D. S. "Photo Therapy as an Adjunct to Group Process: A Project Review of 'Fostering Adolescent Social Interest: A Photographic Approach.'" *Phototherapy,* 1981, *2* (4), p. 177.

7

Seeds of Thought, Arrows of Change: Native Storytelling as Metaphor

Yvonne Rita Dion Buffalo
Storyteller: Yvonne Rita Dion Buffalo

nimosom
Great-Grandfather called me
Ebon, Ebon
(there is no vvvv-sound in Cree)
Ebon is gifted
he said to my mother. . .
send Ebon to school
—*Mike Dion Buffalo*

Medicine healers, or synergizers (as I prefer to call them), pay attention to conditions of health rather than symptoms of disease. The Plains Cree approach emphasizes process, symbolism, and energy flow, rather than the labeling and prescribing characteristic of Western methods of treating people. The traditional Cree approach is also holistic, concerned with and giving equal consideration to an

Note: Special thanks to Monica Dion Buffalo (Gladeau), my mother, for her help with the Cree words that appear in this chapter.

individual's mental, physical, emotional, and spiritual well-being within the Sacred Circle of the universe. The whole cosmic order is imbued with the fire of life; therefore, all animate objects have a spirit, a centrality, an identity of their own. All beings of the universe are intimately knitted together in a pattern of interconnection. This relatedness is symbolized by the Medicine Wheel, which depicts four parts of the self, four colors, four elements, four directions, and four animal spirits. The Medicine Wheel, sometimes referred to as the Sacred Circle, is a symbol of wholeness, balance, and harmony in life. The Medicine Wheel circles clockwise in the direction of the sun. As it turns, it reveals new insights and knowledge. This knowledge is transmitted to us through our senses. However, to understand this, we must remain still and listen.

In order to appreciate the work of synergizers, it is necessary to understand the present state of health for many Indian people. There are both individual and group health problems. Colonialism and neocolonialism have psychological consequences; feelings of anger, fear, and frustration prey on the minds of people who cannot envision choices for themselves. There is a general sense of powerlessness and helplessness. Once this "victimhood" is internalized, depression, anxiety, and other forms of emotional imbalance follow. However, blaming others for our present condition is not the answer. We need to take responsibility and positive action for our own health care needs. Traditional healing methods are useful for working with our current problems. How storytelling, specifically, can be used in healing work is the theme of this chapter.

The Plains Cree medicine people heal individuals by bringing unconscious conflict and resistance to a conscious level where they can be worked with. This is done during a ritual or group ceremony through techniques such as dream analysis, trance inductions, and suggestion using poetic imagery, symbolism, metaphors, and stories. The purpose of these techniques is twofold: first, to support the individual in finding re-solutions by stimulating a synthesis of the individual's unconscious thought form, and, second, to realign the collective and social unconsciousness with the whole cosmic order. Therefore, in contrast to modern, Western psychotherapists, who help their patients build an individual myth with elements drawn from their past, the Plains Cree healers provide the collective with a social myth that is not limited to past personal experiences (Capra, 1984).

The storyteller is a healer or synergizer within an Indian community whose function is to produce sound-words for the listeners so that constricted energy can be released. The synergizer uses picture-words to awaken in the listeners the awareness that they have within themselves all the elements necessary for their own healing. Synergizers are also seed bearers; they plant images in our consciousness that take root and flower. A seed-thought is a conscious impression that comes into being that liberates our mind and livens our imagination. Seed-thoughts have transformation energy because they surprise our consciousness into a new way of seeing (Small, 1982). Storytelling is the vehicle used by synergizers to communicate seed-thoughts.

In the Plains Cree culture, healing is viewed as part of the life process and is incorporated in ancient and modern ceremonies, songs, and stories. Emerging from healing experiences, individuals feel both revitalized and at one with nature. Healing through stories is but one important aspect of synthesizing our relationship with ourselves and with the entire universe. As well as being entertaining and giving a sense of pleasure, stories arouse a heightened mindfulness, a sense of wonder and mystery, and a reverence for life. As the story unfolds, a rapport develops between the storyteller and listeners (Baker and Greene, 1977). Gathering momentum, a storyteller speaks to the spirit through imagery. Jeanne Achterberg (1985) explains: "Imagery is the thought process that invokes and uses the senses: vision, audition, smell, taste, the sense of movement, position, and touch. It is the communication mechanism between perception, emotion and bodily change. Imagery is a major cause of both health and sickness, the image is the world's oldest and greatest healing resource" (p. 3). A good storyteller, therefore, works with therapeutic metaphors to create moods, to form patterns, and to evoke various physical and mental changes. A storyteller uses stories as a teaching tool (Bandler, 1978).

There are professional storytellers among North American Native people because their tradition is an oral one. As invited guests to other people's homes, storytellers enact their gift for entertaining. Wintertime is the best time to tell stories, because, as the

Elders, or wise ones, say, the spirits are far away and cannot hear, so they are not likely to be offended. Special tales are related on particular occasions. Some stories have been learned word for word in order to preserve history and specific rituals and beliefs. Other stories are created spontaneously by the storyteller (Sayer, 1970).

In the Plains Cree tradition, for example, oral storytellers create images, words, ideas, and symbols and incorporate specific stylistic devices when telling their stories. The Cree language lends itself to animate nouns and verbs that convey dynamic meanings and elicit various responses. The specific stylistic devices used for mood and emphasis are pauses, tone of voice, word sounds, and chanting-drumming-dancing. The chanting-drumming-dancing is the vehicle used to transport the listeners to an "eternal" state of consciousness. The chants open the various bodily energy channels; the drums provide the heartbeat sound; and dancing sets in motion one's being in the universe. Stories work best when they move swiftly, like an arrow. Some stories are delivered in less than five minutes.

The kinds of stories told range from allegories and parables to tales about the origin of tribal customs and ancestral heroes. Myths, in a special class of their own, are used by Plains Cree medicine healers and synergizers as a means of communicating spiritual knowledge. In mythical stories, the content takes form or shape in the subconscious and transpires to consciousness. The mythic dimension of spiritual experiences is ordered from irrational to rational knowledge by Indian healers and synergizers who can direct human participation in the spirit world. Since Indian healers have special powers, they are the spirit guides who direct human participation in the supernatural. Myths are, therefore, a means to relay information about the unconscious and spiritual realm. Paula Gunn Allen (1986) explains what is meant by myth: "Myth, then, is an expression to make stories of power out of the life we live in the imagination; from this faculty when it is engaged in ordinary states of consciousness come tales and stories. When it is engaged in ordinary states, myth proper—that is, mystery mumblings—occur. It is, of course, the former relationship between myth and imagination that has caused myth to be regarded as a wholly fictitious story . . . that which has no existence" (p. 105). Further: "Myths are stories that allow a holistic image to pervade and shape consciousness thus providing a coherent and empowering matrix for action and relationship . . . this creative ordering capacity of myth frightens and attracts the rationalistic, other centered mind" (p. 105).

Myths can be viewed as rituals or language constructs that contain the power to transform something or someone from one state to another. Allen believes that the present dictionary definition of "myth" is inaccurate because in Western culture "labelling something as a myth merely discredits the perceptual and worldview" (p. 107). The Native perceptional system and world view has been discredited for just this reason. Downing (1984) states, "There are many variants of every myth and no true version; . . . myths mean attending to all variations and also details in each telling that may at first seem trivial and accidental. We learn to our surprise that a particular detail is essential to the whole" (p. 26). Citing Thomas Mann, she explains, "the myth is the legitimization of life; only through and in it does life find self-awareness, sanction and consecration" (p. 2).

Further in her discussion, Downing speaks about the importance of the myth in personal healing and growth. "The discovery of a mythical pattern that in some way one feels is connected to one's own life deepens one's self understanding. At the same time, the discovery of the personal significance of a mythic pattern enhances our understanding of the myth and its variations. Appreciation of the connection between a myth and my life seems simultaneously to make me more attuned to the myth's unity and to help me understand how moments in my life which otherwise might seem accidental or fragmentary belong to the whole. Indeed, we may thus come to recognize the *mythos,* the plot, the connecting thread, the *story* of our life" (p. 26). So, in essence, the storyteller of today has to be a myth-maker. I would now like to share a personal story, because I firmly believe that I am my own healer and synergizer. I also believe that people have the power to heal and transform their reality with guidance. My story, which follows, demonstrates how I did just this.

> I had difficulty getting in front of a large audience and performing in drama. As a child, I was

> terribly shy. I had a terrible fear that I would forget my script lines. I knew that I would experience embarrassment and humiliation if this should ever occur. In fact, these anxiety feelings did affect my performance, because I could not relax and go with the flow. I did not trust my memory power. Finally, I went to a therapist.
>
> My therapist asked me to put an image to how I felt. I said I felt like I was in a car that had plunged into a lake and I could not swim. Next, the therapist had me go into a trance. I started feeling my body quiver with fright. Then panic set in. I struggled and fought to free myself. I stopped struggling because I knew I had to stop wasting my energy and to try to be rational about my situation. If not, I knew I would die. I looked around, and suddenly I saw a fish that had been swimming around the car. Finally, I asked the fish for help. At that moment, I also saw underwater plants swaying rhythmically from side to side. I felt that they were saying to me, "Just watch me; I'll teach you about the power of rhythm so you can flow with the current and not against it."
>
> Suddenly I knew I had two allies who would help me, and I calmed down. I felt that eventually everything would be all right. My fish ally said that it would stay by my side until I reached the top of the lake. Quickly but deliberately, I freed myself from the seat belt, opened the window slowly at first, then filled my lungs with the air that was left and let myself go. I remembered that I had taken a few swimming lessons, so I could make it to the top. Then I thanked the fish and water plants for their help. Later, I thanked the therapist who had guided me through this synergistic experience. Today, I feel I have more confidence.

The process of entering a trance state, building a story around an image, finding a novel solution, and gaining a new frame of reference can be a healing experience (Rosen, 1982). This was the case with me in my story. In the trance state, I felt less anxious and was, therefore, more open to unconscious associations. My unconscious memory took me back to the swimming lessons I had had when I was young. The outcome of the whole experience was that I found different ways of viewing threatening situations, and I felt less anxious on or off stage. I learned that I could trust my unconscious.

Important lessons are taught by means of traditional stories that are applicable from generation to generation. Some stories have been reclaimed and given relevant interpretations for today. The North American Indian trickster tale is one such type. These trickster tales are laced with important teachings for Indian people on the proper ways to think and behave. They relate a recognition that the sacred dimension in nature has intrinsic meaning and importance. They also demonstrate the law of polarity, teaching that we learn things by experiencing their opposite (for example, that women can be vigorous and men can be affectionate). Trickster tales provide a cathartic experience for the listener. Moreover, a shift or transcendence takes place when the listener understands that change does not occur when people try to be what they are not but does occur when they try to be more of who they are. The trickster is multidimensional; it shows many sides to its androgynous nature, teaching that we, too, have many sides.

The following story of *Wisahkecahk and Mistasiniy** (Ray & Stevens, 1971, pp. 30–31) is a trickster tale (Plains Cree words have been added by the author).

Wisahkecahk and Mistasiniy

> Wisahkecahk was running along a leafy, gladed path in the forest (sakew). As usual, the supernatural Indian (nehiyaw) was looking for adventure; but nothing seemed to present an opportunity for fun. He had not been able to find any geese, Indians (ne-

**Source:* From *Sacred Legends of the Sandy Lake Cree,* edited by C. Ray and J. Stevens. Used by permission of the Canadian Publishers McClelland and Stewart, Toronto.

hiyawak) or animals to torment. Then, jogging along, Wisahkecahk came upon a huge rock, Mistasiniy.

"Tanisi," Wisahkecahk said sarcastically to the rock.

"Tanisi, Wisahkecahk," the big rock grunted.

"You certainly can run quite fast, " Mistasiniy remarked with admiration.

"I am the fastest runner in the forest," Wisahkecahk boasted with a big smile on his face. "Would you like to have a race, Mistasiniy?" asked Wisahkecahk.

Mistasiniy began to laugh, "How could a huge boulder like me race with you? I have no legs like you."

"You can race like this." Wisahkecahk began to shove Mistasiniy and the huge rock started rolling slowly. The slender, supple Wisahkecahk loped along beside the lumbering Mistasiniy. Then Wisahkecahk ran ahead as fast as his moccasined feet could take him. Soon he came to a hill and he started down it. The hill became steeper and steeper.

Behind him, Wisahkecahk heard Mistasiniy coming down the hill. The trees were crashing to the ground under the weight of the big rock. Wisahkecahk ran faster, but to no avail. Mistasiniy caught up with the fleeing Wisahkecahk at the bottom of the hill and stopped on his legs pinning him to the ground.

"Little brother! Get off me! Get off me!" pleaded the fallen Wisahkecahk. There was no reply from the big stone. Wisahkecahk decided to reveal his great patience to the stubborn Mistasiniy. He would wait until the large boulder moved.

The summer moons of the berries (nipin-pisim-minisa) came and passed. Moss and lichens began to grow on the arms (mispitonwak), body and hair (mestakaya) of Wisahkecahk. Leaves fell covering up the prisoner with a golden blanket. Later the snows of winter (pipon) followed and Wisahkecahk suffered terribly from the intense cold. Still the rock had not moved off the legs of its captive. By the start of the second summer, the perseverance of Wisahkecahk was at an end.

"Mistasiniy, if you don't roll off my legs, I will call on my big brother to free me." Silently, the rock kept sitting on him. The bedraggled Wisahkecahk sang and chanted to his powerful brother in the sky. Soon black clouds began to roll and thunder resounded; Binay-sih swirled and a bolt of lightning from his beak burst upon the stony skin of Mistasiniy, splitting him in half (apintaw).

Wisahkecahk jumped to his feet, overjoyed that he was free from the trap of the stone. He cleaned the moss and plant growth from his skin and sat down to smoke an offering to his big brother, the Thunderbird. Then he was on his way again, looking for more adventure in the Nehiyaw world.

This trickster narrative teaches lessons about the different powers of the stone, plant, and spirit world. In the Plains Cree culture, stones are used respectfully in a number of ways. Sacred stones are used in various ceremonies, such as the purification ceremony, and they are used as teaching instruments to talk about the Medicine Wheel. Stones are also used in stories as metaphors to heal one's mental, physical, emotional, and spiritual state. In the Wisahkecahk story, the stone world has symbolic significance relating to Mother Earth's healing energy. The stone itself represents the experience of feeling weighted down or pinned to the ground. The story shows that in times of great need, the plant world, symbolizing growth and warmth, can be used as a resource to protect a person. In addition, plant spirits teach us about balance and harmony in the universe. Another important resource for individuals is the powerful Thunderspirit, to be called on only in times of great need.

A further lesson in the Wisahkecahk story has to do with shamanistic teaching about the death and rebirth process. A person experiences many symbolic death and rebirth processes in a lifetime. The story teaches us that during a period of immobilization, rebirth can be experienced by fasting and by being alone. Further, it teaches that we can seek assistance from the supernatural world; we can ask questions of the spirits, and they will give answers. Thanking the spirits and their spirit helpers by smoking an offering is a way of acknowledging our respect of their knowledge and power.

Names and places signify different elements in an oral narrative. There are naming ceremonies to mark a rite of passage. The names given to people at naming ceremonies usually relate to a special event that a person has experienced or something about the person that stands out. In some tribes, such as the Blood, a name could reflect a physical disfigurement. While this may seem cruel to an outsider, from an Indian perspective, the naming helps people to accept their affliction. Names used in a particular story are also important because they can evoke certain feelings and behavior.

Traditional Indian stories are constructed in various ways. Western Apache stories are constructed around a feature of the Apache language that allows for the differentiation of animate and inanimate things. Both the Apache and the Plains Cree world views emphasize respect for nature and a view of partnership in relation to all life, thus assuming a spiritual base. Apache stories portray the establishing of powerful bonds between individuals and features of the natural landscape. Native names for places or geographical features are important to understand because the names signify events that have personal and social meaning. In other words, the symbolic aspects of geographical features are an important part of the story, encouraging compliance with standards for acceptable social behavior and the moral values that support them. An Apache story serves to illustrate this point.

This story, reported by Keith Basso (1984), is of a young girl who wore her hair in rollers to a puberty ceremony. As this is unacceptable tribal behavior, her maternal grandmother decided to perform a narrative for her. The grandmother's story was about a forgetful Apache police officer who behaved too much like a white man. It occurred at a place called Men Stand Above Here and There. Two years later, the girl referred to her grandmother's story and said, "I know it's me for sure. I sure don't like how she's talking about me, so I quit looking like that. I threw those curlers away" (Basso, 1984, p. 40). Later, when she passed within a few hundred yards of Men Stand Above Here and There, the girl said, "I know that place. It stalks me every day" (p. 40). Both the story and the place haunted her, so she stopped behaving like a white person, as did the Apache police officer.

In describing her telling of the story to her granddaughter, the grandmother used a hunting metaphor: "I shot her with an arrow." Basso reports an Apache Elder's explanation of how stories start working to correct negative behavior:

> They go to work on your mind and make you think about your life. Maybe you've not been acting right . . . maybe you've been trying to act like a whiteman. People don't like it! So someone goes hunting for you—maybe your grandmother . . . so someone stalks you and tells a story about what happened long ago . . . she's aiming it at you. All of a sudden it hits you! It's like an arrow . . . sometimes it bounces off—it's too soft and you don't think about anything. But when it's strong it goes in deep and starts working on your mind right away. Then you feel weak, real weak, like you are sick . . . that story is working on you now . . . that story is changing you now, making you want to live right. So you try to forget that story. You try to pull that arrow out . . . but you won't forget that story. You're going to see that place where it happened, maybe every day if it's near-by . . . if you don't see it, you're going to hear its name and see it in your mind. It doesn't matter if you get old—that place will keep on stalking you, like the one who shot you with the story. Maybe that person will die. Even so, that place will keep on stalking you. It's like that person is still alive . . . the names of all these places are good. They make you remember how to live right, so you want to replace yourself again [Basso, 1984, pp. 41–42].

Storytelling has always been a part of the Native oral tradition and part of the healing process. Stories can be used as seeds of thought or arrows of change for all listeners or as a bridge between Natives and non-Natives. I hope that my own personal story, which follows, will be a seed, an arrow, or a bridge for you, the reader.

Storyteller: Yvonne Rita Dion Buffalo

Cree words escape me
so you laugh.
I left
hurting,
knowing you didn't understand,
so you named me—
"The Woman Who Ran Away."
So here I am.

My name is Yvonne Rita Dion Buffalo, and I'm a storyteller. My family comes from the Plains Cree Tribe on the Hobbema Reserve. It's just south of Edmonton, Alberta. As of September 1985, I was reinstated as a Samson Band member, having previously been denied my status when my mother married a nonstatus Indian. The band members from the reserve my father was from, the Papeechase Reserve, were disenfranchised in the early 1900s. Their land was taken from them. I believe that the government is responsible for the division among families today. Unfortunately, now family members are fighting each other. At present there is a legal suit by Indian mothers, and children will follow, to gain the rights and benefits provided to other Indian and non-Indian people who were Samson Band members prior to 1985. I have always identified myself as a Plains Cree Indian woman. This is who I am. No one can take my identity away.

I want to start off my stories by talking about ceremonies (see Allen, 1986). In a traditional fashion, Indian Elders and storytellers usually begin with a teaching about Indian tradition and beliefs. So I'll start using the same process. Ceremonies serve to integrate the individual into the community, thus developing and maintaining the tribal way of life. Ceremonies are experienced in a holistic way in that through them an individual is able to transcend the ordinary reality and enter into an eternal state of consciousness—into a spiritual realm. At this point, the person sheds her individuality and bonds with the universe.

The crier circles
the encampment
reminding the people
to maintain their
traditional ways,
especially to respect their ceremonies.
Ceremonies heal people
supporting them to accept
rites of passage in their lives.
Over-and-over the word-song is spoken
reinforcing the theme
and focusing on the moment
everyone acts out words
ritual movements
incantations, prayers
in harmony
until the heartbeat, the breath, the thought
are one.

Today, Indian ceremonies involve oral stories and myths that relate to current and past social situations, such as poverty and oppression. At the same time, the stories may emphasize traditions and customs or transition and change, which is why I believe it is important to speak out in writing, in songs, and in stories. With this, I'd like to share some of my personal stories.

This morning as I lay in bed thinking, I decided that I would just let myself be and not worry, just be natural. Today I'll let things unfold themselves and adjust myself to whatever may happen. I want to be aware of my internal being, my feelings, my repressed and expressed emotions. I want to experience sounds from within like the gurgling sounds in my stomach, to sounds I hear from the outside. I want to experience my response to these sounds. Tranquil thoughts, however, pass by quickly. I remember I have a class presentation later in the day. As I start to type, I begin to have anxious feelings. I find it interesting that I get the same feelings when I listen to the refrigerator as it hums. So smug, I think to myself. It controls my appetite. Maybe I'll do something about my weight problem this spring. Pictures of leftover, stale peanut butter sandwiches from the construction camp nearby flash through my mind. I'm certain the poverty situation in my younger days is a contributing factor to my being overweight. Oh, well, I can't deal with that now, so I move forward to better thoughts, happy thoughts, healing thoughts. The birds outside are all chirping, and it stirs intense memories of the imaginative world I lived in as a child. And I'd like to share a short story I wrote.

A Special Place That No One Knows

This special place of mine is very sacred to me. The door is located next to the window so I can control the entrances and exits of others. No one can barge in, although my sister Flora will often come through its invisible walls to tell me something that just couldn't wait. I can distinctly remember telling my brothers and sisters, and there are six of them, that I am not to be interrupted when I am in my home. If Mom or Dad should ask for me, I instructed my brothers and sisters not to tell them where I live. In no case do I allow anyone to come in without first knocking. My goodness, my hair probably needs brushing. My brush is just a piece of stick that I picked up from the ungraveled road that lay beside our tar-papered shack. I am only eight years old at this time.

My playhouse is located right in the forest beside beautiful, tall spruce trees, and there are shrubs all around. I feel safe within this natural setting. Listen, I work hard to keep my house neat and tidy. I always get decorating ideas from the well-read Eaton's catalogue Mom got when she went to town. There are pictures of the inside of homes with checkered curtains in orange-yellow and white. I sneak out pieces of old cloth from my Mom's ragbag, as she calls it, and I hang them up, feeling so proud because I think they look exactly like the ones I've seen in the catalogue. I try to believe that I am wealthy, but deep down inside I know I am poor and that these curtains are poor imitations. "Make do with what you have," I remember my mother saying to me.

Being the eldest, I am often asked to care for my brothers and sisters, or to go fetch water from the construction camp, which is a mile away, or to run to the store, which is even further. Or to wash dishes, or to sweep the floor. There is never any end to the things I have to do. Oftentimes I am blamed for a broken dish, a missing key, or even the smokehouse burning down. I'll never forget that. I love the smell of smoked fish and eating the crunchy bits once it is cured, but I never burnt that smokehouse down. How come I cannot convince my mother that it is not my fault? She doesn't understand me. My dad doesn't say anything to stick up for me, either. When questioned by my mother, my brothers and sisters also remain quiet.

I go sulkingly to my playhouse and make string figures with a piece of string I have found. In anger, I surmise that my brothers and sisters are just nuisances. From this point on, only when they behave on my terms will I allow them to come into my house. Besides, this is my special place. I decide that when we play school, I will be the teacher and they the students. Furthermore, when we play store, I will be the storekeeper and they will be my customers. I conclude that I'll make them take a secret oath. I throw my string aside when I can't make a cat's cradle.

One day, Mom announces we are moving to the city. I feel both happy and sad. Maybe sad first because I am leaving my special place. But happy to leave the tar-papered shack that I feel ashamed of. We don't get many visitors anyway, and the kids at school don't like

> us. I can sense their fear of us. The only friend I have in school is a girl named Margaret, but she only talks to me when no one is around.
>
> I go to my sacred place in the woods one last time to say good-bye. Everything is in its place all neat and tidy. I sweep the floor with my pine branch and touch everything again, one last time. I feel so knotted up inside that I cry. I decide no one should know of this place because it means so much to me. I feel secure here. I resolve that no one will know about my sacred place. It's a secret. So I get rid of every piece of evidence that exists: my special twigs, blade grasses for making sensational sounds, dandelion crowns, innovative drawings from school, different colors of sand, and many stone forms. They are my objets d'art. You know, they showed themselves to me and they all had their stories. I decide to engrave my initials on a tree in case I ever want to go back and find my special place. Maybe one day I'll tell someone the whole story and everything that happened there.

I share this story with a friend of mine, and he says, "Well, how does that relate to what you're going to talk about in your class presentation?" He looks at me, puzzled and unapproving. I go back to the typewriter, and I decide that he is a typical left-brain thinker. And, of course, I smugly think of myself as a right-hemisphere thinker—intuitive, holistic, sympathetic (whatever that means). Pretty rigid thinking, all right. Finally, I decide that making judgments about others and judging ourselves is restricting. Judgment chokes, you know, and tightens, and then you die a little inside.

Let go of old patterns of judgment! "Damn you, Atonement Home! Damn institution!" I scream inside. The image of Christ on Judgment Day comes to mind. Those nuns did a pretty good job of convincing me I was inferior. Pretty hard not to think of yourself as less than human when you spend most of your time on your knees praying for salvation, praying for forgiveness. In retrospect, I realize that I could not comprehend the concept of sin. Going to mass every morning at seven o'clock. Going to evening benediction. Endlessly saying the rosary, starting with I believe, Our Father and Hail Mary. In fact, one time I got water on the knees and had to be taken to the doctor.

Well, what did it all mean? First, there was the whole experience in the Protestant home—one year fighting with the Catholics. And then spending the following five, or was it six, in the Catholic home fighting with the Protestant kids. Who in the hell cares! I don't like thinking about those years. I know I'll have to deal with it sometime. You know, I've always wanted to write a book about a Native child's experience in an institution and how institutionalized one becomes in the process. Like how my real father was replaced by a gray-haired, white, rigid, patriarchal priest. And my mother by a cruel, manipulative, guilt-ridden nun who looked and dressed like a penguin. That's funny! I mean the dressing up, and looking and walking like a penguin. I still remember that pinched-in face with eyes that could see right through me. She had an archaic smile, even when she was punishing me. Yeah, that was Sister Melodious. Listen, I wrote a small script about her.

> "Sister, I have blood in my panties. What shall I do? Am I going to die?"
>
> Laughing, "I want you to ask me should you need any pads each month. Okay, Pocohantas?"
>
> "Please leave my sister alone in the mornings. She doesn't mean to wet the . . . Oh please, yell at me instead. I can take it. She can't help it."
>
> "That's enough. It's none of your affair. By the way, what was that movie magazine and makeup doing under your mattress? I'm not allowing your mother a visit this month."
>
> "But it's my confirmation this month."
>
> "Out. Out. Out, and get the stink blown off of you."

You know, she reminds me of that story that I read by Charles Dickens about Scrooge, who was a squeezing, wrenching, grasping, scraping, clutching, covetous old sinner.

I sing "Ave Maria" to feel better.

Yeah, what do you think of that story? Pretty harsh, eh? Ugly and putrid, I think. Do you know what putrid means? It's a foul odor.

When I was a child, I was called a pig because I was poor. I cringe as I write about that experience, too.

> "I'll have an Orange Crush, please. My Dad gave me ten cents."
>
> "Here's your change. Now, I don't want you hangin' around here. You're filthy, you know. No good Indians. Should all be shot."
>
> "I like your store, sir. You gots lots of pretty things in here."
>
> "Pigs, that's what you are. Squatters, beggars, and stealers. Get out before you know what's good for you."
>
> I hum "Bringing in the Sheaves," wishing I could fly away.

(When I first wrote this, I found it too painful to write it exactly as it happened, so I changed the context. Having written this, some healing has occurred, and I can now say that the incident involved a schoolmate and her mother. I still have some pain to work out before I can tell the real story.)

School was not so great, either.

> "Now open your book to the story of 'Little Beaver Who Goes to the City.' It starts, 'Little Beaver and His Animal Friends.' He was such a wonderful boy and had such a beautiful relationship with nature. Doesn't he, class?" said the teacher as she opened the book to show us a romanticized illustration of a noble savage.
>
> "I wish I could live like him, eating lots of berries, and he gets to go on lots of adventures."
>
> "Did you eat anything this morning? Or did your Dad get drunk again last night? By the way,

someone stole money from Precious's pocket. Would you by any chance know something about it?"

"No! I'm not a stealer."

I sing, "Your Cheatin' Heart," sitting on a branch, high above the ground.

Lighten up, I think. I search around for a poem to help me transcend bad memories. I find a poem by Tennyson and it goes like this:

Willows whiten, aspen quiver
Little breezes dusk and shiver through the wave that
runs forever
By the island in the river, flowing down to Camelot.

Oh, well, I think poems are magical, sometimes. The next poem catches my attention, especially the line which reads:

Music, when soft voices die, vibrates the memory.

I reach for my drum and I start drumming, picking up a moderate tempo. I envision the Yaki deer dancers with their majestic movements. This image triggers memories about my Uncle Narcise.

Uncle Narcise, he always stood apart from other family members. The whole community feared and respected his powers. One of which was to make people laugh at themselves. He would go up to a person and mimic their posture or behavior. This caused a great deal of embarrassment of the person being mimicked as everyone in the hall broke out in a gale of laughter. Also, Narcise would keep dancing when the rest of the dancers had stopped, and he could dance without making any sounds. The ornamental bells tied around his ankles remained still. Then he would look up, pretending to be confused upon discovering that he was alone in dancing. By this time, the crowd was having fun and teasing him. But I remember thinking, "How was he able to defy the laws of nature? Bells were supposed to ring when he moved." Silently, Narcise came near and took off one of his bells, giving it to me as a gift.

He had a wife called Mohco-iskwew, which means silly or funny woman, but not in a derogatory sense. I remember going to see Mohco-iskwew one day when I was young. I said, "Mohco-iskwew, Mohco-iskwew," and she said, "Go on, leave me alone, Narcise will be home soon. I've got to get this washing done and I've got to hang up the clothes." (She hung them on the barbed wire fence near her house.) "Then I've got to make bannock."

"Yeah, yeah, yeah. Burnt your bannock yesterday, hard as rock. Please come and play, Mohco-iskwew. I won't call you Mohco-iskwew any more if you'll come and play. The gophers are playing hide-and-seek, too. Let's go hunting, Mohco-iskwew." She ignores me, so I taunt her, "Fee-fi-fo-fum. I smell the blood of an Englishman."

Startled, she says, "Hey, hey, get away child. Narcise has gone for his medicine and he's getting ready for his next ceremony. Do you still have that bell he gave you?"

"Yeah. But he scares me. He's funny though when he dances. Why does he make fun of people? I think that's mean."

Seeing that I could not sway her from her work, I clamor, "Copy cat. Copy cat. Where have you been? I've been to London to visit the Queen."

Indian tradition teaches that while teasing is okay, it's not okay to be disrespectful. As with the Buddhist idea of karma, a negative act will have a negative consequence. I never saw Mohco-iskwew again.

The last memory story is about my grandfather, whom I consider to be avant-garde. His name was Joe D. Buffalo. He was a singer and dancer. He once acted in a spaghetti western called *Sheriff of Fractured Jaw* with Kenneth Moore and Jayne Mansfield. I remember he was so excited about going to Spain where the movie was to be made. He lived on the Hobbema Reserve and never left the reserve except to attend secret ceremonies "somewhere." You see, Indians could not leave the reserve unless they got a special permit, and that ban wasn't lifted until the late fifties. Indian people couldn't even vote in the early sixties. That's not so long ago.

Grandpa, he stayed with my mother until he died in the early seventies, and here's what he said to me one day when I went to visit him.

I prepared a lunch for him and so I called down because he liked to sit downstairs where it was quiet, so he could meditate and pray.

> "Astam miciso, nimosom. Come and eat, my grandfather."
>
> He replies, "Micisotan chi? Are we ready to eat?"
>
> "Eha, eha. Yes, yes."
>
> "Ceskwa. Wait."
>
> Oh, there goes grandfather. You know, doing his usual kind of rituals. Washing his hands, then he prays, comes into the kitchen and sits down. I pour his tea in his cup and I serve him soup and bannock.
>
> "Sip, sigh. Sip, sigh."
>
> We sit in silence for a long time. Then he says, "Why does all of my family need glasses? There's a curse on this family. None of you, you don't need glasses. Bad medicine, bad curse."
>
> "But my eyes are bad. I need glasses."
>
> "No. No. No glasses! White man cursed you."
>
> Not long after that he went to a secret ceremony at Saddle Lake to have the curse removed.

Grandfather spoke in metaphor a lot of the time, and so it was very frustrating for me to understand exactly what it was that he was trying to relate to me, and it's something that I'm still unraveling, because metaphors are that way. They take a long time to understand. So I try to comprehend the meaning of glasses and what they symbolized to my grandfather.

> Glasses put an artificial boundary between you and the universe. Glasses symbolize assistance for an impediment. Glasses shield you from seeing yourself as you are—warm, generous, and loving or cold, protective, and cautious. Glasses reinforce the dependency cycle for Indian people. Glasses are a white man's material object so they cannot see the Indian person as coming from a sophisticated, complex, and dynamic culture.
>
> As for me, my glasses have been knocked off three times by others who saw me as jealous, unloving, insecure.
>
> "Cousin Weakeyes! Cousin Weakeyes!" I used to be called by one of my teachers wanting a positive response from the rest of the class. But only a few white students laughed, not the Indian students.
>
> So I assume glasses serve to instill fear, hatred, and division. Glasses symbolize racism. And did you know that glasses can take your power away?

Aheiah . . . I do
aheyiahahahah . . . I own
AAHHEEIIYYOOoo . . . my self
Grandmothers
Grandfathers
in-bonded-strengths
I walk
in-shared-wisdom
I hear your voices in the winds
in-oneness-beauty
I find new power

My final story is a personal healing story that came to me as a dream. It came at a significant time in my life, when I had completed three years of intensive psychotherapy, had convocated with a bachelor of arts degree (with my grandmother, mother, daughter, three nieces, and my therapist in attendance), and was now firmly implanted in a graduate program in medical anthropology, happily studying the healing methods of different cultures. I am incorporating the teachings of my ancestors (the ones who have crossed over as well as those still living) with what I'm learning at the university. Indian people consider the imagination to be a great source of power that can be used in everyday life. I have become more confident in using my own imagination as a source of power to aid me in healing from painful experiences and overcoming fear. The following dream is about my personal healing and change and symbolizes an integration of the many parts of me that I have been working with (Vizenor, 1988, has influenced my dream and story work).

Dream: November 6, 1988

Lady Whiteglove is fretting over the fact that her favorite earring is broken. Interestingly, the disc-shaped earring has a wire sticking out from it. She examines it closely because there is something unusual about this earring. She discovers it is alive! The two colors, irridescent gold and sacred black, glow profoundly. "I'll fix it so it will never come apart again," she tells herself.

Trickster sneaks up quietly and snatches the earring from her royal highness. "I want the earring. It is mine, mine, MINE!" (Her/his voice has a deep nasal sound that suggests passion, eroticism and wildness.) "Besides, it looks much better on me than on you." (Her/his voice now has a slight tone of spitefulness because she/he cannot stand Lady Whiteglove's highty-tightyness.)

Lady Whiteglove: "You bitch! Give it back to me." (Her voice is so loud it echoes in the landscape. What she has said horrifies her. Her spontaneity shocks her because she usually keeps a tight rein on her deportment.)

Nun Guiltridden: "Tch, tch, tch, tch. You

know better than that! You know that when you swear you'll go to hell, hell, hell, HELL . . ." (Her voice chastizes the lady real good.)

Lady Whiteglove: (to Trickster, disguising her anger) "PPppplea-ease, give back my earring." (emphasizing "plea" and "ease" because she doesn't want to commit a SIN, sin, sin, sin . . .)

Nun Guiltridden: "Now that's much better." (She feels relieved, knowing she has accomplished her duty, rather, God's duty, in teaching "primitives" how to act "civilized.")

A struggle follows between these two strong-willed, stubborn women.

While Lady and Nun continue their guilt-victim monologue, *Trickster* decides to play a trick on both of them. She/he tousles her/his hair until it sticks straight out like kindlewood on a newly built fire. Then she/he smears Truly Lasciviously Red lipstick all arOoOound her/his already sensuously big lips. She/he looks bawdy and gaudy. Flimflam Ma . . . an? She/he removes the pin that is sticking out from the earring and puts the "animate" disc-shaped object over her/his right eye, wearing it like a monocle. Silently, "There, that should do it. I'll sneak up on both of them—NOW!" Out loud, "Ladies, may I be of any assistance?"

Tribal Community Mongrels howl and kill themselves laughing in the background. Lady Whiteglove overhears one of them, *Dia Metric,* say to his small, roving band of egalitarian followers: "We have to rub out her false consciousness, in particular, her idea that she is so special. It is her notion of 'specialness' that she has to look at. Now, invert this with words like 'nothingness' and 'invisibleness.' Then she may be on to something."

Con Centric interrupts: "It's Guiltridden's 'air of superiority' that is located in the center and her 'inferiority on the timberline' that needs analysis."

Stone Woman: "That's enough! All of you, wapamew . . . go look at yourselves." As the mongrels skitter away with their tails between their legs, she doctors both women from inside out. "Hmmph! The mongrels are so shortsighted; they only see the edges," she thinks to herself. Out loud she pronounces to the Lady and the Nun, "The curse has been removed from *both* of you—the umbilical cord has been cut."

Ekosi . . . that's it for now.

References

Achterberg, J. *Imagery in Healing: Shamanism and Modern Medicine.* Boston: Shambhala, 1985.

Allen, P. *The Sacred Hoop.* Boston: Beacon Press, 1986.

Baker, A., and Greene, E. *Storytelling: Art and Technique.* New York: Bowker, 1977.

Bandler, R. "Foreword." In D. Gordon, *Therapeutic Metaphors.* Cupertino, Calif.: Meta, 1978.

Basso, K. "'Stalking With Stories': Names, Places and Moral Narratives Among the Western Apache." In E. M. Brunner (ed.), *Text, Play and Story: The Construction and Reconstruction of Self and Society.* 1983 Proceedings of the American Ethnological Society. Washington, D.C.: American Ethnological Society, 1984.

Capra, F. *The Turning Point: Science, Society and the Rising Culture.* New York: Crossroad, 1984.

Downing, C. *The Goddess: Mythological Images of the Feminine.* New York: Crossroad, 1984.

Ray, C., and Stevens, J. (eds). *Sacred Legends of the Sandy Lake Cree.* Toronto: McClelland & Stewart, 1971.

Rosen, S. (ed.). *My Voice Will Go with You: The Teaching Tales of Milton H. Erickson.* New York: Norton, 1982.

Sayer, R. *The Way of the Storyteller.* New York: Penguin Books, 1970.

Small, J. *Transformers: The Therapists of the Future.* Marina del Ray, Calif.: DeVorss, 1982.

Vizenor, G. *The Trickster of Liberty.* Minneapolis: University of Minnesota Press, 1988.

8

Reclaiming the Inner Child: Jungian Dream Analysis

Bonnelle Lewis Strickling
Client: "Simone"

It seems to me that a good way to describe the subject matter of therapy is the healing of the inner child. For unless the inner child is healed, change will not take place. There are several aspects to the inner child, and I want to begin by discussing some of them.

We all experience energy appropriately termed "childlike" in our everyday lives. Even the staidest of us sometimes feels a sense of playfulness, of the joy of living, of spontaneously creating something or some way of being, no matter in how small a way. That we experience these feelings as childlike points to the nature of the original inner child, the one who exists before life's difficulties wound her. The inner child is whole, not yet split up into the acceptable and unacceptable, the "good" and the "bad" child, that which can be expressed and that which must be hidden. In *Pornography and Silence,* Susan Griffin (1981) talks about the concept of eros in connection with the world of the undamaged child: "In these acts, we attempt to destroy eros. For isn't it eros we rediscover in the child's world? The beauty of the child's body. The child's closeness to the natural world. The child's heart. Her love. Touch never divided from meaning. Her trust. Her ignorance of culture. The knowledge she has of her own body. That she eats when she is hungry. Sleeps when she is tired. Believes what she sees. That no part of her body has been forbidden to her. No part of this body is shamed, numbed or denied. That anger, fear, love and desire pass freely through this body. And for her, meaning is never separate from feeling" (p. 254).

This child and her body are one; there is not yet me and not-me. She is innocent and feels innocent; she has not yet been mystified into blaming herself for what others have done to her, so she does not yet feel that she must hide her responses to what others do, either from the world or from herself. She can feel and respond spontaneously to herself and others. The therapist wants very much to find this child, to know how much of her has survived what life has brought. The more of this innocent child that survives, the more likely the client is to be able to reclaim herself. Equally important for therapy is the child's hope. She does not expect the world to get worse and worse. She believes that bad treatment is temporary, since she has not given up the hope that her parents will love her someday, if not yet. The success of therapy depends on being able to mobilize this hope. But given the layers of rage and pain, repression and denial of many of those who come to see us, how are we to contact this child?

My own experience has led me to believe that the child can best be contacted through work on dreams rather than purely on the basis of consciously offered material. For people who come to therapy and, indeed, for all of us, it is difficult to give an account of our lives without leaving out a great deal. We naturally describe things not just from a subjective point of view but from a point of view selected by the conscious mind and strongly influenced by our own interests. I don't mean at all to imply anything cynical here—it's not that everyone presents herself to her therapist by representing herself as being right about everything in all her relationships and opinions. Rather, our conscious minds naturally reflect the ego's picture of things, and the ego's picture of things is naturally directed by such things as thinking as well of ourselves as possible, presenting a coherent reality, seeing our own side of the question, and excluding those memories and experiences that are too painful to tolerate. This natural selectivity is a source of great difficulty for both therapist and client. What the client needs is some new point of view, something outside the ego's interests, analyses, and expectations, to provide fresh insight into and energy for struggling with whatever has brought her to therapy. The therapist wants some source of information about the state of the whole psyche, the position of the client's problems in relation to whatever else is going on. In short, both therapist and client need some childlike energy—something spontaneous, unselfconscious, truthful and whole. This energy comes in the form of dreams.

Carl Jung ([1933, 1934], 1964) says of dreams, "Dreams are impartial, spontaneous products of the unconscious psyche, outside the control of the will. They are pure nature; they show us the unvarnished, natural truth, and are therefore fitted, as nothing else is, to give us back an attitude that accords with our basic human nature when our consciousness has strayed too far from its foundations and run into an impasse" (p. 317). And Charles Rycroft (1979), in explaining the title of his book *The Innocence of Dreams,* says, "Finally, I must explain my use of the word 'innocence' in the title. I refer not to any presumed ignorance on the parts of dreams, nor to any presumed freedom from guilt—on the contrary I would maintain that while dreaming we may know more than we know while we're awake and may voice thoughts and wishes that evoke guilt when we awaken—but rather to the idea that dreams lack knowingness, display an indifference to received categories, and have a core which cannot but be sincere and is uncontaminated by the self-conscious will" (p. 7).

Dreams have a childlike quality because they emerge from a part of ourselves with which the child has more direct contact than the adult—the unconscious. The imaginativeness of children, their wonderfully free and spontaneous works of art, reflect this connection with the unconscious. Thus, if we want to contact the child, both from the standpoint of her existence and from the standpoint of the kind of energy she has, we must turn to dreams. Working with dreams allows us to find the other child, the wounded child, the one who still experiences and remembers the events and feelings that have caused the adult's apparently inexplicable pain and anger. She must be able to emerge, to express her reality and have it respected, and find healing for the damaged and split-off parts. This healing process will bring yet another child, the archetypal magical child whose appearance in dreams signifies rebirth, growth, creativity.

The contact, discovery, and emergence of the wounded child, the reclaiming of the whole child's innocence, the subsequent healing and integration as well as the rebirth of aspects of one's being, make up the process of therapy. This is, however, an abstract and impersonal characterization. In order to understand what this process is like, we must look at a real example. (I am deeply grateful to the woman here called "Simone" for allowing me to talk about her work and her life in this chapter.)

Simone first began to see me about two years ago. She came because two things in her life that were very important to her—her intimate relationship and her academic work—had disintegrated or been damaged, and she was extremely depressed. It was the first time she had been so depressed, and she found it very disturbing. The end of her relationship had made her miserable, but the academic difficulties had both made her miserable and undermined her sense of herself. She had always been good at school, priding herself on her competence. Now, because a professor she had trusted had been ruthlessly critical, seeing her and her work in a way almost exactly opposite to the way she did (and, as it turned out, very unfairly), she felt uncertain about her abilities and even her own perceptions of herself. All this together had precipitated a life crisis—doubts about her work, her lovableness, whether there was anything any better in store. She was unable to pull herself out of her depression and was genuinely desolate.

As she told me about the recent events of her life and her feelings about them, I could see that she was very unhappy, but, at the same time, she seemed almost detached. Sometimes she seemed to be speaking about someone else, someone we both knew but who wasn't present. This detachment seemed to me too settled to be only the result of recent events; I tentatively assumed that her depression was not just the result of recent disasters but that these had triggered some much older unhappiness. I was relieved when she told me that she dreamed frequently and vividly, since the dreams would offer a means of getting at more and deeper feeling. At the same time, I felt fairly certain that there was quite a lot of life below the surface because of her clothes. Simone's clothes were really wonderful—colorful and original, with varied textures and styles, worn with beautiful and unusual jewelry. As I came to know her better, I found that sometimes, unconsciously, she would dress in a way that reflected how things had looked or what had happened in her dreams. I looked forward (and still do) each week to seeing what she would wear—there was almost a magical quality to the way she looked. I felt both hopeful and interested as we began our work together.

Almost immediately, Simone and I made some sort of psychic connection. What I mean by this is that somehow we had matching and/or complementary psychic structures and issues, so that I became, in a useful way, a person of psychic significance to her. In order to explain why this is so important, I want first to say a little about transference, especially the kind of transference that can take place between women clients and their women therapists, intensified, as in this case, by the fact that both are feminists.

Transference, from a Jungian standpoint, takes place when contents from either the personal or collective unconscious are projected onto the therapist. Countertransference occurs when the same thing happens from the standpoint of the therapist. In addition, connection can occur between the unconsciouses of client and therapist, so that each has access to the unconscious of the other without realizing it consciously. Jung believed that both transference and countertransference could be extremely creative, with the client using the therapist to bring out undeveloped and previously unconscious aspects of her personality and the therapist learning more about her own psychic life. Thus, Jung did not regard transference and countertransference as in any way undesirable but as a potentially creative process.

From the point of view of the feminist therapist, the transference (negative or positive) can take powerful forms, since at this point in history the needs of women for other ways of being are very great. There are many reasons for this; I want to mention two that seem to me fundamental. According to psychologist Nancy Chodorow (1978), in forming identity in the traditional nuclear family, women do not separate from their mothers as boys do. Lacking the oedipal conflicts, mother and daughter retain strong pre-oedipal connections so that the daughter never quite develops a sense of having a separate identity from her mother. I am speaking here not just of mutual bonds of affection but rather of a kind of tie that, at its greatest extreme, involves an absence of boundary between mother and daughter, a sense that the daughter *is* her mother and has no real right to a life of her own. For such women and perhaps, if Chodorow is right, for all women, one of the major tasks of therapy is the formation of an independent sense of identity. As well, I believe that one of the fundamental tasks of the feminist therapist and perhaps of everyone at this precarious point in history is the rescue of what Jungians would call the feminine. This rescue has already begun through women's insistence on being seen from their own point of view and through the revaluing of those areas to which women have traditionally been relegated. There are new ways of being emerging for women, ways that may not fit with the traditional ways of constructing the feminine. The woman in whom and for whom these things are happening needs more than support; she needs to see real possibilities of other ways of being. Thus, certain kinds of transference seem to me to be attempts on the part of the client to find another way, to see the therapist as embodying those qualities that the client needs to find inside herself to live in a different way. Since many women who enter therapy have experienced profound frustration and disappointment, the hopes that are raised there need to be treated with particular care and attention. If the therapist can affirm them through herself working on new ways, positive transference can be a strong creative force. If the therapist raises these hopes and then frustrates them through trying to maneuver the client back into the old ways or through her failure to work on new ways for herself, negative transference can be not just powerful but explosive.

Simone and I were fortunate to be able to form the kind of connection that gave rise to positive transference fairly quickly. She soon began to dream about me, and, as we worked with these dreams, I realized that a very great deal of her life and energy not evident in her depressed state existed at the level of her unconscious. She had many dreams, filled with vivid imagery and great detail. I want now to tell her story in terms of some of these dreams, spread over about a year and a half.

One of the first dreams Simone had about me was the following:

> I go out to the back of the Hotel Vancouver to meet Bonnelle. She's living in a house (cottage, really) attached to the hotel, which looks at the back like an Italian villa—all terra cotta and golden light. The cottage is small, very charming and lots of fine handcrafting in the details. We sit at a picnic table in the garden. The garden is very lush and beautiful with many flowers. While we're talking, I admire the abundance of food that surrounds us on the table and on the garden wall. Such bounty: a chicken, a crab, many kinds of fruit, vegetables, and so on.
>
> As we're talking, a rainstorm suddenly comes up. The rain (a warm, tropical rain) begins to pour down. Bonnelle begins to dance barefoot around the garden, reveling in the rain. I sit for a moment, not knowing quite what to do, watching B., then I notice that the rain is starting to run the ink on my dream notes, so I move out of the rain under the eaves where B. is not standing.
>
> As B. and I finish our session, some friends of hers are there. All women, all very friendly and jovial. We had rushed to protect some of the food in the rainstorm, and we all set about preparing it for dinner. I feel a part of the group; I feel that everyone's taking it for granted that I should be there, yet I feel a little awkward—I haven't actually been invited to stay, everyone's just assuming that I will. I wonder if I'm intruding at all on B. and her friends, although, apparently, they are very happy to have me there.
>
> We all sit down to a wonderful meal. Although I'm loving the experience, I have another pang of worrying that I don't really belong there. I move to the far end of the table, away from B. My intention is to give her "space," but she looks at me and smiles, pats the seat beside her, and says, "Come here and sit by me."

In this dream, Simone was telling herself and me what she wanted for her life, what she needed to develop in herself, and what she needed in me. Acutely sensitive to the beauty of the world in both a physical and spiritual sense, Simone loved color, beautiful meals, wonderful clothes, bodily and spiritual celebration of life. Her own mother was a woman of limited emotional resources and, as we were to discover later, a capacity for a kind of passive cruelty. Simone received little warmth and attention—bounty, as expressed in the dream, was never a part of her life experience. She longed to fully participate in the aspects of life reflected in the dream, to develop those parts of herself. She lacked opportunity at first through her austere family atmosphere, then, as a result, experienced psychic limitation. In this dream, I seem to represent for her a willingness to affirm and even celebrate the positive aspects of the traditionally conceived feminine. There are no men in this garden; it is full of jolly, sensual women, eating and drinking and, in my case, dancing in the rain. There is also a spiritual flavor to this dream: the garden seems magical and, in a part of the dream I have omitted, there is an archway with magical symbols carved on it. This suggests to me that Simone was trying to connect the spiritual and the sensual, a connection that is made in many feminist spiritual activities, such as the revival of the goddess religion.

In myths that recount the hero's quest for wholeness and individuation, the hero often has two mothers: a natural mother, connected to the world of physical existence and its laws, and a spiritual mother, connected with the world of consciousness and psychic growth (see Layard, 1985, for an excellent discussion of this sort of myth). In traditional nuclear families, women often connect with their fathers as their spiritual "mothers," as representatives of consciousness and as allies in the struggle for identity. This, however, can be unsatisfactory for women, since it can simultaneously undermine our sense of feminine identity. I thought Simone's dream reflected the search for a spiritual mother, someone who could both nurture and offer further psychic development, who could initiate her into further psychic growth. This sense of initiation seems strong in the presence of a group, and in my inviting her to sit by me. She is being initiated into something in which she can participate as an equal, not as a daughter. I invite her to sit beside me, not on the ground or in my lap.

The theme of the spiritual mother emerged even more strongly in her next dream about me:

> I go to keep my appointment with Bonnelle. I notice that her house is right on the edge of the water (or over the water). I notice nearby houses on stilts over the water—almost a floating community. The sun is shining and I notice sailboats in the distance. I think it's very beautiful there, but I ask Bonnelle what happens in a storm, does the water overtake the buildings. I tell her that in the area where I grew up, flooding was a danger. She says no, that never happens here.
>
> She asks if I mind if we don't use the therapy room; some guests are having a party in there. I say that's fine. I also noticed another guest—Bonnelle's client for the next morning—as I had come in. She's from out of town, so she's staying in Bonnelle's spare room.
>
> Because the therapy room is in use we both sit on a bed that's in her kitchen. We sit at opposite ends of the bed. Bonnelle asks me if I'm comfortable. I say yes and snuggle under the covers. We begin talking and I tell her the dream of the night before. As I tell her she shifts up beside me on the bed and I see that we're both naked yet covered by the sheets. As we talk, various parts of our bodies get exposed and sometimes we reach down to cover them up and sometimes we don't. This is done very absentmindedly. I tell her the story of the dream, then abruptly she says we have to stop—the session is over. I'm sitting opposite her in a chair now and I feel frustrated. I feel that part of the dream I was telling her was very important and I want to know what the dream means.
>
> Bonnelle rolls up a magazine then and looks into my nose and ears. She says she's going to look

> into my brain to tell me what the dream means. She tells me that it represents my having been a journalist from New York in the 1960s.

When I first worked with Simone on this dream, my feeling was that the first part of the dream probably had to do with the anxiety many clients have about being overwhelmed by unconscious material and the need for reassurance that all sorts of overpowering and unwanted material will not suddenly rush out and overwhelm them. Now, over a year later, I believe it may have been about something more specific: being flooded with emotion. Simone's family was an emotionally cold one, and she had the role of being "no trouble." She didn't complain, no matter how she was ignored and neglected, and she learned at an early age to retreat into herself and find her own ways of consoling and occupying herself. Even a modest amount of expressed emotion would have constituted a flood in her environment. The first part of the dream may have reflected her anxiety that she would drown in her feelings, that they would overwhelm her and flood the psychic structure she had so carefully built up. Later work made me think that these feelings were mostly feelings of grief and sadness, which other clients have also represented as water.

We were both reminded, in the second part of the dream, of Leonard Cohen's song "Suzanne." In this song, Suzanne is an anima figure (that is, of the soul or spirit, in touch with the inner life) for the poet, but in Simone's dream, something very different is going on. We discussed the sexuality in the dream and agreed that it seemed to be more about closeness and a comfortable relation to the body ("various parts of our bodies get exposed and sometimes we reach down to cover them up and sometimes we don't"), as well as our frank relations with each other. We seem to be seeking knowledge together, talking about her dream, and again there is a sense of equality. We are in the same bed, under the same covers. And, from a therapeutic point of view, I am indeed, like Suzanne, "half crazy" in this dream—there's a party going on in the therapy room, a client in my spare bedroom, and Simone and I are eating oranges and drinking tea (the same things Suzanne gives the poet) under the covers, in bed, in my kitchen. There is a sense of camaraderie and a sense that all these crazy things are perfectly all right. This makes the transition to the last part of the dream even more abrupt.

In the last part of the dream, I turn into a brusque, authoritarian therapist, ending our session suddenly, peering into her head to tell her what her dream means rather than talking with her about it. This may represent her anxiety that I might turn into such a person, might not be trustworthy after all. It may also represent her sense of limitation—that the therapeutic situation is inherently limited, that she cannot stay there with me indefinitely. Or she could be expressing anger—I am capable of a kind of scrutinizing aggressiveness and knowingness. But since in her dreams I represent a potential part of herself, it may also suggest that there is a part of her that knows what her dreams mean in a surprisingly direct way. This is particularly interesting in light of the song "Suzanne"; in it, Suzanne has a special knowledge that, when the poet enters into it, tells him that they have always been connected (lovers). This makes him want to travel on with her because she's "touched your perfect body with her mind." In the dream I do touch a part of her body—her brain—with my mind. Notice that she specifically says "brain" rather than "mind." Perhaps I represent here that knowing part whose ways may be unpleasant, abrupt, and surprising, and with which she doesn't always have conscious connection, but that is there at least sometimes.

Another interesting feature of these dreams, and one that I believe has contributed to our work together, is Simone's use of material from my own life. The issues that occupy her are the issues that occupy me, even to their expression: I do spend a great deal of time in the kitchen, and I find dancing around the house when alone extremely satisfying; "Suzanne" was a favorite song of mine in the sixties. Some clients are extremely sensitive to all sorts of unconscious material; Simone is unusually intuitive in any case, so the fact that she was able to use my inner life in her dreams did not surprise me (Jacoby, 1978, contains many examples of the use by analysands of unconscious material from the analyst). That this is possible makes it particularly important for therapists to do their own work—if the therapist is psychologically rigid and cannot allow anything new to happen or is very cut off from her unconscious, the client may not have the material to use for her own growth. (I strongly suspect that the locale of Simone's dreams—my backyard, my home—is an indication that she was using my psychic material, as well as being representative of my environment.)

Having formed this very positive transference, Simone could feel safe moving more deeply into her own pain and difficulty. An indication that she had finished with the issue of my status as a spiritual mother came when she dreamed that my consulting room needed windows; in the dream, she felt that there was a great deal to be seen outside, if only I'd make some windows. She subsequently left my house and went on a trip in an aerial gondola, seeing the whole of Vancouver and swooping down in various places. She was no longer satisfied with the view from my room; she needed to go out and see for herself. My environment and the way of being I represented had served as a container and a base for developing certain things in herself. Having done so, having found a way to ground herself in that environment, she began to travel into her own world. In the process, a great deal of pain began to emerge; she discovered how radically she had cut herself off from her feelings, though retaining contact with her intuitive side. Simone also participated in my dream workshops, and through this participation, various aspects of this discriminating splitting became clearer to me. She was so connected with her intuitive side that she was in some respects psychic—a great deal of energy seemed to have been shifted to that area. One evening in the group, she participated in an exercise that involved her going around the circle and giving an appropriate (imaginary) gift to each person. As she progressed around the circle, the startled looks on the faces of the other women made me wonder whether she was actually connecting with things that they were thinking about or wanted. This proved to be so—in almost every case, her imaginary present was something deeply appropriate from the person's own point of view and, in several cases, reflected things that the person had been thinking about at the time.

Simone's dreams became more and more magical; imagery from women's rituals, magicians, numinous places appeared. I found these dreams not just psychologically significant but enormously entertaining in the best sense—they were like the most energy-filled and evocative mythology—psychically resonant, rich with imaginative invention, clever. I began to reflect on just how much of her life was lived through her unconscious and, since she had had spectacular dreams since childhood, always had been. This made me wonder whether the dreams were not in part an attempt on the part of her unconscious to enrich her very austere childhood, whether they might have been constructed partly to be entertaining for her in a nourishing way. A poignant picture began to emerge of a little girl with unusual abilities and intelligence, with no one to give her any support and, as it turned out, people who discouraged her in her desires for anything better, more satisfying, more interesting, than her grim life at home. She was told over and over, in many ways, "You don't count, you're not important, don't bother anyone."

I was so used to finding Simone's dreams intrinsically interesting that it took a while to notice that I was beginning to have to strain to concentrate on them; that, in short, I was a little bored. Initially, I gave myself a brisk lecture about attention, but eventually I realized that I had been very caught up in the fascinating imagery of her dreams and had now begun to notice something that had been obvious all along. I was bored not because her dreams were less interesting but because she seemed so emotionally distant as she told them. The imagery was riveting, but where were her feelings? I shared this with her one night as we were working, in a very intellectual way, in the dream workshop. At this point, she had begun to dream about TV families, families whose limited emotional range, arbitrary rules, and fundamental inauthenticity reflected her experience of her own family. I told her that I noticed that the rich imagery of her dreams served as a kind of distraction from her lack of emotional connection with them, or at least the lack of emotional connection as she told them. As a result, we began to focus on how cut off from her feelings she was. She agreed, but the barrier seemed to her to be absolute. She and I agreed that there must be something very powerful indeed going on to make her erect such a strong defense. While she was still in this cut-off state, she had the following dream:

> I am a young reporter on assignment to investigate a young girl who's been very violent. I enter the apartment where she's supposed to live and it's very quiet, too quiet. At first when I had entered the apartment, I

> had felt protected, there had been a protective force somehow near me, but now I realize I am alone with this child. Although I can speak to someone, a friend, while I am in there, and tell what's happening, I am in there alone. I think I know what to expect in the apartment, though I am afraid to confront it. Apparently the girl has been extremely violent, both to herself and others. Even her mother has run from her to seek guidance and protection. I go into the kitchen and the little girl is in front of me. Her anger and violence have been spent, and instead of being a monster as I had feared, she stands before me like a broken creature. Her dark hair is wild and she has painted her face in a very primitive manner. I realize that she is full of sorrow and doesn't know how else to express herself. I feel great compassion for her.

Simone had this dream while she was in the group, and several other members expressed their feeling that it must be very frightening to have such a dream. But Simone was not afraid, just as she was not afraid in the dream. She had been able to keep her defenses in place as long as she needed to and bring the psychic situation to consciousness while they were still there so she could consciously prepare to meet and rescue this anguished child. Notice that, in the dream, the child's natural mother has fled. Simone, who started out in the dream as an investigator, finishes as the potential spiritual mother, full of compassion and understanding. She knows that the child is violent only because she is so sad and cannot express herself in any other way.

After this, Simone's work deepened. She began to remember more from childhood and to become conscious of the dynamics of her family when she was around them. She noticed how she was constantly criticized, manipulated, and asked to pay attention to others. My understanding of the depth of her pain increased a great deal when she began to remember incidents of neglect, of illness and injury that amounted to passive cruelty. Her parents were not just cold but angry, taking it out on her in ways that were not directly violent but still wounding both physically and psychically.

Simone is still working on these issues. She sees how the relationship whose end was one of the precipitating factors in her depression replicated many features of her family life. It was difficult to give up because, even though she hadn't got much attention from her partner in comparison to the amount her partner demanded from her, still it was more than she'd ever got at home. She values her intelligence and ability much more, allowing her creativity to have avenues in waking life as well as being exercised in her dreams. She is beginning to see and to believe that she is someone special, a person of unusual imaginative power and perception as well as considerable intellectual ability. Though her parents have not changed their discouraging ways, she is no longer taken in by them. It has been and continues to be a great pleasure and occasion for learning to work with her as she brings healing to her inner child.

Client's Voice: "Simone"

The rain falls softly
A child cries out in the night
As her eyes open.

I remember when I first put on glasses. I was thirteen and until that moment I had just assumed that everyone saw the world as I did—softly blurred around the edges. I remember the shock of experiencing clarity of vision for the first time.

The process of discovering my inner child has been rather like reexperiencing, over and over again, that first shock of seeing clearly. Only this time the shock is very painful and the requisite adjustment period is a great deal longer.

The focus of my therapeutic journey has been to explore to what extent I was wounded as a child and to what extent I have not yet recovered from those wounds. My dreams guide me on this important journey, as they have on all others. Their images spark memories, and as I remember childhood experiences (or re-remember them in a new light), I confront profound feelings of loneliness, sadness, and despair. It hurts to look at these feelings and it's hard to accept them as mine, even though they're so much a part of me. After all, my major defense has always been to not acknowledge my own pain. I thought feeling sad and alone and unwanted was just a natural state of being. This has been the biggest hurdle—overcoming the belief and the fear that my pain, my wounded child, doesn't count. (Just like I've always felt that my accomplishments didn't count and that I didn't count.) This process for me, as much as anything, has been an affirmation that my pain is real and that it matters.

I don't yet fully know my inner child; we still have some serious reconnecting to do. And that's something I welcome. Some people say they are afraid of the inner child, but I'm not. At present, I feel only love and compassion toward her, and a great sadness for the depth of her pain. Sometimes I am weak with this sadness, exhausted by it. My ego is strong and I function well in the world. But inside, when I'm in touch with her, I feel weighted down, often despairing. I do believe (and I need to believe) that I will once again experience the energy and joy that I know is also so much a part of my child self, but as I write this I know I'm rarely in touch with that aspect of her.

When I feel like this journey will never end and that I'll feel lost forever, frustration sets in. I cry to myself that I want it to end right now! I'm tired. I'm miserable. I'm lonely. I want to forget about this insistent, demanding, and dependent child and get on with my adult life. But even as I say it, I know that in my heart I can never go back to not remembering, not feeling, nor do I want to. My life is finally making sense. I now understand, in ways that I cannot well express, the why and the how of it all. Why I've always felt sad and alone. (Because I cried out as a child and no one answered. No one paid attention when it mattered most.) How I carry that with me. (I experienced so much rejection and loss. Now I hang on to relationships. Don't reject me again. Don't leave me again.)

So with feelings of great tenderness and with the help of a loving therapist, I continue the inward journey, searching for who I was then and what I needed and didn't receive. Despite the inner critic that wants to discount my discoveries, my eyes are opening to the truth. I can recognize now that as a child I had spirit and stamina and I see that these qualities were not honored. I am trying to honor them now. I see that I was intelligent and creative and that these qualities were not nurtured. And I am trying to nurture them now. The list goes on.

I often feel angry and resentful at having to do such necessary caretaking myself: Why couldn't my parents have paid more attention? Why didn't they care more? Why didn't they think I was special? This anger comes in waves, washes over me, then dissipates. I know why they couldn't, didn't. It wasn't done for them. So always under the anger is again, pain and sadness. And compassion for all of us in this together.

This journey hurts and it's hard work, but it heals. Because this is better than not seeing, not knowing. There is freedom in this and somewhere, though I can't touch it yet, there is joy.

A petal unfurls
Weighted down with a teardrop
It drifts towards earth.

References

Chodorow, N. *The Reproduction of Mothering*. Los Angeles: University of California Press, 1978.

Griffin, S. *Pornography and Silence*. New York: Harper & Row, 1981.

Jacoby, M. *The Analytic Encounter*. Toronto: Inner City Books, 1978.

Jung, C. G. *Civilization in Transition*. In G. Adler and others (eds.), *Collected Works*. (R. F. C. Hull, trans.) Vol. 10. (2nd ed.) Princeton, N.J.: Princeton University Press, 1964.

Layard, J. *A Celtic Quest*. (rev. ed.; A. S. Bosch, ed.) Dallas: Spring Press, 1985.

Rycroft, C. *The Innocence of Dreams*. New York: Pantheon Press, 1979.

PART THREE

TRUSTING THE BODY'S MEMORY

9

Voices from the Silence: Use of Imagery with Incest Survivors

Naida D. Hyde
Client: Chris Watson

To shame a woman is to silence her. For the young girl, incest is a profoundly and pervasively shaming experience. It instills a silence in the child that reverberates in the core of her being. Without healing, this profound silence forms the foundation for her lifetime of her being in the world. Healing consists in her finding her own voice and learning to use it by breaking the silence about her shame. She learns to see it as *his* abuse, not *her* shame—and say so, out loud!

But one of the difficulties and frustrations confronting both the therapists doing this healing work and many of their women clients who know that there is something terribly and deeply wrong with them but have no words for what it is is that the clients' pact of silence with their abusers not to tell anyone extends to themselves as well as to the people in their world. They keep the vow of silence

Note: This chapter is an expanded and revised version of a paper on the same topic presented by the author to the annual conference of the American Imagery Association, New York, 1986.

even with themselves, shrouding the words in shame, anxiety, self-hatred, and pain. And for the child who was sexually abused in infancy or her very early years, before language became a central way of mediating her experience, there were no words to understand or communicate what was being done to her, sometimes in the name of love. Her soul and her body registered the violation, expressing it over time in the symptom complexes that are the hallmark of incest: chronic depression seemingly unrelated to external life events, severely negative self-image, specific sexual dysfunction, chronic recurring physical symptomatology, particularly affecting the gastrointestinal and genitourinary tracts, and distressed interpersonal relations characterized by various forms of victimization (Beck and van der Kolk, 1987; Briere and Runtz, 1988; Bryer, Nelson, Miller, and Krol, 1987; Burgess, Hartman, and McCormack, 1987; Hyde, 1984). The secret knowledge is kept in trust for her to access when she feels safe enough and cared for enough to survive knowing and putting words to it.

Although at present there is a burgeoning literature on the incidence and prevalence of sexual abuse, the dynamics in the incestuous family, and long-term effects on the victim, very little has been written on the process of psychotherapy with women incest survivors. There is even less about uncovering the repression and denial and the process of helping early childhood victims find their own words and voice and healing (Hyde, 1986, 1987).

When therapists do not know and recognize the diagnostic indicators of incest or are co-opted by the power of clients' denial and repression, women will leave therapy perhaps having obtained some symptomatic relief but not having been healed. They will then reappear in the same or a different therapist's office when the pain of their symptoms again becomes overwhelming to them. It is sobering to consider that some therapists rarely encounter incest as an issue in their clients, while others, who know what to look for and are not complicit in keeping the secret, encounter incest in as many as 50 percent of their women clients.

The psychotherapeutic use of the woman client's own naturally occurring imagery, imagery in the service of her own healing, is the focus of this chapter. While the term *imagery* is used in a number of different ways, signifying somewhat different processes, it is eidetic imagery, as delineated by Ahsen (1973, 1977), that is the focus here. Ahsen (1977) defines eidetic imagery as "a psychical visual image of unusual vividness. When this image is experienced in the mind, it is 'seen' clearly like a movie image. This inner 'seeing' is accompanied by pressure in the visual apparatus, and a definite change in consciousness" (p. 14). He goes on to describe the psyche as having an eidetic fast-filing system, a system composed of visual units like a library of picture cards, each unit being a replica of an original experience. Each original experience is recorded in the form of a full-blown visual picture, or as ISM: *Image*, portraying a situation; *Somatic* state, representing body feelings and emotions attached to the image; and *Meaning* of the image. The visual image, the somatic state, and its meaning represent a single unified recorded experience. Attention and concentration serve to elicit eidetic imagery in a person.

Imagery has a power and a gentleness that are consistent with the psyche's best ability to heal itself. Used effectively, imagery is not merely a technique or a tool but indeed is part of the fabric of psychotherapy, because it is an aspect of herself that each woman brings to the work, as much as are her words, her feelings, and her thoughts. And she learns over time to feel empowered by and even take delight in the creative and healing use of her own images.

Feminist Theory as a Frame for Clinical Practice

If sexual abuse can be understood at all, it is best understood within a feminist theoretical frame. Sexual abuse is seen as the logical extension in our patriarchal culture of male power, male prerogative, and male inclination to sexualize all relationships. It is one facet, one result, of the misogyny that pervades our lives as women. All women chronically suffer the ill effects of misogyny's double bind: we are shamed from birth because we are born female, and our lives are shot through with the daily corroding effects of being hated and feared by men, but we are not allowed to see it or talk about it (Dworkin, 1974). Our experience of misogyny is denied to us. It is made invisible to us. It is not talked about. It is not labeled. It is not named. And when someone has the courage to give voice to it, it is denied, and the speaker is shamed and punished.

The woman who has been sexually abused thus carries a double shame and a double pact of silence—once for being a woman in this male culture and twice for having been sexually abused. The way back from both these traumas is through making visible the invisible, giving words and labels and voice to the unspeakable, and celebrating the courage of those who storm the barricades of male prerogative.

Because there is such a high incidence of sexual abuse in the histories of women clients, it is incumbent on every therapist who works with women to have developed not only her own philosophy of healing but also her own understanding of the nature of sexual abuse, its dynamics and sequelae, and the process required to heal its wounds.

The Intelligence of the Heart: A Brief Overview of Imagery Literature

Although the clinical and research literature on the use of mental imagery, or "active imagination," has proliferated in the past ten years (Sheikh and Jordan, 1983), none of it specifically illuminates the use of imagery with women incest survivors. However, it does provide helpful ideas and ways to conceptualize mental imagery and the uses of imagery in psychotherapy practice. There is now a *Journal of Mental Imagery* as well as at least two multidisciplinary associations devoted to the study and use of mental imagery in enriching experience and healing.

Horowitz (1970) describes and names different kinds of images, all of which occur in work with incest survivors:

1. Hypnagogic images occur in the twilight state between wakefulness and sleep.
2. Hypnopompic images occur while waking up. Both these and hypnagogic images are characterized by a sense of nonvolitional control.
3. Memory images are a reconstruction of a past perception. They may be quite dim, almost nonsensory in nature, or may be extremely distinct, even projected onto blank spaces, such as walls or paper, in an effort to localize them externally. When

memory images are especially vivid, they are called eidetic images.

4. Unbidden images are sequelae to traumatic perceptions and are the expressions of repressed ideas and feelings.

In his seminal book *Imagery and Daydream Methods in Psychotherapy and Behavior Modifications,* Singer (1974) states that the efficacy of imagery lies in (1) the ability of the person to discriminate fantasy processes, (2) clues for the therapist on ways to approach uncomfortable situations, (3) the rehearsal of alternatives, and (4) consequent decreases in fear in approaching situations that were previously avoided. The person gains competence and mastery in her world through the use of imagery. Singer (1978) goes on to discuss the value of patients using imagery in a natural way in the service of their own healing to adopt the therapist as a kind of imaginary companion, someone to whom they can talk privately in their minds when confronted with a difficult situation.

In *Waking Dream Therapy: Dream Process as Imagination,* Epstein (1981) gives an overview of the history of imagination as an introduction to his "waking dream therapy." He quotes H. H. Price, the English philosopher who elegantly affirms the real existence of the imaginal world: "Paradoxical as it may sound, there is nothing imaginary about a mental image. It is an actual entity, as real as anything can be. Mental images are not imaginary at all. We do actually experience them, and they are no more imaginary than sensations" (p. 15). Epstein goes on to explain that the immersing of oneself in the imaginal realm is in effect the immersing of oneself into emotion. This is, in fact, what is meant by "the intelligence of the heart"—the term used by North American Indian cultures to describe imagination and holistic perception (p. 18). Epstein describes the role of the therapist in waking dream therapy as both instructor and adviser who can give directions to the explorer in this unfamiliar and surprising new spatial terrain. He warns that therapists must refrain from interpreting events either during or after the waking dream, imposing on people's freedom to learn for themselves and allowing either themselves or the patients to "free associate" during or after the work (p. 24). These are wise words, ones that all too few clinicians heed.

Therapeutic Considerations in Using Imagery with Women Incest Survivors

As Beck (1972) says, "You cannot be free if you are contained within a fiction." The inward journey undertaken by the woman client who is an incest survivor to discover the source of her life pain and its crippling effects is a journey of trepidation, driven by desperation and a not quite pervasive despair. It is not unusual for a woman who begins therapy to say that this is truly her last attempt to fix whatever is wrong, that she is too exhausted to fight any longer and life is too bleak for her to continue unless she can find some hope that she can ever feel different. Thus, the therapist must be solid in her own knowledge, gained from experience in this work, that to know one's own early trauma and its effects is better than not to know; that not knowing is what brings chronic emotional deadening, unsatisfying relationships, and recurrent incapacitating physical symptoms. To know brings relief and freeing of energy and the "fitting into place" of a part of a woman's self that has been split off since the original trauma.

Only when the therapist presents a clear, consistent, solid, calm self can the woman client feel safe enough to express and deal with her fears, with the hope that they will be intelligible to the therapist even if they are not to her. The client often expresses her fears by saying something such as "I have always felt that there was something wrong inside me, something deep down, something black and yukky—but what if there's nothing there? Or what if there's something there, but I can't get to it? What if I'm just looking for something to pin my awful feelings on?" The therapist must respond by validating the client's internal experience of her self by saying, "Listen to the wisdom of your own body, pay attention to the truth of your own experience—there must be something there or you wouldn't have felt so truly awful deep inside for such a long time. If you want us to work together to find out what's there, we can do that. If you decide you truly want to know what's there, no matter how frightening it is, it's certainly possible to get to it together." This kind of statement spells out to the client that she and the therapist are participating in a real relationship, that the relationship is an alliance, a working relationship, one in which the therapist is aligned with that part of the client that, despite her intense fears and foreboding, is impelling her toward wholeness. Achterberg and Lawlis, 1980, p. 40, postulate that "body wisdom" or other homeostatic mechanisms naturally allow the return to health if a person is relaxed and in mental contact with his or her physiology—health *is* the normal state. See also Keleman, 1979, p. 10, who describes how a deeper knowledge of his body resulted in an intensifying of feeling and image making.

The Therapist Introduces Imagery

As every feminist psychotherapist knows, women have little experience speaking with their own voice and believing in their own words and perceptions; they have little experience being listened to and believed. The process of any feminist psychotherapy is that process in which a woman comes to appreciate her own thoughts and feelings and to celebrate the emergence of her blossoming self. When the therapist introduces the concept of imagery as a way for a woman to participate actively and creatively in her own healing, allowing a part of her that is usually unattended to speak, women tend to be unsure and timorous and full of fears of failure of not doing it "right." "What if nothing comes to mind?" "What if I can't see what I'm supposed to see?" are typical questions and concerns that mirror every woman's lack of trust in her own inner process and life-given drive toward integrity. I always respond by saying that the wonderful thing about imagery is that the unconscious provides exactly the most helpful, the most healing image for the person at any given time, and that while she may not have faith in her own inner process of healing, I do. The therapist must, of course, believe these words in order to say them. "Allow yourself to be surprised," I say. The therapist's warmth and attitude of friendly anticipation and readiness for an adventure, plus the timely use of humor, help reduce client performance anxiety.

One of the core elements of the incest survivor's trauma is that she was the entirely passive victim of wholly unwanted physical, emotional, and sexual intrusion and violation by her father or other family member. Thus, one of the key elements in her healing is that she learn that she has a right to choices that are in her own best interests. Thus, it is incumbent on the therapist to help a woman experience her active, freely assumed choice, even in small matters. Because any psychotherapy has the potential to be intrusive, it is important that the therapist explain the uses of imagery, its safety features, and the client's right to use it or not, begin it or end it, according to her own comfort and safety level. The therapist must always keep in mind that passivity and compliance have been survival strategies for the incest survivor, no matter how high-powered a professional she is outside the therapist's office.

Additionally, the therapist must keep in mind that betrayal by a loving, trusted person and a consequent enduring state of aloneness are the legacy of the incest survivor. No matter how personable, how social, how verbal, how connected a woman seems, there is every likelihood that deep inside she feels inexorably alone and terrified of any intimate relationship, including the therapy relationship. For example, one new client began several sessions by reporting imagery work that she had done at home alone at night. The imagery content and her bodily reactions were quite frightening to her and reminiscent of old childhood nightmares. Rather than asking her why she was doing imagery alone ("why" questions are intrusive and carry a demand-accountability element), I suggested that when she was ready, we could do some imagery together and that she might feel safer doing it with me rather than alone. She did not respond, but at the end of the session, as she was putting on her coat to leave, she burst out saying that it really frightened her to think of making herself as vulnerable with me as she would have to be to do the imagery, that she was afraid that I would suggest it, and that to be the "good client" (which she had told me was important to her), she would not be able to say no and would have to comply. I told her that I would not suggest it; she knew about the possibility of our doing imagery work together, and when she felt comfortable enough with me, she could suggest it. She left feeling obviously relieved. In my eagerness to present myself as helpful and trustworthy and someone she could ally herself with against her inner terrors, I had momentarily forgotten that safety for the incest survivor resides in aloneness, not relationship. She reminded me. I listened and responded accordingly. To the extent that we can listen with open minds and hearts to our clients, they will tell us what we need to know to help them in their healing. This is the dance of the therapy.

As is true for the psychotherapy process as a whole, imagery work will be effective only if the therapist is able to stay out of the client's way. Imagery work is an opportunity to test our ability to be nonintrusive, verbally and psychologically. The therapist who needs to understand, control, lead, direct, and make sense out of everything presented by the client will soon shut down the process, being left with a rebellious client, an overly compliant client, or no client at all. The therapist must have a deep and sustaining belief in the client's right to her own self-discovery—and must practice this belief! She must be willing not to intrude, to be content to allow the imagery its own integrity, and to resist all her urges toward interpretation and explanation and pushing the client to "see" or "know" or "understand" more than she is ready to.

Thus, when a woman images "a little girl" being sexually hurt by "a man" and goes on to say "I'm looking at them; I can almost see his face," it is all right to ask "Do you know who they are?" but you must believe her when she says no, even when she finishes the imagery by seeing her mother at home in the garden and says "I tried to tell my mother. I thought she knew." A quiet acknowledgment by the therapist—either in the first person, responding to the client's last statement with "I'm sure you did," or to the whole in the third person, "Perhaps the little girl needs to feel safer in order to be able to see the man's face"—is sufficient. The client's use of the third person is defensive and therefore necessary for her psychic safety. For the therapist to intrude and insist on her "owning" the experience in the first person is abusive. The client is quite able to hear her own words and her own voice and see who is in her own images, and she will, as interpersonal safety permits.

Flashbacks

The term *flashback* was first coined in reference to afterimages experienced by people who had taken hallucinogenic drugs. Presently it has two meanings: the subjective sensation of the unbidden return of visual images and an image that is a repetition of a perception from the distant past (Horowitz, 1978).

Flashes of images are often the first memories that present themselves to the woman incest survivor. This may happen inside or outside the therapy session. The flashes are often doubly frightening because of their content and because they are outside the woman's control, coming unbidden and returning unexpectedly. One woman who had a "sense" that her grandfather might have sexually abused her but had no memories of such abuse reported that while playing tennis she had an image of an erect penis lying against a child's body through the midsection. The image remained throughout her tennis game and was very disconcerting to her. The power of unbidden images is accentuated when they come in conjunction with kinesthetic or bodily memories. Another woman arrived late and looked apprehensive, saying she had not wanted to come that day. Later she reported feeling like she had had thick cream in the back of her mouth for the past few weeks. She then said that she had had an image of being held by her father as a baby and his putting heavy cream from the top of the milk bottle onto his finger and licking it off and then putting some cream on his penis and putting it in her mouth and her feeling very strange in her stomach about sucking it. This was a progression, a personalizing of her memory. In the previous session, she had said that she had played pool with her father that morning and that she had felt really "funny" being with him. While she was with him, "flashes" of images had come to mind of a baby with her father's penis in her mouth and a little girl with a man putting his finger in her vagina. She had used these flashes, or naturally occurring images, as the starting point to move spontaneously into an extensive imagery session.

Use of Guided Imagery

To dispel fears about being able to "do" imagery or "do it *right*," I usually start with a simple, straightforward induction and a pleasant guided image. I will outline here the induction that I use, followed by a typical guided image. The client has a choice of sitting up facing me or lying down. Most incest survivors choose to sit up, vigilance and hyperalertness being assiduously developed survival skills. She is then instructed to shut her eyes if she feels comfortable doing that and, if she is sitting up, to put her feet firmly on the ground to help her center and feel grounded. I then say:

> Focus your attention on your breathing and take very slow deep breaths in and out—slow deep breath in . . . slow deep breath out. . . . Notice where you are holding tension in your body and let go of it and allow yourself to be more comfortable . . . just let your thoughts float away . . . use the sounds you hear outside you to deepen your relaxation. . . . Just imagine you have a ball of sparkling white healing light swirling around in your abdomen and as you breathe in, the white light moves up through your body right up to the top of your head sending healing, relaxing energy all over, and as you breathe out, the sparkling white light moves down the back of your head, your neck, your back, your arms, your legs, and out your feet, sending healing energy from the universe all through you. . . . Just take a minute and enjoy the sensations as you experience them."

When the client's breathing has slowed and her energy seems more focused inward, I continue.

> When you are ready, you will find yourself in a warm, comfortable, secure place. It may be a place you have been before, and so will be familiar to you, or it may be a brand new place that you have never been before. Just take your time, and let me know when you are in your place.

I then maintain silence for a minute or two, and most clients will say that they have an image in mind. I then ask them to describe it. If the description is rich and multisensory, I suggest that they take a few minutes and enjoy being there, knowing that because it has come from inside them, they are free to return to that warm, safe, secure place any time they choose. When a few minutes have elapsed, I say, "Take a minute or two to finish off and say good-bye to where you are, knowing you can return any time you need to, and then come back." I sit and wait quietly until the woman refocuses and makes eye contact with me. I prefer to wait until she says something about the experience, but other therapists may not believe that it is intrusive to ask "What was that like for you?" In a first experience with imagery, if a woman does not give much sensory information about her surroundings, I do ask questions, such as "What do you see around you?" "Are there any sounds, smells, is it warm or cool, what time of day, year is it? What do you feel underfoot?" to help her notice what she is actually experiencing, to validate the richness of her experience, and to celebrate with her her creation of that safe place.

"But what if it doesn't go that easily and smoothly?" asks the novice. "What if the client comes up with no image or a frightening image?" If the client reports that there is nothing there, I ask what the "nothing" looks like. The basic rule for the therapist in any psychotherapeutic encounter is to start always from where the client is; imagery work is no different. Often the imagery will progress with the client describing exactly what she is seeing. If she seems anxious or blocked, she may need something for herself before feeling comfortable enough to proceed. Sometimes suggestions from the therapist reassure the woman and let her know that the therapist is really there. For example, one woman was silent for about five minutes before producing an image. (In the following dialogues, *T* represents the therapist and *C* the client.)

T: Tell me what's happening inside.

C: I'm trying to look for an image. I'm trying to look around a sheer curtain as if that's blocking whatever I want to see.

T: There may be something you need for yourself before you can look around the curtain. I wonder what it could be?

Rather than respond to my low-key musing inquiry, the client moved straight into the dissociative state that she had used as a child to "escape" her father's abuse of her. As is true for each moment in psychotherapy, the therapist must be able to "contain" whatever the client presents and must trust that that is exactly what the client needs for herself right now.

An incest survivor may respond to the initial instruction with "There is no safe place." The therapist responds, "Well, if there had been or were a safe place, what would it look and be like?" Or the client might move quickly into a memory of the place she used to hide to keep safe from her father's physical and sexual violence—this was her safe place. It was not the therapist's intent in her instruction, but it is how the client's psyche interprets "safe place," and it must represent somewhere she needs to go in the work and is ready to go or she would not be imaging that place. The therapist must be there to accompany her to that place of safety and terror so that the client is not alone there as she was in her childhood. The therapist must be vigilant not to recapitulate the original trauma inadvertently.

Nondirective Imaging

As soon as the client indicates that she is comfortable with imagery work and has decided that she wants to know what is "back there," I move to an induction that focuses on imagery she produces spontaneously, dependent wholly on her present physical and psychological state. Following the usual induction, my suggestion is, "When you are ready, an image will come to mind that will help you get where you need to go in your healing journey. Just take your time and allow yourself to be surprised."

A variation on this induction includes body focusing. For example, if a woman describes feeling lost, alone, sad, angry, or any other emotion in her present life, I ask her where she experiences that feeling in her body and ask her to put her hands, palms down on top of each other, over that area. For some women, it may take a few sessions to be able to locate their feelings in their bodies; often women incest survivors are so split off from their feelings and from their bodies that they cut themselves off from the neck downward and "think" of their feelings as residing in their heads, rather more like labels than bodily experiences. So they talk *about* feelings but do not experience them, something only a very attuned therapist can often pick up. Bodily clues for the therapist to attend to are shallow breathing and smoking. Because feelings reside down the body's midsection, generally with anger under sadness, and rage beneath anger, with shame hidden deep under them all, shallow breathing and the drug-induced state brought on by smoking tend to preclude access to feelings. This has been a survival mechanism for the incest survivor, but like all survival defenses, over time its cost comes to outweigh its benefits. So the therapist begins the process of reacquainting a woman with her own body and helping her learn to experience her body as her best and most truthful ally in the process of regaining her life and her self. With hands held over a particular place, the instruction is, "Focus on your breathing and breathe right down into that place where you are holding your hands and just see what's there. An image will come to mind when you're ready." If a woman is very out of touch with her self and her body, she may say that nothing is happening. The therapist should then suggest that she stay focused on her breathing and notice what is happening in her body.

C: Nothing is happening in my body.

T: Are you aware of your chest cavity expanding and relaxing as you breathe?

C: Sure.

T: How about the feeling of air going in and out of your nostrils as you take those long, slow breaths?

C: Sure.

T: What else are you aware of in your body?

C: I feel a funny sensation in the bottom of my abdomen.

Because the body is the repository of the woman's incest memories, imaging with a body focus often provides the most direct access to those memories. The above example continues:

T: Stay with that sensation in your abdomen and just see what's there.

C: If you push in, it's a sexual feeling.

T: Where do you feel that sexual feeling?

C: My vagina.

T: Stay with those feelings, let yourself experience them, and see what you're aware of.

C: It reminds me that dad used to tickle us also. Last night when I was in bed trying to think about him, it brought up sexual feelings.

Another woman began by saying that there was "nothing" there and then progressed to:

C: So many pictures that they don't last long enough to talk about.

T: Slow them down and tell me what they are.

C: I'm making my parents' bed and finding something strange and knowing it was sperm and going and being sick to my stomach.

T: I wonder how you knew it was sperm.

C: I was ten years old. I'm not relaxed anymore. I'm tense, and feel incredibly cold.

She then grabbed for my hand and started to shake involuntarily and spasmodically all over her body and then stopped breathing.

T: Take a slow, deep breath.

C: (Crying) I felt a searing pain in my vagina and had to shut it off. I felt like I had a heavy weight on top of me; I didn't feel like I had anything in my mouth.

Calling Forth Allies in Healing

Finding and Healing the Lost Child. It is the inner child of the past who holds the secret of each woman's abuse in a sacred but deadly trust with her offender. Suicide often seems a more viable option than breaking that trust. Whereas loyalty to one's family has been engendered since birth, loyalty to one's own self is an alien and dangerous concept, terrifying to the woman incest survivor. The therapist who tries too directly to help a woman steer a new course through the rocky shoals to self-discovery may find herself relegated to the position of enemy and dismissed accordingly. Her motives will be viewed as highly suspect, and a woman who has come from a family who did not hold her best interests in mind will not readily find it believable or reassuring that the therapist does. The "child" molders in that solitary confinement of the soul (Miller, 1981, p. 8), waiting but not hoping for deliverance.

Through imagery, the adult woman dares approach her "child self." It takes great courage for her to do so, for the child self holds not only the secret of her violation but also the overwhelming anguish, terror, rage, desolation, and self-hatred that have been her unacknowledged companions through life, kept at bay till now by the ingenuity of her defenses. The therapist may suggest that the woman bring to mind an image of her child self, or the woman may spontaneously do so while talking about or remembering incidents from her childhood. Her first reaction may be to push the child away: "I don't want to have anything to do with her, I just want her to shut up" or to feel alienated by her: "She won't look at me, she's over in the corner, curled up with her back toward us."

Only when the woman feels relatively safe in the therapy and experiences the therapist as trustworthy will her child self start to emerge. There is much glib and facile clinical literature about the necessity of trust as the foundation of the psychotherapeutic relationship. It is unrealistic for a therapist to expect a woman incest survivor to trust her; when violation and abuse take place within a context of love, it leaves a deep confusion and mistrust about everyone's credibility, certainly the therapist's.

An imagery session proved to be the turning point in one woman's struggle to allow herself to feel safe enough to align her child self with me in her struggle to bring to consciousness the trauma of her early sexual abuse by her mother. An image came to mind of a deep, narrow swimming pool that she had to enter. It was very dark and very frightening, and she felt both impelled to enter the water and daunted by her fear. I asked her what would make it possible for her to do what she needed to do.

C: Maybe if I had someone else there with me.

T: Who would you like to have there if you could have anybody?

C: For a minute I thought of having my mother there but it's not a good idea—we'll get stuck halfway (long silence). You would be a better person. You're in the water with me—you can just hold my hand and we can kick our legs and just float up top to the sunshine—but it's scary. I don't want to have to depend on anyone. But it feels comforting, too—but I should have done it myself.

T: What would help you to feel the comforting feelings and turn off the thoughts?

C: Just to float there and hold your hand and that's enough. I don't have to do anything else. But that's the fear—that I have to get more involved, more entangled. I can just tread water and hold your hand and just feel safe and comfortable. You don't need my support.

After the imagery, she felt very relieved and clear and said, "I want you to help me but not interfere; I'm so overwhelmed by what I need. It's not an equal relationship, but you're not like my mother. I don't feel like I'm going to be strangled or pulled down." And with hope, "maybe I can have more control in my other relationships—I don't always have to do what they want me to do."

Only when the child self feels nurtured and cared for and listened to and believed will she tell the secret of the incest. It is insufficient, albeit necessary, for the therapist to care for and believe the woman and her child self. The therapist must help the woman learn to truly parent her own child self. The imagery work powerfully conveys the complexity of that process. The following transcript of a therapy session illustrates the dynamic play of forces affecting every incest survivor. One of my clients suffered chronic irritable bowel and anal fissures before accessing memories of molestation, first by a neighbor, then earlier sexual abuse by her father, and then later abuse by her brother. She arrived at my office after several weeks of feeling emotionally better and several months of being completely symptom free, saying she had just come from her doctor and had an appointment with a surgeon because she had such severe pain in her coccyx. This was a signal to me that she had more to remember. When I asked her what she thought her bodily pain was about, she said very reluctantly, "I have a sense that there's more to remember," and then angrily, explosively, "I don't want this shit!" I suggested to her that her body had been using that metaphor for years, but knowing what happened to her seemed to be the only way to get rid of the "shit" and be healed, physically and in her soul. With this, she lay down on the couch, and we began.

C: Image of my father. He looks like he looked in some home movies I remember seeing. Image of him sharpening a knife as he used to when he carved meat—see him in profile. He's concentrating. Image of myself almost overlaid on the image of him—I was eight or nine years old maybe—I'm dressed up for a celebration of some kind. Two separate pictures. I'm behind my dad. I'm acting as if there are other people around. My father is acting as if no one else is around. I see the image from the front—my father's profile—I'm behind his back somehow—like two movies—I have a very open expectant look on my face. I don't look afraid. The child me seems to be coming toward me, but she isn't getting anywhere.

T: What's in her way?

C: I don't think there is anything in front of her, but she's stuck. I have the feeling she would run toward me, but she's stuck with the picture of my dad. It's like she's attached to him—it's like the two images are stuck together. She looks more 3D—my dad looks really flat—like a photograph, except that he's moving in his and sharpening the knife. Now it's all mixed up with that other image, and my father's standing at the end of the table and the baby's on the table and my brother's face is there (image of her memory of being sexually abused at eighteen months of age by her father).

T: The child you has something to tell you, and she needs not to be stuck to her father to come to you.

C: I have a really intense feeling of wanting to hold that child (crying).

T: You can do that.

C: I don't want to let her go—

T: You don't have to let her go, do you?

C: No—it doesn't seem like she wants to talk to me—she just wants to hold on. I have her head right in my neck. She doesn't want to show her face. She feels like any little kid feels when they just cling. Now the image of my father is behind her, and she doesn't want to look back. Like that kid's game we played when we were little and everything freezes—

T: What would unfreeze it?

C: I have to know what she knows and I can't see (crying).

T: Tell her you need to know what she knows.

C: Talking, talking, talking—she's clinging—feels like I'm talking to her hair.

T: What does she need to feel safe to tell you?

C: She needs to know I'm not going to push her away—she needs to feel safe—

T: So can you assure her about those things?

C: I'm trying to—

The imagery ended with her sitting up and leaning forward to have me hold her while she sobbed like a little child.

Some clients, such as Chris, whose story completes this chapter, need no formal induction to move immediately into clear and compelling imagery of their child self and their trauma during a session. Chris's memories all surfaced in this way. Ostensibly out of the blue, but obviously triggered by feeling safe and in the appropriate context to remember her early trauma, she accessed images of her child self. During one session, she had an image of herself as a child lying down on the living room floor on her stomach coloring in a coloring book and seeing her father come up behind her, lie down on top of her, and rape her rectally. She became increasingly terrified as she remembered this and was quite panicky, saying over and over that it couldn't possibly be true, and it didn't make sense that anyone would do that sort of horrible thing to a little child. I agreed that it didn't make sense but said that nevertheless it was true and that she needed to pay attention to her images of what happened and to the intensity and appropriateness of her feelings. She replied that if she had eighteen hands, they would all be pushing the image away and she would be refusing to believe it.

Following several more terrifying and painful memories of her father's violent sexual abuse, working through her own self-hatred and learning to rage at her father for his devastation of her, Chris said that as painful as all the memories are for her, she had an image of the child inside her leaping up and down for joy that finally someone was listening to her and believing her and encouraging her to be free.

Accessing One's Own Spirit Guide. The concept of spirit guides, present within each of us and accessible to us for comfort, wisdom, and companionship, is not a consciously familiar one (certainly it is not one taught in graduate clinical psychology training programs). Nevertheless, there often appear to be a deeper-level familiarity and positive feeling attached to the idea of accessing one's spirit guide. It is indeed a "user friendly" idea. When I learned, in an imagery workshop, to access my spirit guide (a seal—named Lucille), in a matter of a few seconds of delightful conversation with her, she helped me solve a problem that I had been stewing over for months. (The workshop was run by psychologist David Bresler, who prefers the term "inner adviser" to "spirit guide," and whose inductions are used throughout this chapter. See Jaffe and Bresler, 1980.) In that workshop, we did not learn that our spirit guide may appear in some form in real-life situations when we need her, and so I was surprised on a number of occasions when I was lonely or traumatized—for example, just after my dog was run over and killed—to look out at the ocean and have Lucille pop her head out of the water, very close to land, and look right at me. It gave me such a powerful feeling of energy available from the universe to comfort me that a smile invariably began deep in my core and radiated up and out of me to meet her. Since that time, when I have called on the wisdom of the universe, an eagle has come, telling me that I can be as strong and powerful and take up as much space as his beautiful wings. Later, a quiet, serene, and wise woman has come.

How can we understand this phenomenon? Those of us trained in Western traditional thought may be better off not worrying ourselves with the question but accepting the knowledge and wisdom of other cultures.

For women incest survivors, who feel chronically alone and bereft of even the possibility of being truly loved, feeling as deeply unlovable as they do, the idea of discovering their very own spirit guide seems light and innocuous and so farfetched as to not call forth their usual range of self-defeating statements. Calling forth a woman's spirit guide is usually done as an extension of the guided imagery described above, in which, following trance induction through slow, deep breathing, the person finds herself in a safe place where she spends a few minutes. The next instruction is: "Coming toward you, you will see some creature or animal or person; let me know when it appears." When it appears to the client:

T: What is its name—the *first* name that comes into your mind?

The client often expresses enjoyment, interest, and humor at the point of describing the named creature or person spirit guide.

T: Take a deep breath and with its inspiration let a question, concern, or challenge that you need help with formulate in your mind and then ask your spirit guide the question.

Allow a few minutes here. If the client reports the spirit guide saying nothing or just looking at the client, suggest that the client ask the spirit guide what she or he needs in order to respond. This kind of intervention often frees up the system to proceed.

T: (Final suggestion before coming back) This is your spirit guide. You can call her or him up any time you feel the need to commune. Finish off by thanking your guide for her or his wisdom and come back when you are ready.

In *Imagery in Healing: Shamanism and Modern Medicine,* social scientist Jeanne Achterberg (1985) presents instructions for calling forth a spirit guide and then advises, "I would, from my own experience, caution you never to take this exercise lightly. A slightly altered sensorium occasioned by the breathing patterns, the levels of reality that the psyche weaves into the twilight of awareness, and the material that springs up after being embedded deeply in the subconscious (usually for good reason) compose the ingredients for a sometimes frightening, always emotionally charged, experience. Incidentally, you may want to do as the Indians do to test the validity of the spirit ally. Ask it to appear to you in some form in ordinary, everyday, wide awake reality within the next few days" (pp. 206–207).

In imagery work where incest is suspected, the therapist must feel strong and competent and fearless to accompany the woman on her journey inward and backward through time, a journey through the world of her childhood defensive structures and into the world of her terror, aloneness, and deep self-hatred. This is a world that may have been inhabited not only by violence and violation but sometimes by evil. This is not a joyride for even the most experienced therapist, so honest self-appraisal is requisite for each therapist who undertakes to do this work.

To be an intelligent and competent guide helping each woman access and heal her child self requires that the therapist have a thorough grounding in child development and child psychodynamics, as well as in family systems. Many graduate-level training programs do not require students to have experience working with children but consider work with adults sufficient, seeming to assume that adults spring fully formed in that state. When a woman is regressed and in her "child self," the effective therapist must have a conceptual as well as an experiential understanding of how "old" she is and so frame her interventions accordingly.

As feminist psychotherapists helping women incest survivors heal, we must become warriors. We must become whole ourselves and shed our cloak of shame and mantle of silence. We must refuse to be abused anymore in our own lives and so model empowerment to other women. Accompanying a woman through her own birthing into the joy of self-discovery is the legacy of the healer. Imagery offers a vast world of healing possibilities, a kaleidoscope of possibilities for a woman to bring herself to life.

Client's Voice: Chris Watson

My pain is like a river so deep I can swim in it. I am unconnected to anyone, not to this world, not to life. The pain is bigger than I am and it stretches far, far into the future. I feel like I belong to no one, like I am no one. I am a trick person, a pretend body, like an abortion that somehow came to life. I wonder if I was ever connected to anyone or was this profound loneliness all there ever was of me? Was I always this absolutely alone? I feel I am nothing. I will always be shattered glass. Nothing seems real to me. *I* don't seem real.

It's almost as if something's reaching out—in front of me—wanting to take away all memory. It's crazy, but I wonder if I had parents. I know in my mind I did, but the idea of parents seems so far away I wonder if I imagined it. I am sick of being me, sick of life. I have an urge to die and sleep forever. Was I ever connected to anyone? Did I ever belong to anyone? Did anyone ever love me? If I am not connected to anyone, do I exist? I am so alone. If I don't have a mother, who will love me? Why do I hurt so much? I hate this pain. I hate me. I *am* pain. Am I human?

July 1986

It is ironic for me to read Naida's words: "When therapists do not know and recognize the diagnostic indicators of incest or are coopted by the power of clients' denial and repression, women will leave therapy perhaps having obtained some symptomatic relief but not having been healed. They will then reappear in the same or a different therapist's office when the pain of their symptoms again becomes overwhelming to them." For eight years before I inadvertently found her at the counseling service at the university, I searched for someone to put the pieces of me together. The confusion and agony expressed in the diary excerpt above was the norm for me. Although I can't remember not feeling damaged, different, or isolated, the intense pain of being me really started in 1977, when my mom died. How can you explain feeling diffused? It's not logical. You go to a counselor, who tells you you're depressed because your marriage has broken up; you go to another, who tells you you're full of sin and "out of God's will"; you go to another, who has you repeat "positive affirmations"; still another takes the information you so eagerly proffer and attempts to seduce you. In the midst of the pain you live and continue to plod along.

When I think back to the me that existed before I knew I was molested, I think only of a woman who tried *so* hard. I had to be perfect. As a daughter, as a wife, as a mother I had to be not just good but without error; as a returning university student, I had to have straight *A*'s. When I succeeded, it was never real success, just a stay of execution. For eight years I stayed alive only because I loved my son.

When I met Naida, I was in my second semester back at university, an English major with writer's block. Not being able to write frightened me because it was the one thing I had felt sure about. In a sense, I expected Naida to unclog me. I was stopped up; she'd dump some psychological Drano down me; my mind would function again, and I'd go my way. And yet I didn't want to be fixed temporarily. I wanted to be fixed.

I can't recall when I knew just how much I trusted Naida; I just knew I liked her. I'd never had anyone give me their total attention before, certainly not on a consistent basis. I'd never had anyone accept me so unconditionally. I'd never had anyone listen without an ulterior motive. Always when I'd sought help, I sensed an underlying time frame. The counselor was letting me talk, but waiting for the moment when he or she would give me the answer, show me the error of my ways, point me to the path, and present me with the bill. Naida just listened. And waited. Sometimes there were great stretches of silence when she'd just look at me and smile, waiting. It was hard to learn to *listen* to the inside of me. I already knew the words; now I had to learn to hear the feelings, too. Similarly, I was always trying to rearticulate the pain, to *make sure* she understood. It didn't fully register—for months—that she really was listening to me and hearing me. It was just as hard to accept her acceptance of me. She was so kind, so positive toward me. She liked me because I was me. Week after week. There was no "catch," no rug pulled out from under me.

During the summer of 1986, I did get "unclogged." I wrote again, handed in assignments (sometimes even on time), cared for my son, and unraveled my childhood. Much of my journal writing from that period is a welter of emotions. Alone in my room, usually on Saturday mornings, I would wake, write down the dream I'd emerged from, and go from that point into other recollections from my childhood. Sometimes when I'd write it would be almost as if the child-me were writing the experience as it happened. What I remembered amazed me. How could I not have remembered my mom was an alcoholic? Why had I always talked about my wonderful teenage years when these very real memories were so full of sadness? It seemed like everything I'd remembered as my past *wasn't*.

September was the beginning of my last semester before teaching training, my last semester as an undergraduate. Although not a requirement, I signed up for a course in subjective literature. The professor was a follower of Freud; the main author we studied, D. H. Lawrence. That the topic of sex would arise in the next four months seemed more than a possibility!

The semester started as any other. I was overwhelmed with reading, my student loans were late in arriving, the professor I was working for was particularly fussy about how his research should be conducted. There would not be time for anything but keeping up with work. In late October I was to attend my high school reunion (an event I wasn't looking forward to), and in between it all I would continue seeing Naida in an attempt to cope with the increased "antsiness" I felt.

Although I had no explanation for it, I felt at times like I was leading two lives. The student–research assistant–mother was doing her best at doing her best, but the quiet "me" sat up nights trying to figure out the images and feelings. Sleep was one nightmare after another: jumbled images of being terrorized by my parents, hidden away in houses, behind curtains, running away. I'd wake up feeling two years old or nine; sometimes it would take hours to shake the dream. They were so intense I simply had a hard time waking up. It took me at least an hour to get out of bed, and when I did, the dream was more real than the day ahead of me.

The most vivid of these dreams, I believe, was the child inside me simply *telling*. It was right after I'd gone to the school reunion, and fueled, I think, by the many conversations I'd had with people I'd known since I was six or seven. In the dream, my son and I were in what resembled the Catholic church I'd attended as a child. Walking through a doorway, I simultaneously noticed my son was missing and felt hands go down my side, from my waist to my knees. Along with the sensation was a strong image of wood, the same densely grained wood that the doorway moldings were made of in the house I grew up in.

Two days later, the picture of the wood grain still remained in my mind. Oddly enough, I didn't try to analyze the dream. Just as oddly, while doing a routine task at home, I heard/felt a voice in my head: "That's like someone trying to take down a little girl's pants." Still, I didn't make any connection. Instead, I determined to ask Naida about it the next day.

It was while explaining this unusual dream and voice that I experienced my first memory of being molested. From the dream of hands down my side and the unexpected interpretation of it, I suddenly saw a picture in my mind, a picture so real I was oblivious to where I was or what age I was. I saw myself as a little girl on the toilet, placed there by a man's hands. The initial picture was like a soft-focus close-up, then it widened out until I saw the whole room. The effect was much like that at the beginning of a silent movie. The man I saw was my father as a young man! He can't be. No! He can't be. As soon as I recognized him, I pushed the knowledge away. I didn't want to know. Yet the picture unfolded, like a video being turned off and on. I'd acknowledge the reality of one part, then the next scene would be shown. Some scenes I was quick to acknowledge. Others I recoiled from, horrified. Yet as I accepted the truth of each scene, the next was shown, until finally I literally saw the whole picture.

Just as I was seeing the events, I was sensing them. When I realized what I was seeing was true, I immediately felt like gagging and had the sensation of something being forced down my throat. I twisted in my seat, away from Naida, held myself in tightly, and brought myself almost into a fetal position, knees protectively up, body down, arms tight against my chest.

With the reality sinking in, I kept saying, "No, no! It's not true. It can't be. It didn't happen," and yet in the same breath I'd moan, "Why is he doing this to me? I'm only a little girl." Seeing it, feeling it, living it, I explained the events as they occurred, all the while veering wildly between denial and acceptance.

"I am four. He has put me on the toilet, then he puts his finger in my vagina."

Disbelief. This isn't true. I'm making it up. It didn't happen. No!

"He's masturbating, green pants on, black belt, hand inside his pants, finger still in my vagina. He leans into me, pushes me back against the toilet. It's cold. He's pushing at me."

I sit motionless, confused, then start gagging. I'm going to throw up. Instantly: No! He can't be doing this. I watch, horrified, gagging as I see it.

"I'm a little girl, my father's ugly, hard penis pushed into my mouth while he thrusts it in harder and harder. I can't breathe."

Gasping for air: Did this happen, Naida? Did this happen? Tell me it's not real. It didn't happen, did it? She looks at me, wordless. There is wisdom and anger and calmness and strength in her eyes. But nothing that will allow me to say, "No Christine, it didn't happen." "How do you feel? What does your body feel like?" she says.

"Sinking, I'm sinking. I feel like I'm going to throw up. I know it's true." The rest comes. I remember it all.

"He's beside himself in his pushing in and out of my mouth, my head bobbing back and forth with the motion. He holds my head from the back and pushes me forward. Finally, he stops and my mouth is full of gunk. I am choking. He pulls out and throws a towel at me, telling me to clean up. I wipe off my mouth as he goes out the door. I go to the window, sit down on the floor in the corner by the cupboard where my mom keeps the towels. I rock back and forth. I am alone. At night my mom cooks supper. He has told her I am sick and he puts me to bed before she returns. I turn my face to the window and stare at the wall."

My reaction to this memory was quite simply to go into shock. I was jarred and frightened upon leaving Naida's office and increasingly blank as I walked down the hallway. After apologetically explaining to the English professor why I'd be missing his lecture, I found myself in the cafeteria staring at a Styrofoam cup of coffee and forgetting how to drink it. I sat for over an hour, drove home, and began the process of chopping through the denial that had already sprung up.

In the two months that remained until teacher training started (when the little girl and her memories were pushed far into the background), I experienced several other revelations of the same sort. My father using me for oral sex when I was three and so small I had to stand on the chesterfield to do what he wanted. My uncle holding me on his lap, cuddling me; then the shock of his finger up my vagina. I was two then and had no words, only terror and confusion. More memories of my father: stretching himself onto me as I colored on the floor; calling me down to the crawl space to show me "what Santa had" for me, then forcing intercourse on me; an isolated image of a penis across my abdomen.

It would be nice to say that the trauma of remembering stopped with ensuing memories. It didn't. Each time I remembered a different episode it was like the first. The denial and terror and confusion were there with every memory. Each time I'd be horrified, unbelieving, convinced I was crazy, and each time it would take about two days to come out of the daze the memories left me in.

At times the intensity of my reaction was so strong I'd literally be incapacitated. It was as if everything I'd ever believed was suspect, not just my relationship with my parents. I didn't know what to believe about anything, anymore. It was like being dismantled.

Reverberations echoed in every part of my life. Most people I dared to tell listened politely but seemed shocked. I felt tainted. The professor I'd seen immediately after the first memory gave me an *A* for the paper I wrote, "Images of Incest in the Rainbow," agreed I'd come up with credible proofs, and told me I should stop going for counseling. My closest friend of nine years, an incest victim herself, stopped communication altogether, unable to look at her past.

Another dropped me because I'd become "too intense after that incest stuff."

Finally, I stopped talking and thinking about it entirely. With a year of teacher training ahead of me and the need to acquire the professional veneer of a teacher, there was no time or energy for the emotional turmoil therapy involved. So the little girl was silenced, her memories put on hold. I had to survive.

Since graduating as a "real" teacher (with no veneer, alas), I've had only one memory, but my relationship with the child has flourished. When I first learned she existed, I was angry. She hadn't been protected as a child, she was the one intensifying all of my painful feelings, and Naida and every book I read advised me to begin nurturing her. Great. First I have my mom and dad to nurture, now this invisible child. When would it be my turn?

Gradually, however, I began to like the little girl. She was quiet, but spunky! After finally getting the chance to be heard, she made up for lost time. Polite enough to wait until I graduated, she then began making nightly appearances in my dreams a week later. Often now I wake up conscious only of her presence. In an odd sort of way she's relieved the loneliness I've always felt, and I now feel the mother of two children, not just one. Before, I never understood how to do nice things for myself; I was good only at pleasing others. Now in conscious awareness of meeting my child's needs, I inadvertently meet mine.

There is, of course, still much in my life that is unfinished and unexplained. My relationship with my father still exists, though I no longer try to win his approval or love. It is a deathwatch for us both. Nothing of the past is mentioned, nor, for that matter, of the present. He is eighty-one years old, a facsimile of the man who repeatedly raped me. His denial is rock solid, far more impenetrable than mine ever was. I know that to utter the words "I know that you abused me" would be to engineer my own downfall. He still can make me feel shamed, worthless, a fool; the child within cowers in his presence.

To avoid confrontation is not cowardice. It is—again—a matter of survival. At thirty-seven I have still to deal with the loss, the sadness, and final acceptance of the childhood I never had, the adulthood I was almost robbed of. I may never confront my father. The decision is mine.

References

Achterberg, J. *Imagery in Healing: Shamanism and Modern Medicine.* Boston: Shambhala, 1985.

Achterberg, J., and Lawlis, G. F. *Bridges of the Bodymind: Behavioral Approaches to Health Care.* Champaign, Ill.: Institute for Personality and Ability Testing, 1980.

Ahsen, A. *Basic Concepts in Eidetic Psychotherapy.* New York: Brandon House, 1973.

Ahsen, A. *Psych eye: Self-Analytic Consciousness.* New York: Brandon House, 1977.

Beck, J. *The Life of the Theatre.* San Francisco: City Lights, 1972.

Beck, J. C., and van der Kolk, B. "Reports of Childhood Incest and Current Behavior of Chronically Hospitalized Psychotic Women." *American Journal of Psychiatry,* 1987, *144* (11), pp. 1417–1476.

Briere, J., and Runtz, M. "The Effects of Childhood Sexual Abuse on Later Psychological Functioning: Defining a Post-Sexual Abuse Trauma." In G. E. Wyatt and G. J. Powell (eds.), *Lasting Effects of Child Sexual Abuse.* Newbury Park, Calif.: Sage, 1988.

Bryer, J. B., Nelson, B. A., Miller, J. B., and Krol, P. "Childhood Sexual and Physical Abuse as Factors in Adult Psychiatric Illness." *American Journal of Psychiatry,* 1987, *144* (11), pp. 1426–1430.

Burgess, A., Hartman, C., and McCormack, A. "Abused to Abuser: Antecedents of Socially Deviant Behaviors." *American Journal of Psychiatry,* 1987, *144* (11), pp. 1431–1436.

Cantela, J. R. "Covert Conditioning: Assumptions and Procedures." *Journal of Mental Imagery,* 1977, *1,* pp. 53–64.

Dworkin, A. *Woman Hating.* New York: Dutton, 1974.

Epstein, G. *Waking Dream Therapy: Dream Process as Imagination.* New York: Human Sciences Press, 1981.

Horowitz, M. *Image Formation and Cognition.* New York: Appleton-Century-Crofts, 1970.

Horowitz, M. "Controls of Visual Imagery and Therapist Intervention." In J. Singer and K. Pope (eds.), *The Power of Human Imagination.* New York: Plenum, 1978.

Hyde, N. D. "Long-Term Effects of Childhood Sexual Abuse." *British Columbia Medical Journal,* 1984, *26* (7), pp. 448–450.

Hyde, N. D. "Covert Incest in Women's Lives: Dynamics and Directions for Healing." *Canadian Journal of Community Mental Health,* 1986, *2* (Fall), pp. 73–83.

Hyde, N. D. "Uncovering the Repression: Some Clinical Considerations in the Psychotherapy of Women Incest Survivors." *Alberta Psychology,* 1987, *16* (3), pp. 3–12.

Jaffe, D. T., and Bresler, D. E. "Guided Imagery: Healing Through the Mind's Eye." In J. E. Shorr, G. E. Sobel, P. Robin, and J. A. Connella (eds.), *Imagery: Its Many Dimensions and Applications.* New York: Plenum, 1980.

Keleman, S. *Somatic Reality: Bodily Experience and Emotional Truth.* Berkeley, Calif.: Center Press, 1979.

Lerner, H. "Guided Affective Imagery: An Account of Its Development." *Journal of Mental Health,* 1977, *1,* pp. 73–92.

Lerner, H. "Basic Principles and Therapeutic Efficacy of Guided Affective Imagery." In J. L. Singer and K. S. Pope (eds.), *The Power of the Human Imagination.* New York: Plenum, 1978.

Meichenbaum, D. "Why Does Imagery in Psychotherapy Lead to Change?" In J. L. Singer and K. S. Pope (eds.), *The Power of Human Imagination.* New York: Plenum, 1978.

Miller, A. *Prisoners of Childhood: The Drama of the Gifted Child and the Search for the True Self.* New York: Basic Books, 1981.

Sheikh, A., and Jordan, C. S. "Clinical Uses of Mental Imagery." In A. Sheikh (ed.), *Imagery: Current Theory, Research and Application.* New York: Wiley, 1983.

Singer, J. L. *Imagery and Daydream Methods in Psychotherapy and Behavior Modification.* New York: Academic Press, 1974.

Singer, J. L., and Pope, S. (eds.). *The Power of Human Imagination: New Methods in Psychotherapy.* New York: Plenum, 1978.

10

Recovering the Past: Using Hypnosis to Heal Childhood Trauma

Cheryl Malmo
Client: Betsy Warland

When the body has been wounded and broken, the flesh must be carefully cleaned and disinfected, the bones set straight, and the affected area protected. All this must be taken care of so that healing can take place with the least amount of scarring and so that maximum functioning can be restored. Such is the case with the healing of the psyche after psychological trauma. In psychotherapy, the healing process involves first an emotional cleansing—the identification and release of forgotten, hidden, or repressed feelings that have been locked inside the body. These feelings may have been locked away because there was no one to listen to them, because they were not permitted by parents or authority figures, because there was no recognition of their importance, or because the person understood that it would have been dangerous for her to let them show. Setting straight in psychotherapy involves the achievement of a healthy self-concept in relation to one's personal dynamic and to others and a conscious awareness of one's place and rights in the community.

In adults who have been abused as children, healing may require the removal of guilt that cripples the spirit, the directing of responsibility for the abuse to the perpetrator, and the confronting and overcoming of fears that cripple both spirit and behavior. Irrational, destructive, or false beliefs must be changed to rational, healthy, and enlightened ones. In psychotherapy, this change is sometimes called reframing, restructuring, resocialization, or reparenting. In feminist psychotherapy, reframing also involves consciousness raising about how women, by virtue of being female (and perhaps also by belonging to a particular class or ethnic or racial group), have been restricted and devalued within patriarchal society. The psychological consequences for women of their having been restricted and devalued must then also be identified and overcome. Additionally, new rules for survival based on the assumptions of worth and of having equal rights must replace old rules that were born out of trauma, fear, devaluation, and limited options. Protection in psychotherapy is provided by the safeness of the therapist's understanding and nonjudgmental attitude, respect for personal boundaries, and the support given while the client learns new skills and behaviors for living beyond the survival mode.

In my work with adults who have experienced the childhood trauma of emotional and/or physical neglect or physical, psychological, and/or sexual abuse, I have found that I can facilitate the healing process by using hypnosis.

Hypnosis and the Healing Process

Classical definitions of hypnosis are varied and somewhat vague. Hypnosis has been described as a trance state, a state of hypersuggestibility, or an altered state of consciousness. Therapy using classical hypnosis, sometimes referred to as traditional or authoritarian, describes the therapist as inducing a trance and giving direct commands or suggestions to inhibit symptoms or to instruct new behavior by means of posthypnotic suggestions. Whatever happens seems to happen because the therapist makes it happen. The control is seen to be with the therapist, and the power differential between therapist and client is magnified. The danger inherent in the assumption that power and control rightfully belong to the therapist is obvious to feminists, who are keenly aware of how women's lack of personal power and control undermines their confidence and self-esteem. The authority of the traditional hypnotherapist may also reinforce women's mistrust of their own experience and abilities and, thus, reinforce the devaluation that they have already experienced in so many ways in a patriarchal society.

A tremendous change in the practice of hypnotherapy occurred as a result of the work of Milton H. Erickson and his followers (Rossi, 1986, 1987). Erickson believed that hypnosis is a natural phenomenon that can be used in therapy by the client and the therapist in numerous ways. According to this approach, sometimes called naturalistic hypnosis, control of the trance state is assumed to be with the client. The therapist is understood to be simply a teacher, a facilitator, and a companion, guiding or accompanying the client into and through her own natural healing process. Hypnotherapists who favor naturalistic hypnosis generally agree that hypnosis is a natural state of consciousness, a state of deep relaxation combined with a heightened concentration and awareness, a state that can be used to great advantage by a skilled therapist for psychotherapeutic work. Additional definitions will give the reader a clearer idea of what hypnosis is and how it can be used in psychotherapy.

One definition of hypnosis is that it is a natural phenomenon experienced in everyday life that provides a pathway to the subconscious mind, the seat of emotions, feelings, sensations, and habit patterns, or automatic behaviors (Mann, 1986). This interpretation of hypnosis maintains that all hypnosis is really self-hypnosis, because entry into and control of the trance state remain at all times with the person who is hypnotized. Hypnosis has also been described as a tuning into right-brain consciousness, which controls memory, feelings, creativity, intuition, and other functions of the unconscious mind. The language of the right brain is that of symbols, images, dreams, associations, metaphors, stories, and bodily sensations. And it is through these modes of communication that healing occurs. Left-brain consciousness, on the other hand, controls analytical thinking, decision making, judgment, criticism, and other functions of the conscious mind and uses the language of words and logic—the language of cognitive therapy (Rausch, 1984). Alternatively, hypnosis is defined as a special kind of introspection in which the mind is focused on inner, subjective experiencing and that occurs when the parasympathetic nervous system is activated by relaxation (Negley-Parker,1986).

Erickson, who challenged traditional psychoanalysis with his unorthodox use of hypnosis, defined hypnosis as a natural phenomenon—a special psychological state that can be used in therapy as a period of creative reorganization. (Erickson's view that hypnosis is a natural phenomenon should not be confused with the idea that all hypnotherapy should be nondirective. For a further explanation of this point, see Hammond, 1984.) He advised therapists to capitalize on this natural state when they perceived it in their patients or to facilitate their patients' finding it. It is at this time, he maintained, that the therapist can assist patients to reassociate and reorganize their inner psychological complexities in accordance with their own experience, resulting in an inner resynthesis. Erickson viewed therapy as taking place on an intrapsychic level, at the moment when the inner self makes a significant shift, not when external change is noted by the therapist (Rosen, 1982; Rossi, 1987).

Most recently, in his book *The Psychobiology of Mind-Body Healing,* Rossi (1986) has defined hypnosis as a natural and comfortable state akin to the rest period of our ultradian rhythms, which are basic one-and-a-half hour cycles of activity and rest periods regulated by the endocrine and autonomic nervous systems. Each time we attend to our natural rhythms and take a break, our systems normalize themselves and in doing so undercut the process of psychosomatic illnesses at their psychological source. A perceptive and sensitive therapist will use a client's natural, ultradian rhythms in therapeutic hypnosis, which, according to Rossi, involves two processes: (1) accessing lost information (images, thoughts, memories) through feeling states that are located in the body and that he calls state-dependent memory learning behavior and (2) reframing the experience or belief. The result he is working toward, as was Erickson, is a resynthesis.

Hypnosis and the Feminist Perspective

The assumption in naturalistic hypnosis that the client is in charge and that she has the ability to enter hypnosis and to heal herself, guided or accompanied by the therapist, is compatible with feminist beliefs about the need for women to experience their own power and to value their own abilities. Of course, even naturalistic hypnosis can be an abusive experience for women if the therapist holds stereotypical notions about what is proper or expected behavior for females and males or otherwise speaks or behaves in a sexist manner. This is the case with any therapeutic approach, however. That feminist values and beliefs about equality, about women's need for personal power and control, and about the importance for women to learn to attend to and trust their own experiences and abilities are compatible with naturalistic hypnotherapy, and specifically with the affect bridge technique, should be obvious throughout the rest of this chapter.

Using the Affect Bridge in Hypnotherapy

Hypnotherapy can take many forms. Louise Oliver (1987) has documented how hypnosis is used as a therapeutic technique by traditional healers in South Africa. Terry Tafoya (1985) has compared the drumming and storytelling utilized by North American native medicine people to the hypnotic storytelling of Milton Erickson. Within the traditional fifty-minute session in a psychotherapist's office, hypnotherapy can arise spontaneously (as in the case of a client focusing on a body sensation, tracking a feeling, seeing an image in her mind's eye, recalling a memory, and so on), or it can be planned (either the therapist or client can suggest a formal or informal induction in order to facilitate a particular piece of emotional work). In any case, the hypnosis can still be naturalistic insofar as it is the body movements or sensations, feelings, images, dreams, or memories of the client that determine both the content and structure of a therapeutic session. Once the state of hypnosis is achieved and therapy commences, the therapist can engage in the same range of responses and behaviors as is open to her in any other therapy situation. She may at different times be inquiring, exploring, reflecting, directing, giving support, seeking or giving information, confronting, reframing, and so on, as the situation requires.

A formal and structured hypnotherapy technique that can be very useful for uncovering repressed memories from childhood in women (or men) who have been traumatized by physical, sexual, or psychological abuse is the affect bridge. This technique, first documented by John Watkins (1971), involves the regression of a client to the time of trauma, using a feeling experienced in the present as a bridge to a time in the past when the same feeling was experienced. (When a bodily sensation is being tracked, the technique is called the somatic bridge.) Hammond (1988) suggests that the affect or somatic bridge is appropriate to use "when a patient is experiencing emotion (e.g., depression, anxiety), compulsion, or physical sensation (e.g., pain) of unknown origin." He cautions, "The patient should be judged stable enough, and the therapist experienced enough, to constructively handle an age regression where intense emotion may well be experienced." I would add that the therapist should also know the client well enough to anticipate what experiences or feelings might be uncovered by this powerful technique. Hammond further indicates that prior to initiating an age regression using the affect bridge, a therapist should obtain permission for this exploration, both before (from the conscious mind) and after (from the unconscious mind) the patient has entered hypnosis. This practice is in keeping with the feminist concern that control of therapy, its content, structure, and timing, be put in the hands of the client. (I wish to acknowledge here Corydon Hammond's work with the affect bridge technique. I have been fortunate to observe him at work and to learn from him how to use the technique in a sensitive and respectful way.)

Probably all therapists who use the affect bridge technique have developed a favorite way to structure the experience, in keeping with their beliefs about the therapeutic process, their personal style, and the needs of their clients. The following outlines my version of the affect bridge and the preparatory work I do with clients before I assist them to explore disturbing feelings in this way. My feminist values, beliefs, and consciousness are apparent at every step in the process, I believe.

Preparation for the Affect Bridge. **Step One:** My first task as a therapist, whether I will be using hypnosis or not, is to get to know my client and what she perceives to be her problems. Depending on how aware she is of the reasons for her problems, how aware she is of her feelings and motivations, how able she is to express her feelings, how much she trusts herself (in other words, how emotionally healthy she is), and how supportive and stable her current living and work situation is, I will have an idea of how slowly or quickly we will be able to proceed. I usually inform clients early in therapy that hypnosis is one of a number of techniques I use. Also, I indicate that not I but she is the best expert when it comes to knowledge about herself; that she, not I, has the answers to her problems; and that she has everything that she needs to be healthy. I will simply help her to know herself better and to look in the right places to find her answers or solutions. I take this position because I believe it to be true, and I inform every client of my belief because I believe that this knowledge is empowering to them.

Step Two: In keeping with my feminist belief about the importance of a client being in control, I explain to my client before using hypnosis that hypnosis is a natural, psychological phenomenon. I give examples of how she might have already experienced being in a state of hypnosis without realizing it. At this time, I clear up any misconceptions about hypnosis derived from a client's experience with stage hypnotists or party demonstrations. If a client has experienced hypnosis before, I ask about this experience and what it was like for her. I make clear, before we ever begin, that this is her experience, under her control. I will simply be a guide who will show her how to use this special and powerful aspect of her mind and a companion in her explorations. I will also do or say whatever is required to keep her safe psychologically.

Step Three: With the client's permission, I teach her how to enter a hypnotic state. I usually begin with a rather formal induction, the content of which varies depending on the client's preference or what I know about the client and on my mood (whether I feel like relaxing into something familiar or adventuring into a new metaphor). The induction involves my assisting the client to shift her focus from the external world to the world inside herself by providing various suggestions for relaxation. A typical formal induction that I use to teach an uninitiated client would sound something like this: "You can close your eyes, if you like, and begin to focus on the world inside you. Concentrate first, if you like, on your breathing, and as you breathe in, breathe in relaxation, and as you breathe out, breathe out tension. I'm going to count from one to ten, and as I do you can imagine yourself walking down a hill, or riding down an escalator, or moving down deep inside yourself. And with each count, you are moving down, becoming more and more relaxed, so that by the time I've said ten, you're down at the bottom, feeling very, very relaxed. One. Going down, beginning to relax" (and so on). If the client has had previous experience with hypnotherapy and has a preference for how she will enter the hypnotic state, I either instruct her to go ahead and hypnotize herself and indicate to me when she is ready to begin working or assist her to enter hypnosis in whatever way she requests. The choice is hers.

Step Four: Included in the initial induction is the identifying of a safe place where she can go to in her mind. I would say something like the following: "I'd like you now to go to a safe place in your mind. This place can be real or imaginary, it can be a place outside somewhere—on a beach, by the ocean, in a field, in the mountains, in a grove of trees, in a park—or it can be in a room somewhere—from the past, from the present, or an ideal place in the future. It doesn't matter where it is, just so long as it's a place where you can feel safe, comfortable, relaxed, at peace with yourself." After a safe place has been located, I provide visual, auditory, olfactory, tactile, and kinesthetic suggestions for being in this place. This is done in order to engage as many of the client's senses as possible in the experience. I then explain that many kinds of work can be done from the safe place and that she can return to this place whenever she wants, with a professional whom she trusts or by herself. Sometimes I teach self-hypnosis so that the client can practice going into, being in, and coming out of this state. Finding a safe place can be viewed as a deepening of the hypnotic trance or as part of the therapy. In my experience, the finding of and going to a safe place is useful for many clients, either as a means of relaxation and stress reduction, for ego strengthening, or as a place from which to venture out to explore more dangerous feelings, images, experiences, and so on.

The safe place is an especially important feature to build in for a client who has been sexually abused. It serves to give her more control over how much pain or fear she uncovers at a time (she can move between the safe and scary places as she feels ready or feels the need to do so). It also teaches her to identify, value, and trust that place in her mind that exists apart from other people's demands and expectations (past, present, and future) and in which she can find peace, strength, self-love, and self-nurturance. Sometimes a client cannot find a safe place. This seems to happen especially when a client has been extremely neglected or abused, when the abuse was ongoing, or when in her attempts to cope with the abuse she developed a tendency to be always on guard. Sometimes a client will go immediately in her mind to a scary place or will find that the place that she thought would be safe suddenly is not. If this happens, I ask the client (again, giving her control) whether she would like me to help her to find a safe place. Usually the answer is yes. Sometimes, however, a client prefers or feels compelled to explore the scary place first, and so this is what we do. With some clients, a safe place is achieved only after some fearful experiences have been worked through, at the end of a therapy session, or even at the end of a series of sessions.

Step Five: Typically, once a safe place has been established, I introduce the idea of a special container. My patter would sound something like this: "If you look around your safe place, you may find a special container that has been left for you to use to store anything that would interfere with your being totally relaxed and comfortable. I don't know what kind of container it will be; it may be an old chest, or a bottle, or a box, or a vase, or a basket, or a pail, or a garbage bag, or something else. Look around now and see whether you can find your special container. It has been left for you, so that you can put into it any disturbing feelings, images, thoughts, or memories that would interfere with your being totally relaxed and comfortable." When the client has indicated to me that she has found the container (I have never yet had a client who did not find one), I instruct her to put any feelings, images, thoughts, or memories into it that she wishes, so that she can be even more free to be totally relaxed and comfortable. When this has been done, I instruct her to place the container outside of her safe place or out of view. Usually this has the effect of ensuring that the client's safe place is free from worry, responsibility, fears, and so on; of increasing her comfort; and of deepening the state of hypnosis. Sometimes, however, a client will indicate that she can't put all of the things that disturb her into the container. When this happens, the therapist can give the choice of finding a larger container or of exploring what it is that will not fit into the container. If the client chooses to explore what she cannot put into the container, the emotional work for this session has probably begun.

Step Six: Often in hypnotherapy, especially when the client has experienced severe trauma (childhood or otherwise) or when I see indications of a tendency to be self-critical, I will teach a client about the presence of a spirit guide which resides in a place nearby (if her safe place is outside) or in an adjoining room (if her safe place is a room inside). The concept of the spirit guide is akin to the adult in transactional analysis but has the added dimensions of being spiritual and nurturing as well as rational. Attending to the spiritual dimension reflects a growing awareness in psychotherapeutic practice of the importance of this realm in the clients' healing. Attending to nurturing is very much a feminist concern resulting from the awareness that women have suffered from too little nurturing and need to learn how to nurture themselves. (For further information about the concept of the spirit guide, see Chapters Nine, Twelve, and Fourteen.)

The identification of and introduction to the spirit guide might take place in a therapy session following the teaching of hypnosis, the safe place, and the container, or it might take place in a later session when I judge there to be a specific use for it. After the client has entered a hypnotic state, I explain: "This spirit guide is very wise and loving, is always ready to listen, will always be understanding, compassionate, and supportive, and will give good advice or otherwise meet your needs. It may take a human form, female or male, or it may be androgynous; it may be very old, or about your age, or it may be very young; it may be a kind of creature, or an animal, or a magical kind of being. It may be like a bright light, or it may be someone who was close to you but who has died. It may be you when you are very old and wise, or you when you were young and pure, unaffected by others' expectations, behavior, or problems.

Or it may be a part of you now, deep inside. But whatever form it takes, it will always be there for you." The client is first instructed to imagine her spirit guide and then, if she wishes, to visit and talk with it about whatever is on her mind at the time. Clients often have a very strong sense of who or what their spirit guide is and of what they most need from it. The introduction of the spirit guide initiates or reinforces in the client the development of a nonjudgmental and nurturing attitude toward self, as well as a sense of her own strength and power. While the teaching of the spirit guide concept is not a necessary step in order to proceed with the affect bridge technique, it can be utilized very effectively to facilitate healing in the resocializing, reparenting, or reframing phase of a therapy session, once a forgotten memory has been uncovered and the feelings expressed fully.

The Affect Bridge. **Step Seven:** When a client has practiced on her own and feels comfortable with being in a hypnotic state, we are ready to begin the work of hypnotherapy. (Some clients find self-hypnosis difficult, so we proceed without their home practice.) When a client talks about having been extremely upset by an incident (or a thought, dream, image, movie, book, conversation, and so on) that may appear from the outside to be fairly harmless or neutral, or when a client has experienced a disturbing feeling that seems out of context or out of proportion, the affect bridge technique may be an appropriate way to explore the feeling further. Either the client, myself, or both of us may have a sense that the feeling belongs somewhere in the past. The key to the appropriateness of the technique is, however, the client's identification of a disturbing feeling.

Step Eight: I assist the client to enter a state of hypnosis in whatever way is most comfortable for and meaningful to her. As explained previously, both prior to and while she is under hypnosis, I ask the client whether it is all right with her to examine the disturbing feeling. In effect, I ask permission to proceed, ensuring that control is with the client.

Step Nine: After the client indicates that she is sufficiently relaxed in her safe place and is ready to explore the identified feeling, I instruct her to allow the feeling to come into her awareness now. The client may have had the feeling when she walked into my office that day, or she may not have felt it for several days. To assist the client to allow a nonpresent feeling to resurface, I may instruct her to imagine that she is in the place or room where she most recently experienced the feeling, recalling the time of day, who was there, what was said, and so on. This going back to a time when the feeling was recently experienced is actually an initial age regression. Sometimes a client who is practiced in hypnotherapy will come to a session without being conscious of anything in particular that she wishes to examine that day but will ask to use hypnosis to find out what to explore. If, after relaxing in her safe place, she allows whatever is most pressing to surface and is confronted with a disturbing feeling, we may decide to proceed by using the affect bridge to explore the feeling further. I say "we" because I may decide that this is an appropriate direction in which to move, but I always ask the client whether she wishes to do so, and then her decision as to whether we proceed determines the direction the therapy will take.

Step Ten: I instruct the client to allow the feeling to be there even more strongly, to allow it to be with her so intensely that she seems to be overwhelmed by the feeling. This instruction assists the client to focus on the feeling inside her rather than on the incident that precipitated it, and it also helps her to safely experience the feeling in its intensity. If a client experiences difficulty in allowing the feeling to be more intense, instruction can also be given that she identify where in her body she is experiencing the feeling and to focus on this place. Hammond (1988) further instructs his clients to intensify the feeling to the point of feeling confused or disoriented. I have found that this additional step may be helpful if I sense that a memory is going to be particularly difficult to uncover, but I usually do not find it necessary.

Step Eleven: I instruct the client to travel back in time, to a time in the past when the same feeling was experienced, back perhaps to the first time when the feeling was experienced, using the feeling as a bridge to the past. This is the crucial age regression, which will likely lead to uncovering a repressed memory. Various metaphors can be used in place of the bridge to suggest going back in time. Hammond uses the idea of traveling back into the past on a railroad track that consists of the particular feeling. I sometimes use the image of "walking down a road that takes you into your past" or "standing on the path of your life and walking back down the path into the past" or "looking at the book (or photograph album) that tells the story of your life and turning the pages backward, reviewing the past, seeing yourself at a younger and younger age" or "viewing a film about your life and running the projector backward, seeing yourself smaller and smaller." Next the client is instructed to stop at a time (place/page/picture/frame) when she experienced, perhaps for the first time, the same feeling she is experiencing now.

Step Twelve: The client is then encouraged to identify where she is and what is happening in her mind. The therapist can ask questions such as "Where are you? How old are you? What is happening?" Sometimes clients know immediately where they are and what is happening, and sometimes they become aware of this information very gradually. Depending on what is uncovered, I may decide to do some healing work with the memory or to continue the regression to an even earlier time. This decision would, of course, be made with the permission of the client. The healing work that takes place at this time is much the same as the healing work that takes place at any other time. What has happened is acknowledged by the therapist with calmness, understanding, and compassion; feelings (confusion, hurt, anger, fear) that were repressed are identified and expressed and verbalized fully; needs of the young child are acknowledged and taken care of; inaccurate or destructive beliefs about the self that result in guilt or low self-esteem are reframed or replaced with healthy ones; resocialization or reparenting is accomplished. If the client has already developed a healthy, constructive, supportive adult self, I will instruct the adult self that she is today to join the child in the memory and to assist her in whatever way the child needs. Or, alternatively, I may suggest that she call on her spirit guide to assist the child by making her safe again, listening to her feelings, giving her physical comfort, reframing her beliefs about her responsibility or guilt, answering her questions and giving reassurance, or whatever the child needs. If the client has not yet developed a strong adult self or a spirit guide, or if she is uncomfortable with or bewildered by what the child needs or is only partially aware of what the child needs, I will enter the scene, too, and ask questions, offer suggestions, or proceed with reparenting. Obviously, an awareness of child development theory and experience in working with children are very beneficial, if not crucial, for work involving this kind of age regression.

Probably the best way for the reader to understand how the affect bridge works is to consider some examples of how it has actually been used. The following are examples of how the affect bridge technique was used by three of my clients and me to facilitate their healing.

The Case of Gloria. I first worked with Gloria in a workshop on compulsive eating and body image that I taught for the women's program at the university. Through the exercises and discussions, Gloria discovered that her cycle of starving, binging, and vomiting began with severe self-criticism "for not having made right decisions in the past." She learned that she would need to be more accepting of herself and to pay more serious attention to the messages her body gave her about what she felt and needed.

Two years later, Gloria came to me for therapy, explaining that she was worried because she had been unable to get pregnant and thought that this might be because she still felt guilty about having had an abortion several years earlier. She felt isolated, explaining that she did not communicate openly with her husband and that she had "closed off" from her friends who had children. Because Gloria was leaving shortly on an extended vacation, we had to work very quickly. I encouraged her to be more open in her communication with her husband, to focus on her friendships with her friends rather than on the fact of their having children, and to accept herself whether she was to have children in her future or not. Then I made a hypnosis tape for her to take away with her. On the tape was a formal hypnosis induction, instructions to go to a safe place in her mind and to use a container, and the option to speak with her spirit guide if she wished. In addition, I instructed Gloria to locate a special healing light that she could focus on any place in her body that needed attention. In the session with me, she focused the light on her lower abdomen, where, she explained, she felt pain and saw negative images. Then off she went on her travels.

Sixteen months later, Gloria came to see me again. She now

had a six-month-old baby and believed that it was the safe place and healing light that had enabled her to relax enough to get pregnant. She also reported that on her travels she had found the safe place that she had fantasized, exactly how she imagined it. Gloria's current problem was that since having her baby she didn't want to have sexual intercourse or any other kind of sexual activity with her husband—it felt invasive. She thought that the reason for this might have something to do with the fact that she had been sexually assaulted in childhood by at least three men: her brother, her cousin, and a hired man who worked on her uncle's farm. She was also concerned that previously she had been able to have an orgasm only if she fantasized about little girls being forced to have sex with older kids or their being observed in sexual activity.

Because Gloria was so ready and so motivated at this time to do whatever emotional work was necessary in order to make specific changes, she worked very quickly. In only six sessions (including the first session, in which she identified what the problems were), she was able to confront the reality of her childhood sexual abuse, identify and express her repressed feelings, shift her focus from the needs of the males who abused her to the needs of her child self, act from her adult self to protect and comfort the child, reclaim her sexuality, develop a positive fantasy about herself as an adult woman initiating sexual activity, and communicate to her husband about her sexual feelings and needs (first saying no, then saying yes). In sessions two, three, and four, Gloria confronted the reality of her abuse through age regression using the affect bridge; in session five, she age regressed spontaneously as she was imaging the block she was experiencing with regard to sexual activity with her husband; in session six, she reported her success and satisfaction with the changes that she had made in her sexual relationship with her husband. Further, she made specific plans to confront her brother about the effect on her of his abusive behavior and to speak to his daughter. The following is an account of Gloria's second session, in which she experienced age regression using the affect bridge technique for the first time.

We began the session by inducing hypnosis in the way that was already familiar to and comfortable for Gloria. I counted slowly from one to ten while she imagined riding down in an elevator.

When she got to the bottom, she went to the safe place in her mind (a wooded area next to a pasture, with blue skies, fresh air, and warm sun) and relaxed there. I then instructed her to "allow the feeling of anger that you experienced in your dreams last week to be with you now." She reported that her throat felt tight. I asked whether it contained any words that needed to be spoken, and she replied that the words that seemed to fit the feeling were "No! Stop it!" After a few seconds, Gloria reported that her legs felt tight and that her right arm felt like pointing at something. Traveling back in time, with these feelings providing a bridge to the past, Gloria found herself at age five in the bathroom of her family home where her brother and his friend had taken her to take down her pants and look at her genitals. She recalled that a baby sitter had caught them and reacted angrily, sent her brother's friend home, and put Gloria and her brother into their separate bedrooms. Gloria felt angry toward the baby sitter, believing that it was unfair that she was being punished, because she had done nothing wrong. In the regression, I asked her to express this anger to the sitter, and she did.

Gloria then began to feel a tightness in her shoulders. Using this feeling as another bridge, she traveled in her mind to another incident when she was also five years old and had been left on her uncle's farm. She was now remembering and reexperiencing the hired hand putting her up onto a horse and then putting his hand into her pants. She continued sensing the same tightness in her shoulders and felt confused and afraid. I instructed Gloria to go back to this scene as the adult woman she is today and see what was happening to the child. (At this point, we began to incorporate ego-state therapy into the hypnosis session. For a further explanation of this type of therapy, see Chapter Fourteen.) Immediately she extended her right arm, pointed her finger, and stated in a loud and angry voice to the hired hand, "You stop that! Get away from her! Go into the house! I'll deal with you later."

From this point began a positive interaction between the adult Gloria and the child Gloria. In response to my directing her to "Look at the child. Notice what she is feeling. What does she need?" the adult Gloria held and comforted the child and told her it was okay for her to say "No!" if anyone touched her in a way she didn't like. I also directed the child to speak and tell or ask about whatever she wished. When the child asked "Why did the man do that?" the adult explained that he needed help. I noted that as the adult, Gloria was being a little too focused on and sympathetic about the man's needs, but I did not say anything about this to Gloria at this time. She continued with her imaging and the dialogue between her adult and child selves. Together, the child and adult decided that the child would confront the man, and they entered the house to do so. The child spoke in a little-girl voice, saying, "I didn't like that, and I don't want you to ever do that again." The adult added that if he ever did that again, she would tell her uncle and the police and that he should get help. At this point, I intervened and said that the police must be told now, because the man had committed a crime and the law was very clear that our first duty was to protect children. The adult had not been aware of this but agreed. The child reported that she now felt safe, secure, and protected by both the adult and the law. She also reported that her body felt soft and relaxed around her vagina.

I instructed Gloria to return to her safe place in her mind, to relax there, and to think about the experience and what it meant to her before returning to an alert state. Her comment to me at the end of the session was that it had felt very important to her both to be able to express her feelings and to experience the feeling of being protected. She further explained that until now she had not understood how important it was to put children's needs first. She wondered about the safety of her brother's daughter and about a child at her workplace who had reported having been touched sexually. Her final comment that day was that she had had a very difficult childbirth because her uterine muscles had been so tight and she felt that they were more relaxed now.

Although Gloria is no longer in therapy with me, she continues to work toward integrating the learnings from our sessions into her everyday life. In addition, she and her husband are seeing a marriage counselor to assist with their communication problems. The case of Gloria illustrates how the affect bridge can be used to do very concentrated healing work with a client who is aware of having been sexually abused. The case of Betsy, which follows, illustrates how the affect bridge can assist a client to uncover abuse where there is no conscious memory of it.

The Case of Betsy. Betsy came to me for therapy because she had heard from an acquaintance that I used hypnosis to work with incest survivors. She had been in therapy previously and was satisfied that she had resolved past and present issues with her parents and was in good shape psychologically, emotionally, and physically. She enjoyed her work and was involved in a loving and supportive relationship with a woman whom she respected and trusted. However, Betsy was concerned that she might have been sexually assaulted by a particular family member, for two reasons: she felt generally estranged from this family member and felt distinctly uncomfortable in his presence, and she had no awareness of her own sexuality during adolescence or in her early adulthood. I worked with Betsy for a period of only six weeks, because she was leaving the city for an extended vacation and then moving back to Vancouver. We had a total of six therapy sessions during this time.

In our first session, Betsy reported details of her life and past therapy, and we got to know each other. In the second session, I taught her how to enter a state of hypnosis and how to practice self-hypnosis at home. Her safe place was a little "house" made of hay bales in the loft of the barn on her family's farm. She could enter the enclosed space through a small hole that she could cover from the inside, and no one would know that she was there. A soft light came through the boards, and she could smell the fresh hay and hear the sounds of animals and people coming and going below. Betsy needed to experience only two age regressions to get enough information to do the healing work she wanted to do. What follows is an account of her first age regression using the affect bridge.

Having entered a state of hypnosis and relaxed in her safe place, Betsy allowed herself to feel the tense feeling that she experienced around the family member who had assaulted her and then allowed it to become stronger and stronger. With her permission, I instructed her to leave her safe place and to imagine that she was looking at a book of her life, turning the pages backward, keeping the feeling with her as she moved back across time. Slowly but steadily, she made her way to a time when she was eight years old and felt the same uncomfortable, tense feeling. She was in her family home, and she was being baby-sat by two older family members. They told her that they were going to play "hotel" and that she was to stay in her bedroom and wait for "room service." Alone in the bedroom, she could hear them laughing in the next room. She felt scared and wanted to leave but couldn't. Her male relative then came into her room with an erection. She continued to feel afraid as he told her to get into the bed, got in after her, and proceeded to rub his penis on her until he ejaculated. Betsy felt afraid, confused, angry, and humiliated. I directed her to speak her feelings (again, louder) and she did, repeating in a louder and louder voice, "Stop, I don't like this! I'm angry! I'm angry!" I then instructed Betsy to return to her safe place and relax. After she returned to an alert state, I warned her that she would probably need to continue to be with these feelings before our next session and that she could help herself by allowing time for them and by writing about them or talking about them to someone she trusted.

In the third session, Betsy continued to process her feelings of hurt and anger. In the fourth session, she underwent another age regression and this time reexperienced her fear. In the remaining two sessions, she continued to process the feelings of fear, to integrate the now conscious knowledge of her abuse, and to make sense of different incidents in her life, given this new information. Betsy was able to do this work as quickly and effectively as she did, I believe, because she had already done substantial emotional work on the issues that were a consequence of her abuse, because she had a very secure and healthy self-concept, because her present life was satisfying and relatively free from stress and conflict, and because she was obviously ready to investigate her hunches. Like Gloria, she continued after she left therapy to integrate this new knowledge with her ongoing life. Betsy's account of her experience in hypnotherapy follows at the end of this chapter.

The next case study illustrates how the affect bridge was useful in the midst of long-term therapy with a woman who had layers of feelings and behaviors and who had many complicating problems to work out.

The Case of Susan. Susan came to me for therapy after attending my workshop on compulsive eating and body image, as had Gloria. She was aware that her compulsive eating behavior masked many feelings that she was afraid of but nonetheless wanted to investigate. She was also aware that she was comfortable being overweight, fearing that she would too easily become sexually promiscuous if she were "thin and sexy looking." Slowly, over the course of a year, using Gestalt body work and imaging to assist in identifying and expressing feelings and ego-state therapy to explore conflicting parts of herself, Susan began to develop greater self-awareness. During this time, she was also dealing with current problems in her marriage, with her children, with her work, and with relationships with family members. Friendships with women were foreign to Susan, but she tentatively began to take risks in communicating openly with a couple of colleagues and a sister-in-law.

Susan worked through feelings of having been abandoned and neglected by her mother and of having been psychologically and sexually abused by her father. She could recall having been bathed and fondled by her father as a young child, his making denigrating comments about her mother's and other women's bodies, and his telling her lewd sexual jokes and playing strip poker with her when she was an adolescent. Susan had coped with the psychological trauma of these experiences by living in a fantasy world that was at times more real to her than her world with her family. For example, she had fantasized having two different boyfriends whom she would meet and spend time with, and she had actually convinced some school friends that they existed. She herself had been convinced that she had become pregnant by one of these boys and had fantasized leaving home with him. In addition, Susan coped by splitting off into different ego states (a child, a whore, a mother, and a career woman), each of which represented different experiences, feelings, and behaviors. These ego states were conscious of each other, so Susan could be described as having dissociated but not as having a multiple personality disorder.

Several factors pointed to formal hypnosis and the affect bridge as a useful way to proceed with Susan's healing work. Susan had large memory gaps and sensed that they served the purpose of keeping painful memories unconscious. She also felt a great sense of terror that she perceived as inappropriate to the memories she had thus far uncovered. Further, she had flashes of images that left her feeling very disturbed and that she had feared to investigate in therapy. She hoped that hypnosis would allow her to examine more comfortably whatever it was that seemed to her so foreboding and dangerous. After several sessions in which Susan first decided to investigate her disturbing feelings, then hesitated and avoided "taking the plunge," she arrived one day and said that she felt so miserable she could no longer stand it and so was ready to "dive in." She had been experiencing severe uterine cramps for the past six weeks, suspected that this pain was psychologically based, and felt that she had no choice but to do whatever emotional work was necessary to feel better. After ensuring that Susan would see a medical doctor to have the pain checked out, I proceeded to assist her with the emotional work that she said she was now prepared to do.

Susan allowed herself to relax in her safe place and then gave permission for me to direct her to reexperience a feeling of black terror that was connected to a recurring image of a child's face. She traveled back in time on this feeling to an age she identified as two or three, finding herself in her crib in a bedroom that she could vaguely remember. Gradually, a scene unfolded in which she became aware first of a large shadow, then of being touched, then of a sharp pain as a hard, wooden-like object was inserted into her vagina. Finally came the recognition that the man who was assaulting her was her father. With these images and sensations came extremely intense feelings of pain, fear, and helplessness. Susan had successfully uncovered the horrific memory that she needed to make sense of and had created a place for the intense, overwhelming feelings of terror that prior to this had seemed to her so inappropriate.

Susan needed to return to her safe place three times throughout the session as she confronted the awful memory and the feelings attached to it. She would indicate to me each time that she wanted to go to her safe place to calm herself and would indicate again when she was ready to explore further the scene that was unfolding. She knew at every step what she could handle, and I perceived that my job as her therapist was to listen and watch carefully so that I could follow her lead, be with her, and assist her to make the transition from her safe place to the scary place and back again. The uterine cramping had completely stopped by the end of the session. It returned from time to time with diminished intensity over the next couple of months (usually when Susan was ignoring a feeling that she needed to pay attention to, she explained), and then it gradually faded out.

This session marked a turning point in Susan's therapy. With the reclaiming of this lost memory, integration began: over time, the helpless baby ego state was seen as legitimate rather than as whiny and was accepted and cared for by the mother ego state that had previously despised and rejected her; the mother learned to nurture herself as well as the baby; the whore ego state decided that it was more fun to go out to work with the career woman ego state than to play at seducing men in order to be powerful; and the career woman began to acknowledge the feelings of the other ego states and to accept her own feelings and vulnerabilities. Susan separated from her husband for several months as she continued to work with me on making changes in her life that were in keeping with her newly integrated, healthy self-concept. She stopped eating compulsively, changed jobs, and, after her husband had worked with me in therapy to make some changes on his own, began to rebuild her marriage with the help of couple counseling. For Susan, the emotional work that she did using the affect bridge was a relatively small but crucial part of her therapy that precipitated a significant internal shift and resynthesis.

Client's Voice: Betsy Warland

Memory goes back to the Indo-European root *smer-,* which the word *mourn* is also derived from.

This is about memory. A kind of memory that a great many of us have fiercely repressed. A kind of memory that we have no awareness of. That profoundly shapes our intimate lives without our understanding. Without our assent. It has no relationship to formal education or "remember when. . . ." This memory is the interface (inner face) of a self-induced amnesia. Sometimes it occurs when, as adults, we suffer some horrific event alone. More frequently, it occurs when, as children, we suffer a deeply disillusioning event alone. It has to do with being victimized, usually an invisible victimization. No witnesses. No visible scars.

So why seek out this memory? Why not leave "well enough" alone? So, you've happened to build your house on top of a toxic waste deposit: just don't dig around, stir things up, or plant a garden. Sell and don't tell. Not possible.

A brief bio. I spent the first thirty years of my life with practically no sexual sensations or feelings. Certainly no orgasms. No self-exploration or self-stimulation. Yet I was a very passionate person. Deeply involved in all other facets of my life. After an eight-year marriage, I felt compelled to determine if, in fact, I was a lesbian. The marriage ended. I did fall in love with a woman. We were lovers for four years. My sexual, sensual self became very much alive. I concluded that my repressed lesbianism had kept my sexual self in the deep freeze for all those years. Yet there were problems with this new sexual intimacy, too. Eventually, my lover betrayed me by having an affair. I fell into a profound depression, experienced a primary sense of abandonment. Realized that I had been terrified of this happening my whole life. Wondered why. Moved away and began my life over. But just before my departure, I happened to see a video. A video I attended only as a gesture of support for a friend who had arranged its public screening. It comprised six incest survivors talking to one another about their processes of coming to terms with their incest. By the end of the screening, I knew this video had something to do with me. I knew it clearly, but had no idea as to how or who or when.

The next four years I spent reading, talking to incest survivors, looking over childhood family photographs, and asking my one sibling I'm close to (who has a good memory) about the sexual dynamics that were operating in our extended family. The tracks had been well covered by us all, but there were pieces of the story here and there. Only fragments. During these years the backdrop filled itself in. No plot. No central characters. Then came the shock of another family member who, under great distress during a familial crisis, revealed being a victim of incest. Suddenly, this family member's chronic and maddening fear of being taken advantage of made sense! The hiding of valuables and then the accusing others of stealing them (having forgotten the original hiding). The resentments so deeply held.

You are probably aware by now of my use of nonspecific nouns for my family. I still feel compelled to protect them as individuals. They are caught in the net-of-never-tell. Only I have decided to write this.

With this revelation of incest, I finally had evidence. Affirmation that I hadn't been imagining things. Incest did exist within our extended family. This was the point at which I began to work with Cheryl. Though I had only a brief period of time before I moved back to Vancouver, I knew I was ready. Ready somehow to unearth my own memories. Fortunately, Cheryl recognized this, and agreed to fit me in on a short-term basis. We had six sessions. She suggested that she teach me self-hypnosis. Since I sensed that this might be the only way in, I agreed. There was a practicality about this approach and about Cheryl's presence that I found reassuring. Through self-hypnosis, I regained my ability to establish my inner place of safety. The very place, I suspect, that was trespassed and violated in me as a child.

In the second or third session, my first memory reconstructed itself. I say "reconstructed itself" because it seemed like that. It initially felt like a very bizarre process. I trusted it, however, because I felt safe, essentially in control, and I had a reliable witness. My body led the way. Chest tightening with panic as I fell backward in time. Everything was black. Like a movie theater with all the lights out. I think now, that terrible nothingness was the thick membrane of amnesia I had to pass through. The first fragment surfaced on my mind-screen; the word *hotel.* What did that mean? Lights on again. It seemed so bizarre. Cheryl urged me to keep trusting myself. And I sat in the nothingness and waited. Then the scene of the upstairs of our house flashed in front of me. Where our bedrooms were. Lights out again. Chest painful from constriction. And so it went. This jerky motion like an old silent film that kept stopping and starting, skipping numerous frames but somehow allowing the central images of the story to appear. When it was over, I said what all incest victims say, "I must have made it up." Cheryl responded, "Why would you do that?" We talked. Through the talking I began to accept this unfamiliar memory process, the way these bizarre pieces string themselves together even though they seem, at first, to make no sense. During our last sessions, we spent most of the time exploring the impact of my reconstructed memory and discussed what I needed to do to continue my healing process. The most valuable comment Cheryl made to me was that incest doesn't come out of the air: it is a learned behavior, and the family member who victimized me was very likely victimized by someone else first. This insight was critical in focusing my attention and anger on the dynamics of my extended family instead of simply singling out one of its victims.

I now believe that both people are victimized by incest. The nature of the victimization is different, however. The one who is taken advantage of is left considerably more powerless and more terrorized. I still rage at the prevalence of this invisible brainwashing of young girls. See rape as a "refresher course" that reminds women to always wear this fear of unprovoked attacks like chains around our necks. This is a method of enslavement. But the *perpetrators—perpetrate, "to perform in the capacity of the father"—* suffer damage too. I cannot speak for them. Only know that they must work to heal themselves, as well.

As well. Well. Memory is like a . . . ; yes, I am . . . , thank you. More accurately, I am getting there. Two years after working with Cheryl, I wrote to my perpetrator. It was a confronting letter about our incest, our family's pattern; but it was also a letter that was written with love and concern. In my letter, I urged this family member to begin to work toward personal healing. If incest is to stop, everyone must take responsibility for healing themselves. In response to my letter, this family member accepted the premise of my confrontation but admitted to having no memory of it. True regret was expressed as well as the assurance that "I will undoubtedly keep thinking about this for a long time to come." It takes a long time. It has now been six and a half years for me. Seven years is said to be the average length of recovery time.

Since those sessions with Cheryl, other memories have surfaced periodically. Finally, I knew how to recognize them. Some came through hypnosis, others through dreams or associative experiences. The plot and characters gradually filled themselves in. Although some incest survivors do vividly recall their experiences, most of us don't. With Cheryl, I understood that the recovery of my experience was never going to come back as a whole, intact memory.

The imprint of unresolved incest on our adult lives is very real, very tangible. Tangible, once you learn to recognize its shape; sense its presence; remember its gestures. You catch yourself incest-shadowing current associative dynamics with your intimates. This shadowing is very subtle and very subversive. This is why it is imperative that we do "dig around." But first, establish a safe place. Find someone who has experience with incest survivors, who has the skills to work with your amnesia. A counselor or therapist who knows how to witness, who recognizes your reconstructing fragments. Include your intimates in your process, because your healing has repercussions on them.

My repressed lesbianism is not what put my sexuality into the deep freezer for thirty years. In talking with other lesbians, I grew to realize that nearly all of them knew an active sexuality within themselves (fantasy and self-stimulation) and with others (female and/or male), before they came to terms with their lesbianism. No, it was the freezer door of incest that slammed tight. It has taken me perhaps half of my life to pry it open again. I write this with the hope that it won't take so long for you.

References

Hammond, D. C. "Myths About Erickson and Ericksonian Hypnosis." *American Journal of Clinical Hypnosis,* 1984, *26* (4), pp. 236–245.

Hammond, D. C. "The Affect or Somatic Bridge." Unpublished short paper circulated to workshop participants at the annual meeting of the Canadian Society of Clinical Hypnosis–Alberta Division, Banff, Alta., May 1988.

Mann, H. "Describing Hypnosis to Patients." In B. Zilbergeld, M. G. Edelstien, and D. L. Araoz (eds.), *Hypnosis: Questions and Answers.* New York: Norton, 1986.

Negley-Parker, E. "Physiological Correlates and Effects of Hypnosis." In B. Zilbergeld, M. G. Edelstien, and D. L. Araoz (eds.), *Hypnosis: Questions and Answers.* New York: Norton, 1986.

Oliver, L. "The Use of Hypnosis as a Therapeutic Technique by Traditional African Healers." Paper presented at the European Congress of Hypnosis, Oxford, England, July 1987.

Rausch, V. Lecture material presented at workshop at the annual meeting of the Canadian Society of Clinical Hypnosis–Alberta Division, Devon, Alta., Feb. 1984.

Rosen, S. *My Voice Will Go with You: The Teaching Tales of Milton H. Erickson*. New York: Norton, 1982.

Rossi, E. L. *The Psychobiology of Mind-Body Healing*. New York: Norton, 1986.

Rossi, E. L. "Altered States of Consciousness in Everyday Life: The Ultradian Rhythms." In B. Wolman and M. Ullman (eds.), *Handbook of Altered States*. New York: D. Van Nostrand, 1987.

Tafoya, T. Lecture material presented at the Third Annual International Congress on Ericksonian Approaches to Hypnosis and Psychotherapy, Phoenix, Ariz., Dec. 1985.

Watkins, J. G. "The Affect Bridge: A Hypnoanalytic Technique." *International Journal of Clinical and Experimental Hypnosis*, 1971, *19*, pp. 21-27.

11

Let My Soul Soar: Touch Therapy

Joan Turner
Client: Carol Rose

[oh], let my soul
soar above my room
let her dance on walls
to songs of violins
leap rooftops
to pages of poetry
praise
    an orange, a house
    a mountain, a breeze
let her transcend all limits
of my small life

—*E. Starkman**

Walking down the road in the valley of my childhood, I notice, for the first time in a long time, the scar on my left arm. The memories of a hot kerosene lamp suddenly shattering, the burning glass piercing my forearm, flood into my consciousness. Some scars show forever on the outside, but for the most part the experience fades and is forgotten.

The scars from abscessed tonsils, the hideous mask thrust over my face, arms and legs tied down in place, the cruel nurse ordering my mother home . . . the time my teenage friends and I jumped from a truck to avoid being raped . . . the trauma of birthing a child alone while simultaneously grieving my father's sudden death. Those scars do not show visibly on the outside. I know them well—they have marked me deeply. Tongue-tied, silent, unable to speak or to write for myself, looking to male experts to explain the way life is. Eventually I discover that women speak my language, and I theirs.

My therapeutic style of work may be called therapeutic massage, counseling, healing through touch, body work. I think in time we may find better labels. My clients, Di and Carol, and I, in our own words, describe the process. It is the process and the discovery of the self that is important. Action, movement, change will follow the discoveries: that is our experience.

Ten years ago, more or less, I began to change my life significantly. I was a university professor of social work, married, mother of two daughters, living in a modern home in suburbia, jogging to keep fit—unhappy, miserable, scared, pretending. The child in me felt beaten down, confused, uncertain. One day I looked in a mirror and saw myself, the old woman. I did not like what I saw, shrivelled skin, tense tight body, weary eyes. But I studied the image, feeling impelled to do so, while the chaos of fighting children went on about me (relative's children, left with me for the day, permission not even requested). I felt powerless, sad, used. There I was, old and wizened. She clearly was me, no mistaking, and she seemed to speak as I studied her. "Change," she said, "You are aging prematurely, you spirit is dying, your body—just look at your skin becoming old and sick, dis-eased. Or perhaps you will go crazy, a patient on the psychiatric ward. This is sickening. Play the martyr or take action. It is your life, craziness, or death we are talking about."

I put this information together with the other image of myself—successful professional, competent at work, athletic, reasonably well-liked, eldest daughter modelling the good life. But I was in pain and I was scared. I did not like the way I looked and sounded. Needing help, I decided with difficulty to go for counseling, choosing a man, hoping I would involve my husband in the counseling process, which I eventually did. The couple counseling was an educational process. I learned how it is to be on the other side of the desk, experiencing my hopes for the marriage and my disillusionment, being blamed for everything that was wrong, feeling alone, not really understood by the counselor. I experienced how my love and feeling of being loved was dying, dead. Little warmth between us now. It was painful to see and know.

I could not even have imagined that ten years later I would have my own name, not my ex-husband's, be doing body work, healing work, and writing about it. Opening the door to life may mean doing what we never dreamed of doing, becoming a person different than anyone we have ever known. It is exciting and scary.

I have never written about my therapeutic work beyond one line, in *Perspectives on Women* (Turner and Emery, 1983). I find it hard to think of myself as just possibly a healer. It seems that I have been "found out" by the senior authors of this book, women I have never even met. I am challenged. I review my own healing journey and my professional experiences. I ask my clients for help. They respond in writing, with telephone calls. They tell me about their healing in their own words.

Di's and Carol's responses are being published, too. I feel very vulnerable. Up to now, there has been intimacy, privacy, confidentiality, in my work in the little pastel-colored room with the stained-glass window and the sturdy massage table with its breathing hole. I look out at the apple and lilac trees, a huge brown squirrel scurries up the neighbor's elm, a bird alights and I see the blue sky beyond. Sunlight floods in. I feel strong and centered in this room. I work for hours without tiring, bare feet quietly moving about the table with tai chi ease. Ideas flow from inside. My hands guide me. I bring forth into the work all I know and am, including what I know from living in a woman's body for half a century. I know it is a partriarchal world. Sometimes in my work I use the language of feminism—sometimes not. For almost twenty years, I taught social work skills in a large bureaucratic institution where, of course, men hold the power. Through painful life experiences, much of it feeling as if I was hitting my head against a brick wall, I became a feminist. Gradually, feminism became reflected in all that I do. My energy, time, and interests became focused on work with women. I moved away from a rather traditional form of social work practice that emphasized comprehensive social assessments and empathetic listening skills with individuals, groups, and families to the alternative form of practice that I use today. I work primarily with individual women. I emphasize caring. I do care. I believe in the process of opening, of discovery, of the gentle unfolding of the budded flower. I believe in change and the body's need for change and motion.

Once my body, like many women's, suffered from trying to be thin (thinner is better, isn't it?). I took up little space. I spoke only when invited to do so, and only when it was appropriate. I was very good at being polite and proper, and I was rewarded with success. Society appreciates women who know their small space, seems to care little whether it is an oppressing prison, limiting potential, breaking women's spirit, consuming time and energy.

Now I encourage women to unfold, to take their rightful place, to express themselves. In the one and a half hours of our appointed time together, we shut out demands and expectations from others and the world, focusing on the body, involving the mind, spirit, soul. The entry point to the body space and inner child is through the muscles. The technique I use is deep-tissue therapeutic massage. With my hands, my thumb or fingers, I focus on the muscles that are "needful"—tight, sore, knotted, numb. They respond by softening, relaxing. The breath slows and deepens. The body feels lighter. Awareness deepens.

Jane is a new client. We talk, at first exchanging information. I clarify whether she is open to being touched, to doing body work. If she seems unsure, we move more slowly, without touch. I respect her need for space and time to test whether she can trust me. I realize that body work not only seems but *is* powerful, enhancing the likelihood of change and the fear of change.

Long ago, from wise women social work teachers, including author Helen Perlman, I learned the importance of beginning where the client "is at." What is Jane hoping for through working with me? Where does she want to begin today? The answers of women like Jane are varied. Most women want freedom from physical and emotional pain and a full and meaningful life. Some examples are: "I have headaches, and my shoulders ache. I want to see if I can at least reduce the frequency of the headaches and the extent of the aching. You helped my friend." "I don't feel anything but numb and depressed. I am tired of living this way." "I have writer's (artist's) block. I want to write (paint) again." "I am burned out. I cannot go on. Please help me." "I want help in opening; to feel more joy, to be more spontaneous." "I need help to understand the trauma of my childhood." "I feel locked inside, and I am tired of being sick." "I am an incest survivor, and I need to know more." "I need to heal my hurt child. She is beaten and scared."

Jane and I agree on the use of touch and body work. I introduce her to the massage room and ascertain that she is not allergic to the body lotions and cream I usually use. We turn on soft instrumental music to promote relaxation and as a bridge through the stillness. I leave the room, giving her time and privacy to undress. If she is uncomfortable, we will begin with her fully dressed, perhaps sitting on the floor or in a chair. The process of working directly with the body, muscles, skin, may be a gradual one. The more I work through body work, the more that is my reputation and the expectation of clients. But it is not the only way we work. Breathing and relaxation exercises, Gestalt, talking—listening empathetically, journaling, drawing, photography, pounding pillows, and screaming are all possible, instead of or in addition to the body work.

When I enter the room again, Jane has quietly slipped under cotton sheets and is lying on the massage table. She is trying to relax. Her body is anxious, her jaw tight, her coloring relatively pale. She feels cool. I add a light yellow blanket and turn on the heater. We begin with her feet, massaging the tight spots. Most women do not feel particularly vulnerable through their feet.

Using open-ended questions, I invite her to tell me about herself. For example, are there parts of her body that have experienced trauma, accident, surgery? I want to be particularly sensitive to those places, for wherever there is accident, trauma, surgery, that part of the body usually has a painful story to tell. Muscles, like the mind, hold memories that can be triggered through touch. I do not want to trigger too much too soon, before I am sure of her strength, that she has at least one or two caring people in her life, and that we have a connection that will feel supportive to her. I do not want her out on a limb in a difficult world where people and institutions often really do not care about the particular life or journey of a woman or about women collectively. I learn as I proceed into the massage that Jane has survived many traumas and has important coping and survival skills. At the moment, she seems more aware of her problems and weaknesses than of her strengths. As I massage her legs, I ask her the stories of her legs, what they might say if they could talk.

I massage her hands, arms, shoulders, neck, and face, then ask her to turn over so that I may do her back. We are silent now. Her breathing has relaxed and deepened. She is present in heightened awareness with her self, the outside world irrelevant in this time and space. As I hold my warm hands gently on her lower back, she begins to softly cry. Her little child feels rocked and tended to, gently, lovingly. I represent now the adult who loves and cares. Perhaps in the beginning, there was at least one unconditionally loving adult present, perhaps not. This time there is. As long as I experience through my hands Jane's openness to receiving, I experience myself as a giver, nurturer. When we have finished, I cover her once again with the sheet and blanket and indicate that for today we will end there. I leave the room appreciative of Jane and of myself. Our journey together has begun.

This first appointment is clearly a beginning. I ask Jane to make two more appointments, after which we will evaluate whether she wishes and needs to continue. We set her appointments one or two weeks apart, depending on a number of factors, including our schedules, her financial situation (for she pays me a fee), and how quickly she intends to move with the therapy. She leaves her first appointment with most, if not all, of her body feeling warm and relaxed, free from pain and tension. She knows that she will sleep well tonight.

I encourage Jane to give the rest of the afternoon and evening to herself, imposing few, if any, tasks upon herself. It is a time to be with oneself as much as possible. For some women, the massage-body work time with me is their only protected personal time.

Beth is my next client, a composite of many clients, most of whom are white, at least high school educated, city residents. When I enter the massage room, Beth is lying on the massage table trying to relax. Her body, she says, feels anxious. She has a vague but disquieting feeling that she is on the edge of a deeper layer of knowing her inner child. She feels tightness, particularly in her shoulders, jaw, and neck, and hopes that today's session will at least ease that physical discomfort. She knows from experience that we cannot anticipate the body's personal messages. Maybe this session will hold emotional pain and release as well as knowing, challenge as well as discovery. Perhaps she will go deep into the well, into darkness, finding light; perhaps not. We try to set aside expectations.

I massage her left hand, arm, and shoulder; then her right hand, arm, and shoulder. Beth tells me about her busy week. Like most women, I hear that she has many care-giving responsibilities. She struggles to balance her need to be financially self-supporting with her need to be creative, to let her spirit soar, to heal the pain of old wounds, to let go of old expectations and patterns, to grow and develop personally. She would also like to complete the university program she began several years ago. She wants to be treated with respect, to gain credibility, to be taken seriously. She would like to have enough money not to worry every month about how the bills will be paid. Her relationship with her partner is challenging.

Beth is concerned that she is moving, changing, growing, but her partner is rooted in maintaining traditional patterns. She cares about her partner deeply, but worries that the difficult edges in their current relationship are warning signals that they may move away along different pathways. She cannot *not* see, hear, grow, now that she has begun.

She is propelled along, nudged and nurtured by other women. The faint glimmer of the possibility of a full creative life for herself and, more probably, for her children, glimmers in the dark—a world of peace and justice, where women are respected and equal. Maybe this is possible!

I move behind her, softening the knots, the stiffness, in her neck. I ask her to focus on her breathing: long, deep, full breaths, drawing up from her abdomen through her chest, up into her face, behind her eyes, then out, blowing out through loose jaw (as my friend Karen says, "Let your jaw fall like a moose"). We laugh. Laughter is good medicine, naturally massaging the muscles. I coach her with a few gently spoken words. Her eyes begin to tear, rivulets trickling down her cheeks. She is letting go, trusting in herself to find her way inside and back again, trusting me to facilitate, support, and guide. We know that the answers are inside of her.

Beth worries about violence everywhere. This week a friend's daughter was assaulted. She feels angry but dislikes the anger. Memories of her own experience have been triggered. A lump is in her throat. Her coloring heightens. I invite her to scream, but nothing comes. Her body stiffens. It learned a long time ago that expression of anger was forbidden for women. The anger moves inside, blocking her again. I feel her fear in coldness. There are goose bumps on her arms. I am watchful of body changes, acutely present, encouraging the process of going deeper. She is in touch with her inner child. I stay very present, moving very little. Beth is seeing and knowing at a deep level. Perhaps a caring adult was present then, perhaps not. I aim to be there—present, focused entirely on her, noninterfering, supportive. It is her journey as an adult back into her childhood.

Like Beth, I may see images, hear words, see colors; feel heat or coldness; experience muscles that are like knotted fists, holding on, resisting the emotional pain of knowing, or softening, transcending into new depths, expanding into poetry, art, songs of life and living. I encourage the expression of sounds and hear the cry of babies, the plaintive aloneness of five-year-olds, and the outrage of inner teens.

In Carol's statement, at the end of this chapter, she describes how she "sees" and "hears" her mother and grandmother and later how she sees a mountain and a waterfall. We cannot predicate how or in what form—be it in images of people, of nature, of colors, or words—we will experience our inner child or teacher. What I try to provide is a way to that inner power, to that way of knowing.

Sometimes the action that must follow knowing for change to actually take place requires that we dialogue after the body work and develop an action plan. Most often the first steps are clear from the experience of the body work, and the time and personal space are most important. I ask my clients to rest for five minutes or more before preparing to move back out into the world. I caution them to be careful, to move in the world aware that they have been on an inner journey and their reaction time has been slowed. I encourage attention to nurturing and regularly exercising their bodies between appointments.

Di rides her bike to her appointment. Mother of two, graduate student, teacher, employee, poet whose book *Questions I Asked My Mother* has been published (Brandt, 1987), Di first came feeling burned out. We have worked together over time. Today, I begin by massaging her shoulders. They are tight. She had been working and studying intensively. I encourage her to breathe deeply from her abdomen. Her breathing slows and deepens. She remarks how good it feels to be breathing deeply, to be touched, to be in this safe place that she has come to know over time. The exams that she had been worrying about, her concern about the state of this difficult world, the politics of the university, all seem to float away. Her body is . . . Time and space are . . . She is finding herself again. I stay present, listening, seeing, encouraging. Later she brings me this gift.

i'm finding myself again in the healed heart
(for Joan Turner, with love from Di Brandt
—Winnipeg, 1988)

& suddenly i'm little again so little i daren't
breathe or make a sound i'm staring through crib
bars at a blank wall the room is big & far away the
world is full of wonder if i move or make a sound it
will happen again do what he says the voice
whispers in my ear do what he says or he will kill
you i'm locked frozen with fear i'm too little to
understand fear my whole being trembles with
shock what is happening do what he says the voice
whispers & i'll watch out for you i'll watch don't
make a sound remember this for your life remember
& suddenly you're here in the room with me i'm a
grown woman i'm so little lying on this table
huddled in my crib why don't you make some
sounds you say your strong soft hands stroking my
back i'm frozen with fear my whole being trembles
with shock now that you're grown up & can break

the rules you say again your hands stroking my back make some sounds i'm scared i've waited all my life for this moment & yes & i let it come up a huge ancient cry a wail from somewhere deep inside me deeper than my bones deeper than my womb a cry of children left alone in the night the cry of women with torn bellies screaming pain the cry of trees ripped from the earth in huge furrows a cry of oceans reeling with blood i cry my small loneliness my betrayal my fear i cry all my years of numbness & confusion i cry my father's anger his knowledge his cruel hands i cry my mother's silence her fear i cry the joy of the earth's own wanting it washes over me in a great wave it'll break my bones washing over me i think it'll break the world smash the crib bars shatter the table but i'm after all only a baby my grown woman's pain comes out a small baby's cry so little the cry spills out of me like rain like laughter onto the table into the room & suddenly i'm laughing my baby's body shakes with laughing you bastard i laugh i gurgle i crow you thought you could break me possess me own me you thought you could make me live in fear on nothing past your grave past your dying forever you didn't know someday i'd get free & i'm smiling smiling full of light & over my shoulder I see her the watcher her beautiful calm face her radiance her deep eyes & suddenly i see that she is me & the moment i see this the moment i know myself she is gone & i feel an opening in my chest i'm finding myself again in the healed heart & my father's spirit is beside me blessing me with his tears my father who cried with such anguish when he knew what he'd done & he didn't know even then after death my father he didn't know such an outrage such a great wounding could be undone & he's glad the split years roll away my father is no more the hole in my heart closes gently my mother does not move

the trees outside the window shiver their ancient secrets   you cradle me in your arms tenderly   you cover
my nakedness with the cool scented sheet   you touch
my cheek   hold me miracle fairy godmother my
sweet   grown woman   little child   the room is so big
& far away   the world is full of wonder

Client's Voice: Carol Rose

Working with Joan has taught me how much material is available to me from my own treasure house of information, my body. Our work together invites every body cell to come alive and reveal what it can from its own personal memory bank—a source often unrecognized until the massage therapist urges into consciousness the fullness of its knowledge.

In our particular case, the therapy follows a unique pattern—one that reflects, I believe, the personal preparation of the participants. Both Joan and I have studied and explored a variety of healing techniques, gaining respect for the significance of creative imagery, especially as a tool for greater self-awareness. We share and respect the language and the rhythm of this inner "picture making" process. While we have never discussed our particular pattern of working together, it seemed to evolve out of our very first session, and it has continued to unfold organically, informing and enlightening each subsequent session.

We generally greet each other warmly, with Joan asking me where I would like her to begin. As Joan massages, I enter into a state of "relaxed concentration" where body sensations trigger images and memories. When I feel that I have gone as far as I can, alone, with these "picture stories," I turn to Joan and ask her what she has been perceiving/sensing while silently working on an area of my body. She shares what she has encountered in the muscle, tissue, limb, or spinal column and I try to connect this information to the experiential material I have "seen." Occasionally her insights validate what I have become aware of; often, too, Joan is able to give my vague images a clarity or direction that I might have missed or ignored. Sometimes we talk at length about what has come up, particularly if it is an issue that relates to women or if it is an experience that many of us share. Other times there is a deep, respectful silence after we have each shared our particular insights from the "body teacher." These are precious moments—holy moments—moments when we are humbly aware of the "source of all knowledge." The entire process is reverential, respectful, receptive, and deeply personal. Intimacy of the highest order, I believe, is possible at times like these when the therapist and the recipient are in sync and are finely tuned to the wisdom of the other.

To illustrate the ways in which my work with Joan has helped me, I will use selected journal entries. These begin in December of 1985 with the following affirmation:

> It is the end of the calendar year and I am feeling ready to come to my own center; to "know what I know"—consciously. To do so, I will begin working through the body, that part of myself that feels most neglected, dishonored, ignored. Often I feel as though I live "despite my body"—now I wish to live in harmony with her. I am aware of how my work with Colette [my teacher] has radically changed my heart, my mind, my spirit. Now it is time to invite my body to participate in this challenge.

The journal entry of that very first day continues with an appraisal, as it were, of Joan herself:

> She is small, strong, mature. I feel her to be very real, alive, working hard to sustain the certainty that her hands emit as they begin their exploration of my body. She seems to have spent much time honing her spirit. There appears to be a respect for my work, as well as for my desire to grow, though we have not exchanged many words. During the massage, I am aware of Joan becoming very transparent, concentrated, and focused. I feel invited to participate at this very deep level of awareness.

The first real insights I had from my body teacher are very apparent, I believe, in the following entry:

> As Joan begins today's massage journey, I "see" my mother and my step-grandmother fitting me for a skirt. My body is sending me signals of pain, of having been humiliated at this time in my childhood [I am about nine years old]. My step-grandmother notices the first indications of my scoliosis—one hip is slightly higher on the right side than the other and there seems to be some slight twisting at my waistline. My step-grandmother comments to my mother about this, complaining that she will have to work hard to make me "look good." My sense is that she is accusing me of being less than perfect and that this is a *judgment* on her part, not an observation. My mother seems helpless, embarrassed—as though she is, in some way, unfit because of my "deformity." As Joan continues the massage, I experience my own hurt, my own anger. After all, I'm only a child, a child who is growing, who is in the process of growing, and I feel absolutely no appreciation from my mother or from my step-grandmother for this process. They seem to have formed their opinion of me as though I was already complete—finished—and forever to be seen in this way.

Joan asks me what I am "seeing," and I tell her. She asks me what I have learned from this, and I explain that "this helps me as a mother. It helps me to see all of my children in their own processes of development. I feel that I am being cautioned against judging them prematurely." Joan asks me to apply what I have learned to myself, gently urging me deeper into my own awareness again. I reply, "I see that I am still changing—still in process and truly able to "straighten myself out" with work and with will. I am aware that I must not push with my will exclusively, but that I should *pace* myself, trusting the work of massage as a means of coaxing the body, educating the body and inviting it, in turn, to teach me what it is holding on to and why." I feel, at the end of this massage, that I have made the first step toward "healing the child within." I have found what my body has registered, and I am learning to read it accurately—accepting only what fits for me now and releasing what no longer suits my needs or my reality at this moment.

At another stage of massage healing, I experience the body as a messenger of "transformational images"—images that appear as one thing and then become another, or images that themselves contain change. I note the following examples taken from several journal entries:

> Joan works on my upper left side and I am surprised by the pain. Suddenly I see reeds or a web of fibers, moving fibers—and at the end of this web, an eye, looking at me. It feels like the eye of a frog, like a bull frog, or like something not quite born. I experience myself being born then and I observe my physician's eye peering into my mother's birth canal, trying to watch my birth. Still this is not the whole picture. I see the fibers changing and becoming external, like reeds. I feel like I am behind reeds—watching (like Miriam watching behind reeds as Moses is saved). I like this biblical image—an image of change, of something new about to occur—yet somehow out of my reach.
>
> I ask Joan what she has been sensing. I am especially curious because I have always thought of my left side as "healthy" and now it is quite painful. I tell her that because the left side is straight I've always assumed that it was pain free. Joan talks about the left side as my coping mechanism—keeping me conventional—allowing me to live under difficult circumstances—supporting me. She says she has experienced my "gypsy" or my "old woman" in prison. Perhaps the reeds are prison bars, I wonder. Somehow Joan's image carries a truth that I recognize.

> Today again the frog and the fibers (or reeds) appear as Joan works on my upper left side. I think of the "frog into prince" myths, but realize that the frog is for me the symbol of living in the conscious (on

land) as well as the unconscious (in water) levels of reality. The frog is now very large and it wants me to come into the water. Before I do this I know I have to step into "a darkness" and as I do, I meet and take with me a large blackish/brown bear. I take the bear by the hand and realize that it is "the darkness" itself. I am amazed at how easily I can take the bear—how gentle and playful and youthful it is. I take the bear and settle it behind the reeds so it can watch me as I go toward the frog. The frog is sitting on a lily pad, waiting. It wants me to lie down on my back so it can put the lily pad over my face and then sit upon the lily pad. I do so and then sit up and look at the bear (behind the reeds) and then again I look into the water. There is a white flower floating on top of the water. I know that I have to put my face into the flower and wear it as a face mask because it will help me breathe under water. It provides me with oxygen, like a scuba mask, as I go deeper and deeper into the water. I see many gems on the floor of the sea, mostly turquoise. The stones are so lovely that all I want to do is look at them, but I know that I must stay alert. I look closely and see an arm, a small, slim arm buried under all of the turquoise. I pull it up, expecting a child to be buried there. Instead I pull upon a wing and, as I tug, the turquoise releases a small owl. I am still concerned that there was a child down there, a child that I couldn't rescue yet, but I treasure the little owl.

The images all seem so powerful. The bear, an earthly creature, well covered and protected, able to walk on four legs as well as on two. The frog, a creature of both the land and the sea; and now, under water, a little owl—symbol of wisdom, one who is awake during the night, during the darkness. A being who lives above the land, high in the trees. One who calls out "Hoo-Hoo" or "Who-Who?" I stare at the eyes of the owl and they remind me of the eyes of the

> frog. Somehow as I do this the owl transforms and becomes a white dove with an enormous wingspread. The image seems to be born of the owl and yet, at the same time, it springs from my own heart. This dove who soars in the skies above all the others—in the heavens; a messenger of peace, discoverer of a safe space to begin a new life. The images appear to be very complete.

As an illustration of another facet of the healing of massage, I would like to share images of learning to accept the inner teacher. This, I believe, represents an important message for women who have been taught to acquire information, skill, and general know-how from the outer world exclusively.

> Joan is working on my right side and suddenly I see myself in a huge library. Books are piled up high, up to the ceiling, and I am sitting in my father's lap in a deep, comfortable leather chair. I am very young—three or four years old. At the entrance to the library is a young soldier, somewhat like the American war heroes of the 1940s–50s. He is a sentimental, gentle soldier—not cruel or warlike. He is telling me something important: "you must never leave this room. There is no need to, for everything you will ever need to know is in this room. The accumulated wisdom of all the ages, from everywhere in the world, is in these books. It would be very foolish for you to leave since anything that anyone needs to know is in here. It would take a lifetime to know what is available in here. Going outside would be foolish! You could learn things outside but it would be much harder, and therefore, ridiculous to pursue." I realize that I am no longer in my father's lap but that I have sunk deeply into the leather chair and that I am a teenager, perhaps. I realize how very deep and comfortable this chair is. I know that what the soldier is telling me is his way of protecting me—but it is not my way of learning. It is

> hard to leave. My eyes are drawn to the highest shelf of books. Big volumes are almost tumbling down and I am interested in those. I keep thinking that though this is, perhaps, the safest way of learning, it is certainly not the only way to acquire knowledge.
>
> Today I see the soldier again. This time I decide to leave and I tell the soldier that I am going. It takes tremendous energy to rise from the chair and pass the soldier who is still guarding the doorway. It is very dark outside the door and it takes a great act of will to pass through. I pass through the darkness, which I realize is temporary, and enter a new place beside a pond. There, the frog awaits my arrival—inviting me to enter the water.

Today as Joan works in the chest and abdominal areas, I find that it is easy to become centered and energized again by focusing attention on my breathing. Joan often concludes the massage by working with the "energy field" surrounding the body—bringing light and healing from the center of the body itself. As she draws this healing energy up, I am aware of another presence, a spirit guide or teacher.

> I see the side of a mountain just below a waterfall. Carved into the mountainside is a perfectly shaped cave or cavern. Looking closely, I see a young woman who has assumed the position of the half moon shape of the cavern. She gracefully moves herself out of the cave enclosure and walks to the edge of the ridge upon which she resides. With "dancelike" movements, she seats herself on the ledge and, as though engaged in an ancient ritual, she tosses her hair over her head and over the mountainside. The waterfall gently washes over her, soothing the back of her neck and bathing her long dark tresses. Gracefully, she lifts her hair and smooths it back over her shoulders as she rises and returns to her place in the cavern. As she fits herself

back into the cave, I realize that this is the ear—that she lives in the inner ear and that I may meet her whenever I wish, simply by listening. This awareness gives me great joy and it reminds me to heed my own inner teacher.

The work of massage therapy requires trust and commitment. It is hardly passive, demanding the fullest possible involvement of both parties. It calls upon every resource, every sense, indeed, every pore. Because it invites the whole of a human being, it has the potential to heal in wholeness. It is organic, like all real growth, and it respects the integrity of the individuals involved. Its unique feature seems to be its ability to involve clients and therapists in nonviolent change—change drawn from the very inside rather than change that is determined and superimposed from without. It is esthetic, peaceful, and calming, yet extremely powerful and transforming. In order to *reach* the child within, in order to *heal* her, we have to be able to *touch* the child within, to *stroke* her, to *caress* her, and to make her feel *loved* and *capable*. Capable, able individuals seek their own growth, find their own cures, and, ultimately, heal their own wounds.

References

Brandt, D. *Questions I Asked My Mother*. Winnipeg: Turnstone Press, 1987.

Starkman, E. "Prayer." In M. Cohn Spiegel and D. L. Kremsdorf (eds.), *Women Speak to God*. San Diego, Calif.: Women's Institute for Continuing Jewish Education, 1987.

Turner, J., and Emery, L. (eds.). *Perspectives on Women*. Winnipeg: University of Manitoba Press, 1983.

Recommended Readings

Downing, G., and Rush, A. K. *The Massage Book*. New York: Random House, 1972.

Greenspan, M. *A New Approach to Women and Therapy*. New York: McGraw-Hill, 1983.

Johnson, D. *Body*. Boston: Beacon Press, 1983.

Niddell, L. *The Book of Massage*. New York: Simon & Schuster, 1984.

PART FOUR

HEALING THROUGH INTEGRATION

12

The Therapeutic Journey: A Guide for Travelers

Jan Ellis
Client: "Eve"

My basic assumption in working with women in therapy is that all of us have been abused. No one escapes the world's prevailing attitude that women and children are less valuable than adult males. Within each of us is a child whose development was short-circuited. I find this to be true for both male and female children. The critical difference is that for males, there is the promise of a time of power. For women, there is no such promise. It is only a matter of time until a woman discovers that the plan for her is to remain limited. The horror of the plan is that she is also to smile and accept this graciously, to join the belief that this is all that she deserves, and that she is to do this in silence.

Think about when this happened to you. When did it really sink in? How many of the early messages or clues did you ignore until it really got through? For some of my clients, it started in infancy and very early childhood with tremendous violence and deprivation. For many, it didn't occur until puberty, when they learned to be ashamed of being female. For a few who led relatively protected and cherished childhoods, it happened in adolescence as they began to plan educations, search out occupations, or make love for the first time. A tiny minority made it all the way to early adulthood only to experience the sudden blow of marriage, motherhood, or the ugly realities of the workplace. For each of us there was a message to stop our own growth, and we did. If we're honest with ourselves, we know that there were subtle and overt messages all along. The thread goes all the way back to childhood.

The child who is within each of us controls the life force energy. Until she is reached, heard, and healed, the woman cannot flourish. She is too busy with survival. As I meet each of my clients, I am wondering: When did it happen to her? At how many ages will we have healing to do? Sometimes I think of my therapy as a giant rocking chair where I will rock her back and forth in time. Back in time to reclaim the child, forward to claim the wise old woman. Back and forth in time until she can discover the strength for the present tense. I wonder, how long will it take for this one?

Each of these women will need a lot of strength, for each one is attempting a task of truly mythic proportions—nothing less than a transformation, a creation of a personal reality where she has room to live and grow. She will be finding a child that she is deeply ashamed of and feels is worthless and unlovable, a child whose spirit has been trampled. And she will be required to discover that this wretched small person is, in fact, the divine child, the goddess within, her soul, the mystic child who solves riddles and teaches wisdom, the heroic child who liberates the world from monsters. It will be a giant leap, and it will be arduous.

Some of the work we do together will seem silly, some of it will seem awesome, and much of it will be painful. It will require every skill, technique, and intuition at my disposal to create enough safety for her to gradually challenge every belief she holds and to throw most of them out the window. The beliefs and lies that women hold about themselves are often deadly. For each one, I assume that healing will require core changes in her belief system. My operating paradigm is that we are seeking a rebirth or resurrection: "Out of the union of soul and spirit a child is conceived—the Jewel in the Lotus, the new consciousness dedicated to the possibility of Being. The child is the new energy that steps out of the past and turns its face to the future with hope, but lives in the now" (Woodman, 1985, p. 169).

The woman on this healing journey will also require an introduction to the crone to sustain her through the transit of menopause and old age. Her new reality must contain a more positive image of aging, a continuation of growth to the last breath. Older women in our culture are made powerless through our tendency to experience them as insignificant or invisible. The cult of youth will make this introduction even more difficult than reclaiming the child. She will need an empowerment that is unshakable for the terrors yet to come. "Once upon a time a wise old woman named Crone lived at the entrance to the forest. Her job was weaving, weaving the roots of the trees into the earth, the branches into night sky. She held the sun in its white orbit with the orange threads she spun from fire. Corn was woven from the silk of her hair and life itself was the thread of her vision which she spun, twined, tied, knotted and cut. . . . But the finest thread she spun, was the unravelling of her heart" (Metzger, 1978, p. 183). The child within is very wise. It knows that there is no point in making the effort that will be necessary unless the path is cleared. A path that ends by decree at fifty is no path at all.

Most of my clients are either incest survivors or women with cancer. A surprising number are victims of both. This means that the issues I work with daily are sexuality and death. It has often been as terrifying to me to listen as it was for my clients to speak. The code of silence and secrecy attached to these histories is immense. You might say that I was driven into the use of such transformation metaphors by the sheer weight of my own terror and shame at feeling so inadequate. Fortunately, it also led to humor. When one is faced with the unfaceable, when hurling into the abyss (mine or hers) is a daily possibility, one gets to learn that there is sometimes nothing left to do but to laugh at the absurdity of it all. Laughing with me, laughing at herself, and learning to laugh in the face of anyone who ever asks her to desecrate herself again are also part of this healing.

Last summer, I fell in love with a pink and black print in a local women's bookstore. The print, by Winnipeg artist Marni Kalef, said "GIVE ME LIBERTY OR GIVE ME VALIUM." This phrase rattled around in my head for weeks. It eventually dawned on me that I could use this phrase to describe the process of feminist therapy as a series of stages.

Stage One: Give Me Valium

Most clients arrive at my office in pain and anguish. They've heard how therapy helped a friend. Secretly, they hope that the first hour with me will take away the pain of a lifetime. It never does. Listening to her story will give a little relief and some new hope. The first few sessions will be like the early stages of a romance, full of warmth and discovery, excitement and rosy optimism.

The first phase of the work is safety. She will be breaking the rule of silence that she has carried since childhood, and she will be giving up secrets, both her own and those of her family. She holds extremely negative beliefs about herself, and they are well entrenched in her conscious mind. We will need many side doors to get around her logical traps and extensive taboos. After many years of sound defeat by massively maladaptive logic, I finally realized that imagination is the beginning. To begin her sense of safety and trust, I begin by assuming that she has no safety. If she has cancer, she lost whatever shreds of safety she had the day she received her diagnosis. If she is an incest victim, she has never known safety in the real world. If you can't hide under the covers in your own bed, nowhere is safe. So I ask her to create a safe place in her imagination.

I persist until she imagines a safe environment where no one can enter without her permission. It is to be constructed of any natural elements she finds comfortable. It includes a physical shelter, an outside, an impermeable perimeter, places to have fun, and places to rest. It has any sounds, smells, weather, textures, objects, tools, food, animals, or magical beings that she needs or wants. It will take her several tries until she gets this safe place completed, and even longer until she learns to use it regularly.

To solidify the image, I will then ask her to draw this place. On blank paper, she is simply to allow her hand to choose any crayon before her, trusting her hand to go to a color, and begin to draw the shapes and textures of her sanctuary. If she moves into this easily, I will hand her another page with a large circle inscribed on it. Then she is to choose the most significant images from the exploratory drawing and place them in the circle, adding anything that feels important. This is the foundation of her safety mandala, a concentrated image that she can use to focus on whenever she needs to interrupt a heavy emotional state or for simple relaxation. If the blank circle is too threatening, I give her a sheet with a classical Tibetan meditation mandala design on it (see Figure 1). I suggest that she trust her hands to color in the spaces until the design evokes the feeling of her safe place. I then ask her to redraw the mandala at home until she is fully satisfied with it. Then I ask her to put it in a place where she can see it frequently throughout the day with little effort.

Mandala in Sanskrit literally means "circle and center." Its traditional design uses the circle as the symbol of the cosmos in its entirety and the square as the symbol of the earth or human world. "In Tibet the centre, the abode of the deity is contained within the square—the palace of inner being—surrounded by a circle or series of circles, each symbolizing a particular phase of initiation or level of consciousness" (Arguelles, 1972, p. 13). In forming the sanctuary and the mandala, we have thus begun her ritual of carving out space for herself. These are early steps in her learning to place herself in the center of creation.

The mandala and return to safety will be powerful centering devices as she weathers the storms to come. I frequently will suggest that she use this one to help her learn to fall asleep more easily. If she has insomnia, I will suggest that she draw whatever her feelings are until she can let go of the day.

The second phase of her initiation into safety is the creation of a guardian spirit. (Most incest survivors already have one, and they are pleased to have permission to talk about the hidden friend.) If she already has one, we work in her imagination to get this figure more fully experienced and available. If we're creating one from scratch, we try for a female figure. It is all right for the guardian to be male or to be an animal, as long as it's a trusted figure. If she is less experienced at constructive imaging, we might begin with a guided fantasy to a sacred spot where she will encounter a wise woman. Or we can construct a fantasy of the ideal mother. For

Figure 1. Mandala.

women who are quite attached to the ordinary world, I might ask that they use an admired figure from their own life or from any time in history or a character for a novel or movie. If she reads as an escape, I might even send her to the library to research goddesses and to choose one that she would like to have on her side.

Once she has the guardian spirit, she is instructed to consult the guide any time she feels scared, confused, or lost. She is to bring the guide into her presence whenever she cannot reach me or a trusted friend. Then I ask her to draw the spirit guide in any way in which she can get her essence onto the paper. Shapes, colors, and textures will do for a start. She will refine it as she gets to know the guide. Now she has the second step of her initiation of safety. The guardian spirit symbolizes the forces gathered on the threshold of transition between stages of evolution or progress. She is the keeper of the treasure, the protector of her deepest self, and the kernel of the development of her crone.

The next phase of her initiation is a technique that I learned from Sandra Butler (1985), the construction of a secure container for her overwhelming feelings. In her mind's eye, she will take the pain, rage, violence, despair, loss, and betrayal, remember all of it, and build a container for it. She will make it as large and strong as it needs to be to hold the feelings completely. It is to be opaque so that no one can see inside. She will construct only one way in and out, which she can open only in the presence of the spirit guide. She is never to go in alone again. Then she is to place it anywhere in the universe, as close or far away as she wants. She is to know the location. Then she is to make the container beautiful. I remind her that she may revise it as many times as she needs. And she is to practice using it until she knows how to find and use it quickly. As before, I ask her to draw it until she is satisfied with the representation on paper. I make particular use of the Tibetan mandala walls as examples of sturdy construction and sacred gates. The construction of her container is the symbolic act that introduces her to the possibility of boundaries and control of her own feelings and eventually is a template for physical and psychic territory that belongs only to her.

Following this initiation, we move into drawings that are ways for her to project her experience for herself. One method that I find quite useful for diagnosis is to ask her to draw me what kind of tree she would be. This one is given as homework. When she brings the completed drawing, I ask her about the trunk, the branches, the leaves, the roots, the soil. These features tell me about her basic power and strength, her ability to reach for sustenance from the environment, her personal stability and reality contact, and her general state of health. Using the tree image, I can ask her safely what kind of tree she is, her best and worst part, what she needs the most to grow, whether she's more alive or dead, whether she has seeds, how she handles changes in the weather. The trunk in particular will give me some special clues. Scars and holes in the trunk often mark the age of significant traumas, with the base calibrating infancy and the top her current age (Wohl and Kaufman, 1985). Since I work with severe abuse cases, the drawing of multiple trunks or several trees will be one of my first signals to look for multiple personality.

There are volumes of books on interpreting this drawing procedure. I assume the tree to be a basic symbol of life and growth, and I add to this perspective Deena Metzger's transformative definition of healing love: "TREE: transformative and revolutionary love, created in one body and exerted toward another. Despite distance, proximity, danger, obstacles, ignorance, disease, or aggression, TREE can keep that body from harm . . . converted into beams of energy . . . sent and received . . . can sustain, nurture, protect, heal and cure. . . . Here we must be most sensitive to the civil liberties of the psyche, and even in matters of life and death, we must not impose upon another in the body, psyche or heart without an invitation. But once accepted we can begin" (Metzger, 1978, pp. 198, 203).

For beginning to isolate issues, I ask her to draw a circle for each difficult area in her life. She is to let herself draw as many as seem right to her. Then she is to go back and name the problem for each circle. It's okay to be vague or specific. Then she is to give each circle a color, texture, sound, feeling, shape. In deciding which one to work with first, she can use any criterion: easiest, least threatening, best understood, most pressing, most curious. After she chooses one, we can elaborate it and fill it out with questions, such as what is stuck, what feels frozen, what repeats, what moves, what the circle needs, what will change when it is resolved.

If she happens to have cancer, the preliminary drawings will include a picture of her cancer and a picture of her treatment. I ask her to imagine the cancer cells and how her treatment deals with them. She is free to construct these images in any metaphor she can understand. It does not have to be scientifically accurate. Then she is to draw what she experiences in the mental imagery. These pictures will document her beliefs about her illness at this time.

With these preliminary imaginings and drawings, I have a map of her strengths and problems. At this stage, the drawings are the most reliable reporter of her core experience. Fortunately, abusive families and cultures are never successful in prohibiting these unconscious devices. Combined with whatever she has been able to tell me verbally, the information from these steps gives me some idea of how severe is the damage, how many resources are available and active, and how extensive are the secrets. In completing this process with me, the part of her that wants to heal has found a way to let the process begin without an excessive amount of taboo breaking.

Stage Two: Give Me Liberty

As the Valium of the early sessions wears off, we get down to what needs to change in her life to decrease her discomfort. She will spend quite some time here vacillating between her strong drive to get perfect and a new drive that insists that her liberty depends on some change in her husband, lover, parent, child, boss, income, or job. She assumes that she must be set *free, that someone else needs to do the work. She even begins to get quite adamant about it (much to the chagrin of anyone close to her). She is shocked that I expect her to examine her own behavior and feelings. Her own inner life cannot possibly be what drives her. Her feelings are unacceptable; she couldn't possibly be powerful enough to do such hard work herself. Secretly she wishes that I would just wave my magic wand and heal her.*

The second phase of this work involves many trips into dangerous territory. She will be releasing as much information and feeling as she can, retreating from the edges of many terrors, and discovering the first throbs of her extensive anger and rage. We will be finding the places where she has no voice and is terrified of silence. Since this phase will be exhausting, she will need to learn to relax. The ins and outs of her explorations will require both psychic and physical time out. Most of my clients have a running inner dialogue that is harsh and demanding. As their activity level decreases, the negative voice gets louder and more insistent. They are most vulnerable as the day begins, between tasks, and late at night. Sitting still is unbearable, and genuine relaxation is either unknown or a dim and distant memory. Performing even the simplest relaxation exercise will bring on anxiety or panic. Silence is a terrifying absence of control. They often live in homes where the television is on constantly. To remove the background noise causes the sudden onset of the deep gulf between themselves and any safe contact. They attempt to avoid the horrible lack of intimacy and trust between them and their family.

For these women to learn relaxation, a lifeline with sound is necessary. We start with my asking her about music. What kinds of music does she listen to that can energize her when she does housework, what kinds soothe her, what types does she play if she's feeling blue, what types make her feel like dancing, what kinds can clear her mind? Then I ask her to find the music she already has at home and to play it for herself, in the background at first, while she does any task or activity. If she does not find music comforting, we begin this step with tapes of environmental sounds, such as ocean waves, streams, rain, or heartbeats. Providing herself with a safe auditory surround is essentially the beginning of her own lullaby, basic training in nurturing herself.

To accomplish this simple task, she will experience many ripple effects. Making time to do the assignment, using the stereo for herself, fending off questions and comments from her family or friends, and noticing her own responses to the sounds will cause many dilemmas. One of the more difficult parts of this task will arise as she is instructed to move herself into a private space in her home and listen through headphones. It may take weeks or months until she discovers how to keep the door closed, unplug the phone, and stop finding excuses for letting other people's needs take precedence over her healing. The exercise is a major lesson in the setting of boundaries. It also contains the seeds for learning to say no, learning to change her feeling state by herself, learning to let go, learning to ask for help more frequently, learning to pace herself, learning to make choices on her own behalf.

Using music to cushion her begins to soften the internal barriers that she had to create in order to survive. It can give her a subtle message that there is a road out of the silence, a detour around her noisy internal demons, a pathway to her own truth. This second stage is the telling of secrets, the breaking of silence, the discovering of her own story and her wounded inner child, and the finding of her inner walls. She will often attempt to get through this very quickly. Perhaps if she tells it quickly, it won't hurt so much, or perhaps she won't get caught in it. She does not understand that the barriers are protective; she wants to rip them away and be well. If cancer is silence, then she will tell all and be well by Saturday. She does not yet realize the extent of the maze of everyone's participation in keeping the family lies.

> Probably everyone has secrets, but when you stop and consider it closely, there are no such things as secrets, only people who keep them. . . . To find them out takes energy. . . . Often it is painful. . . . The only thing more painful than finding them out is not finding them out.
>
> Secrets means barriers, and bad-mouthing barriers really is a mistake. Barriers deserve a place of honour, respect and attention. You wouldn't have put them there without a reason—probably many reasons. The fact that barriers may cause pain is no reason to assume that the original placement was in error. No, the reasons were probably once valid. Many reasons, many secrets, many barriers.
>
> What is a barrier? It is that which protects a secret. But also it is that over which we trip and fall again and again. It is a limit to possibility, infinite possibility, our own possibility. Still, if it is there and if it has to be there, it should be cared for and watched

> . . . a gathering of strength . . . is necessary [Fisher, 1985, p. 23].

We will spend a long time here, rocking her into the past to retrieve her story and comforting her as she finds out that the telling will not be enough. Rocking her into the future, I will play her songs written by women who made this journey successfully, to sing to the child that she will not yet comfort on her own. Her present tense will contain many rough times. There will be nightmares, flashbacks, and sudden onsets of fear, rage, and grief. She will be scrambling to avoid the intensity of pain that is yet to come. If she has found part of her voice, she will be demanding changes from others with a forcefulness that they will concede to in shock or sympathy. There will be her own shock as she discovers that others cannot sustain the changes. She may make use of whimpering or whining to get sympathy and attention. And she will despair as she finds that it is not enough. If she uses her voice in this mode too often, she will get angry or depressed as she finds people avoiding her.

In her efforts to stay away from the distraught child inside, she will even try to convince me that she deserves to be this wretched. There is something intrinsically bad about her that is beyond loving. The energy she uses for avoidance is extremely powerful, and she will demonstrate the extent of her maladaptive logical schemes to justify her claim. She will try everything she knows to wriggle away from even accepting that she needed these strange beliefs to survive. As she sees that I will not agree with her claim that she is worthless and unlovable, she will try to test me. There will be late arrivals, missed appointments, bounced checks, and self-destructive behaviors. There will be a series of crises in her personal life that she wants advice about and that she makes more important than her own healing. She will go very far in her attempt to get me to express the strong feelings for her, to rescue her, to feed her fantasy of a magic cure.

As I stay with her through all of this, I will be repeating myself often. She will be furious with me for leading her back to comfort and safety. She believes that there is no safety for her. The music, drawings, container, and spirit guide are sure to be inadequate, her therapist is inadequate, and she is certain that *she* is inadequate to complete this task. She is terrified to learn her own truths and keeps insisting that she will be helpless forever. She is furious with me and the world, especially with me, for insisting that there is a way out of this mess. She hates hearing about loving herself. "Everything reminds me of silence, of telling secrets, of protest, of screams which have to be uttered. Sometimes the briefest conversation is seditious, anything which posits love is against the state" (Metzger, 1978, p. 214). She has found her inner child, and she is a holy terror, a sniveling waif, a screaming animal in a leghold trap, a disgusting slimy creature, a ghostly fog, a rotting corpse, clinging by a thread to life. Surely she can't be expected to love *that!*

Stage Three: Give Me Valium

As she becomes aware of the enormous size of her task, to grant herself a full-scale identity, she vacillates between rage and despair. She does not yet believe that she can find sustenance for a personal universe. One week she will act on her own behalf, and the next week she will sabotage herself with every bad habit and old guilt at her disposal. If she progresses in her emotional life, she will numb herself out with a physical setback. She cannot see that there is enough energy in her fury to get her through this dark place. All of her secrets are out in the open, and she flops into despair as she realizes that they will never stay put again. If we make it through this stage, she will complete the healing transformation. But she will be sorely tempted to stop here, to give up, to die. There is just a subtle shift in balance to make here. Maybe everything about her is useful. Maybe she can make it without a fairy godmother after all. Maybe. She is sure by now that I'm not the fairy godmother.

As she enters phase three, she submits to the prospect that there is nothing left to do but feel her feelings. In the first few attempts, she will be riding on the familiar old submission, giving in to a larger force. No one has ever gone into this territory with her before, but she must try it. She will make several tries alone, until she trusts me as a guide. She will grudgingly make me some drawings.

The drawings in this stage are the pictures of her abyss: canyons, tunnels, deep wells, basements, dungeons, pits, or graves. It may take several tries before she can even give it a shape. This place starts in formless blacks. She will be terrified of the familiar sucking force that pulls her to the edge of this place. The child is down there, alone and helpless. She will recoil in horror. This is it. The dark place she has been afraid of all her life. Death, abandonment, pain, betrayal, and grief. So many powerful feelings, such a little girl. "Resurrection is difficult. . . . Three days in hell between crucifixion and resurrection. Wasn't the crucifixion bad enough? No one discusses the three days in between. Do you think no one knows what it's like? Everyone knows. I know I am not going to talk about it. It is so awful, if we looked it square in the face, we would go blind. . . . Give me darkness, and silence, put out the lights" (Metzger, 1978, p. 189).

I will be cautioning her to use her spirit guide, to hold my hand, and still she will try this alone. The training we give women goes very deep. She will surface from the first attempt panting, breathless, sweating, wishing she could scream, wishing she could shake off the bone-chilling coldness, shaking her head to throw off the image, shaking. She closed her eyes so tight she couldn't find the guide. The throbbing in her ears was so loud that she couldn't hear me calling to her. She goes home exhausted and, if she could, she'd throw up.

Now she knows I mean it. We will be facing everything. She will have to change her beliefs about herself and about me. She will now see that she must have help to get through this place. She still doesn't trust me fully, but I sound like I know this place, her guide is urging her on, and she has nowhere left to hide. She is now sure what people mean when they say "leap of faith."

She finally consents of her own free will to explore one tiny portion of her abyss. She hangs onto my voice for safety, and we begin to find out what she needs to get to the child. She will bravely make many descents in this scary place. She will be somewhat dazed that she can come back out. She always thought she would be stuck there forever. "The woman leans back into the circle of arms which have kept her safe, feels the soft limbs against her back, allows herself to be rocked by all those arms. She is happy for a moment, she knows that no one has any more than this moment, none of us has any more than a while. Forty, eighty years is only a while. Whenever we die, it's today. Whenever we live, it's now. Anyway, at this moment, it is very clear that she is very much alive" (Metzger, 1978, p. 213).

To relieve some of the stress of this time, we may spend several sessions in light conversation. She is in a hurry, but she must rest often to complete this phase. She must learn that even the abyss takes time, even in the abyss there is room to laugh. One of our side trips will be another rock into the future. I will ask her to imagine that she is having tea with her ninety-year-old self. What is she like? How does she look? What has she done in her life that she is proud of? What does she regret? Ask her to tell you how you survived this time in your life. What richness or depth followed this period? What does she say to the younger you? What is there to look forward to?

I will encourage her to read the myth of the goddess Inanna's descent to the underworld (Perera, 1981). I will read her Ursula Le Guin's article on menopause, and we will cackle together over this part: "Women . . . by imitating the life-condition of men, surrendered a very strong position of their own. Men are afraid of virgins, but they have a cure for their own fear and the virgin's virginity: fucking. Men are afraid of Crones, so afraid of them that their cure for virginity fails them; they know it won't work. Faced with the fulfilled Crone, all but the bravest men wilt and retreat, crestfallen and cockadroop" (Le Guin, 1976, p. 109).

She begins to take some of her power. She makes some small changes. She beams as she reports them. She meditates regularly. She insists on having the most talented lab technician to do her blood work. She starts to exercise. She prepares healthy foods for herself. Then the undertow sets in. She gets sick, she has strange pains, she has a car accident, she pulls muscles in her legs and back. No problem, she thinks; these are all coincidences. She does not want to know that her body learned all the messages that her brain did. She makes a few more changes, small ones. She takes a day off. She teaches her children to do their own laundry. She learns to leave her briefcase in the car.

She gets sick again. There is no improvement in her latest bone scan. She stops walking and swimming. She is having headaches and insomnia. She begins to think of stopping therapy. She may even become suicidal. She is tired and longing for escape again. There will be more missed appointments. She is now extremely vulnerable to any fast-cure story.

She is at the point where she finally realizes that she will have to take herself seriously. She will have to do these self-caring processes forever. She must question every belief and suspect that they will all need revision. She has been feeling more powerful, but she does not trust herself to sustain this change for a lifetime. She is appalled that I challenge her to imagine what would happen if she stopped. She is shocked that I ask for a no-suicide contract. If she already has cancer and is considering moving toward death, she is amazed that I give her permission to give up, to stop everything and see what happens. She is right at the edge, and I am pushing her.

> Come to the edge.
> No, we will fall.
>
> Come to the edge.
> No we will fall.
>
> They came to the edge.
> He pushed them, and they flew.
>
> —*Guillaume Apollinaire*

Some of these women will fly right out of therapy at this point—some with my blessing if they ask for a break here. Pacing is important, I say. Some will fly into the arms of any guru they can find who promises faster results. I'll bless them, too, if they give me the chance. Maybe their intuition is finally working better than mine. A few of my cancer patients die at this place. Going to funerals was never in any psychology class I took. I bless them, too, and cry a lot. Easing people into death is not my favorite task, but that's where we go if they want to get off the path permanently. Rebirth in this lifetime is not on everyone's agenda.

Stage Four: I'm Taking My Liberty

One day she walks in and reports that she doesn't quite yet understand what happened, but she has quit the job, left the lover, filed for divorce, changed doctors, or hung up on her mother. And the world did not stop, and no one died. She is a little embarrassed that she feels so good. She has room to breathe, the pain in her head and chest is gone, and she is full of energy. She is finally ready to use all of her resources and to learn whatever else she needs. She feels that she has done something so right for herself that she can feel it right down to her bones. She trusts herself. She is new, and the world is full of opportunity. She can now experience me as a consultant. Our work is easier. She can predict the rough spots. She is occasionally scared that someone will sneak up on her and steal it all away. She is extremely inexperienced at feeling good this often.

Ah, now I can relax. We can use just about anything now to help her heal. This is the easy part. She is much more comfortable at noticing what works for her. We talk with the child to make sure that it is healed. She will giggle as the child tells her directly what is left to do. We consult with her spirit guide and crone to find out where she needs to grow. When she blushes, I know that we are ready to work with her sexuality and reclaiming her body for her own pleasure. "The wound is there and part of our experience. So we have to learn to accept and live with it, and yet relate to new healing possibilities. This requires an active effort, a willingness to go into our depths and to listen and speak out of our feminine experience" (Leonard, 1983, p. 169).

She can now use all of her past, her present, and what she can imagine in her future to complete herself. Our sessions are now lessons in what she can handle on her own, what she will use her friends for, and what part of her she can open to new help. The child has grown to occupy her larger adult body, and she does not fall down the rabbit hole anymore. She still wavers a bit under stress. But now she can read her own danger symptoms earlier. She has her own wise woman to consult. This phase is to increase her flexibility, review any weak areas, and solidify her integration. "It is not enough to bring about a little change for a while, it must be a stable experience" (Tsong-kha-pa, as quoted in Arguelles and Arguelles, 1972, p. 126).

At this point, I will ask her to create a ritual for herself to mark her transition into health and wholeness. If my video colleagues are offering workshops, I will urge her to put this ritual on film for herself. Or we can do it in my office, or in any setting of her choice. There must be at least one witness, and she may invite others. "Ritual is rooted in the intuitional realm of vision—our deeper nature. The essence of ritual is an impulse that originates deep within us. The ritual is used to investigate and open the centre, and to grant identification with the cosmic forces and their source" (Arguelles and Arguelles, 1972, p. 83). If she has strong spiritual ties, she will find herself using something about her religion in a way in which she has never used it before. This time it will feel empowering. If she is like most women, keenly distanced from organized religions, we will simply make it up, trusting herself to include anything that she needs, allowing her own inner voice to guide her.

Stage Five: Liberty and Strength

Now it's her turn to surprise me. She may make large moves: world travel, advanced study at a university, complete change of friends, a new job suited to her skills with a large salary increase. She is vibrantly alive and healthy. It's time to say good-bye.

She will often take a long break between stages four and five. Most of the time, I will learn of her big leaps with a letter, a phone call, or an invitation to lunch. She finally seeks me out as her equal to celebrate her joy. I take great pleasure in these return connections. It gives me a chance to initiate her into the feminist pact: When you get the chance and have some extra strength, reach back and pull out one more woman or child. You don't have to be dramatic. Telling just one that there is help for her is enough. Just point her toward help.

My approach includes what I love about the feminine assumptions about life. Everything is connected. There is no power in isolation. To tug on any part of the complex web of life will affect it all. To categorize, separate, and exclude is to invite destruction. When one of my clients heals, she knows down to her cells that she is the web, glistening in the morning light. And she is the spider woman, free to move on, free to spin as many webs as she needs for a lifetime.

Client's Voice: "Eve"

I have come to think of my work with Jan as a spiral. There are times when I return to the thoughts and feelings I experienced when I first began with Jan, and there are times when the spiral spins me forward and I see the light at the end of this very long tunnel. After three years, the times spent "back at the beginning" are fewer and farther between—more a reminder of how far I have come and how I continue to creatively heal in my work with Jan. The times at the other end of the spectrum are exciting and invigorating—times where I am my most creative and truly in love with the whole of this wondrous world.

How do I begin to describe Jan's and my work together? I have decided to include some of the song writing that I did during my work with Jan from November 1984 until 1988. The messages in each piece are an accurate description of our process together and certainly a window into what I call my soul. It is in this deep place, which is sometimes dark and scary, that I have learned to find my music—and therefore the light.

I wrote "Daddy's Little Girl" before I started to see Jan in November 1984. I wrote in my journal: "I have been thinking about 'Daddy's Little Girl' . . . a powerful song about a little girl's incest experience. The incest survivors who have heard it cannot believe that a person with no incest background could have written it. I never play that song, because I wrote it in a style suited to a bolder performer. It's ironic in that everyone thought I was daddy's little girl because I took such good care of him. . . ."

Daddy's Little Girl

Chorus: Everybody runs to the door when daddy gets home
How come you're the only one who doesn't go
Why are you so quiet in the evening
Aren't you daddy's little girl?

Verse: For twenty-two years this darkness has been with me
Never understood the locks around my heart
Came to me in dreams of utter terror
Dreams where the trust of a child was torn apart.

Verse: Why did he ever have to use me
Never get back the price I had to pay
Cost too much in years of lost childhood
Years where the trust of a child was torn away.

The secrets about my incest experience were buried deeply indeed. It took four months before I felt safe enough with Jan to begin to even hint at what really happened in my house. I wrote "What Would It Be Like To Fall" at some point during those four months. The song gives some idea of my fear of losing control of all the feelings I had kept secret for so long.

What Would It Be Like to Fall

I walk a high wire
Fifty feet below me
I can see the water running

I walk a tight rope
Each step in balance
With each foot forward I wonder

Chorus: What would it be like to fall
What would it be like to tumble
What would it be like to lose control
What would it be like to fall

It's a fine line
Marks my limits
All the rules that I live by

Such a fine line
I live within it
And I question its control

(Chorus)

(Instrumental)

I continue
Walk a straight line
Don't look left or right

Only time I
Let the walls down
Is late alone at night

(Chorus)

We began a long series of sessions on safety, safety, and more safety. Being able to create my own safety is one of the most empowering skills I developed in my work with Jan. We used mantras, healing stories where I created my own spirit guide, visualization, and a number of relaxation techniques. I still use a number of these techniques for myself regularly. They continue to work for me in my own work as a massage therapist. They help with stage fright when I perform, and they have allowed me to explore other forms of therapy work in a way that I can always access my safe place.

As my feelings of safety increased, my dreams became more and more vivid. After a particularly scary and pornographic one, Jan offered me a book called *I Never Told Anyone* (Bass and Thornton, 1983), with a gentle suggestion that I might want to look at it. I remember being overwhelmed with a feeling that I had some choices here. To this day, I still am constantly amazed at how wonderful it is to make choices. I also am aware of how secure I felt that I was the one setting the pace in our work. I chose to read the book and for the first time saw parts of my own experience for what they were.

I wrote "Where Do You Draw the Line" shortly afterward.

Where Do You Draw the Line

Where do you draw the line
When do balanced steps
Fall into crazy
You can learn to walk the wire
It's the balance of survival
Of a child

Chorus: If I ran a million miles
What would you have thought
Without water made you an island
Would it have made any difference (No)
Would it have made any difference (Oh No)

And where do you draw the line
When does gentle touch
Turn into error
You can learn to hide your fears
Pretend it doesn't matter
Sleep like a child

(Chorus)

And where do you draw the line
When does anger
Turn into fury
Comes with the passing of time
I can learn to share the secrets
Of a child

(Chorus)

Where do you draw the line
When do balanced steps
Fall into crazy
You can learn to walk the wire

It's the balance of survival
Of a child

Where do you draw the line

The song describes my confusion about what types of behavior were appropriate and inappropriate for my father. The chorus, in its original form, did not have the word *no* in it and was therefore a sort of helpless questioning of a child, thinking she should have been able to make some sort of difference or change the fact that her father was sexually abusing her.

When I showed Jan the song, her first response was that there was something missing in that chorus. When she asked me what could be added, I remember I whispered the word *no*.

Pushing farther, she asked, "No what?"

I said for the first time, "No, I could not have made any difference. What happened was not my fault."

I changed the song—and for me it speaks of the incredible power of the word *no*. With this change, Jan gave me the gift of anger, and our work became an exploration of this healing emotion.

With the rage came my voice, and I began to perform my own material. I also did a ritual at that time that acknowledged my own voice and marked the recognition of my deep dark secret. I wrote "Speak Your Mind" as part of the ritual. It was wonderful for me to have Jan see that ritual because so much of the song talks about her skills as a healer and the healing that all women can offer each other. I was also very much influenced by the work of Sandra Butler. She dances in these lines as well.

Speak Your Mind

Speak your mind,
For the secrets you carry,
Might not kill you,
But they'll wound you for life.
Silence becomes habit, habit vices,
Before you know it, you carry lies.

Chorus: Speak your mind, know your heart.
Speak your mind, know your heart.
Speak your mind, know your heart.

Speak your mind,
There is so much inside you,
It's a shame you hide it,
You think they won't hear.
Spread your wings, it's time you tried flying.
Your own truth is dying, inside of your head.

(Chorus)

Speak your mind,
I am right here beside you,
There are many things as women we share.
Take my hand cause I've been through the forest,
Use my light to guide you,
I'll help you through there.

(Chorus)

I have begun to see Jan again after a long break. The spiral continues. Our sessions have changed, much like my music has changed. I am much more able to speak and give voice to my feelings, and there is more humor and light.

I feel very much that, as a result of my work with Jan, I have been able to make significant changes in my life. I have learned a great deal about my own value, and it is no longer so necessary to seek world success to make me okay. I have been able to risk leaving a full-time teaching job and only work part-time. In the other part of my life, I am developing my own massage therapy business and working on my music. When I read in my journal about "Daddy's Little Girl," I celebrate that I now seem to be performing at least once a month—the empowerment of voice.

I now use my music to express that part of myself that was so badly wounded. My songs offer hope—because for me, music is hope. I have heard from a number of women across Canada and in the United States that my music has touched them in a very personal way. The songs have often been a gateway for many women to begin their own healing. Somehow that makes the work all the more worth it.

I feel as if my work with Jan is at a critical place. It marks a time where I am becoming ready to give up the whole of my secret. The work is not easy, and I struggle with wanting to stop. Even though it is very difficult, Jan and I have been in difficult places before, and where there is absolute blackness there must be light. I am using my spirit guide, I am trusting my dreams, and I am taking long walks to "remind myself of the beauty of the world." Jan says that to me a lot. My writing reflects this place.

Took Her by Storm

And he took her by storm
Sometimes it's hard to read the weather,
It changes so quickly.
And he took her by storm,
Sometimes it's hard to know your father,
There's so much pain.

Chorus: And somewhere there's light here,
And somewhere there is light,
And somewhere there's light here.

And he took her by storm,
Sometimes it's hard,
To take the nightmare from the dream.
And he took her by storm,
Sometimes it's hard to say what is real,
I know.

Chorus: And somewhere there's light here,
And somewhere there is light,
And somewhere there's light here.

And he took me by storm,
Sometimes it's hard to read the weather,
It changes so quickly.
And he took me by storm,
Sometimes it's hard to know my father,
There's so much pain.

Chorus: And somewhere there's light here,
And somewhere there is light,
And somewhere there's light here.

Postscript: It has been five months since I gave Jan my initial writing. Since that time, a number of events have taken place regarding my experience with my father. We have gone through another painful confrontation—lots of anger, frustration, and tears. My family has struggled through with both hope and courage. As a result, my father wrote the postscript that I include here. I am deeply moved by his process and feel seen, heard, and believed. It means a great deal to me to have him claim responsibility for his actions.

> In January of 1988 at the age of seventy-three years I learned that I had sexually abused my daughter on four occasions nearly twenty years before when she was thirteen years old. This means to me that in the ensuing years she had that memory and lived with the possibility that I would do it again. In spite of this, she supported me in many, many ways.
>
> I was horrified. I covered my face and eyes and ears with my hands, and bent over and cried out in disgust and shame. I could not remember abusing her but I knew that for a period of years I drank very much too much and that that might account for my not remembering—or I might have "repressed" the memory. I had no doubt that she was telling me the truth.
>
> I was physically stiff with horror at what I had done and I asked for help from a friend who was a therapist. I felt that I was going crazy and I felt very

frightened of going crazy. I did not want to hunt for ways to excuse myself, such as "Well, I was under a lot of stress in my life" or "Well, I didn't know what I was doing because of the drinking" or "Well, she has developed wonderful new talents by working through her problem with me." I wanted to find some way to live with the knowledge that I had done this.

A few weeks after she told me what had happened, my daughter gave me her account of her work with Jan as it is published here. When I began to read it, I found I could not go on for more than a page by myself—my body froze into stiffness with horror. What she had written I took with me to my therapist and read it aloud in her presence, where I could cry and shiver and sometimes cover my face and where I knew help was nearby. So I came to understand a little of what she had been through. And I came to appreciate how much my daughter loved me—perhaps too much.

As I neared the end of my work with my therapist, I began to feel I could tolerate knowing what I had done and nevertheless go on living and growing and working. I could not leave that knowledge behind—erase it—put it into some hidden compartment never to be noticed. I could even perhaps use this knowledge to understand and write about what goes on between persons in this human world, even to help me in my chosen work of psychotherapy. Understand a little, but never understand completely. Explain a little but *not* explain away.

Also towards the end of my work with my therapist, my daughter talked with me about publishing what she had written about her work with Jan. She was not at all sure that she wanted to do so. I found that my mind went quickly to thinking about the reaction of my family, my friends, my professional colleagues, imagining their anger and disgust with me as well as their pain at their association with me. I talked

> with my therapist about this. She said to me "When you first came to me, you were very much concerned to be sure to take on your own shoulders the responsibility for sexually abusing her. What do you *mean* by this 'taking the responsibility on your own shoulders'?"
>
> I put answering this question together with answering two questions that my daughter asked me: "Do you think it is a good thing for me to publish what I have written in the book where Jan describes her therapy?" and "If I publish it, would you like to write a postscript?"
>
> So—I found that one very important meaning for "being sure to take responsibility for my actions" is *not* keeping this information secret. I do not mean that I shall try to advertise it to everyone. I do mean that my answer to both of my daughter's questions is "yes." And as I write this postscript I am sad and ashamed about the very great distress I have caused not only my daughter but others among my family and my friends.

I am also filled with deep sadness that this has occurred in my life with him. I hope that those who read this publication use the information in a healing way. My father and I chose to share this story for that purpose.

I feel able to give Jan this work now with a very deep sense of compassion and love—for myself, my father, and all those who have shared this healing journey with me. As I have reread it I see I have moved from feeling mostly anger and confusion to feeling a very much deepened and opened heart. Surely this is what healing means. The tears I cry now are ones of relief as I feel complete and able to move on in my life. I wish the same for my father and all others who are encouraged to pursue their own healing as they read this work.

References

Arguelles, J., and Arguelles, M. *Mandala.* Boston: Shambhala, 1972.
Bass, E., and Thornton, L. (eds.). *I Never Told Anyone: Writings by*

Women Survivors of Child Sexual Abuse. New York: Harper & Row, 1983.

Butler, S. "Counselling Issues and Techniques for Working with Abuse Survivors." Workshop held at Counselling the Sexual Abuse Survivor Conference, Winnipeg, Man., Feb. 1985.

Fisher, A. "Connection." *The Sun,* Jan. 1985 (110), pp. 20–27.

Le Guin, U. K. "The Space Crone." *Medical Self-Care: The Co-Evolution Quarterly,* Summer 1976 (10), pp. 108–111.

Leonard, L. *The Wounded Woman: Healing the Father-Daughter Relationship.* Boston: Shambhala, 1983.

Metzger, D. *The Woman Who Slept with Men to Take the War Out of Them & Tree.* Berkeley, Calif.: Wingbow Press, 1978.

Perera, S. B. *Descent to the Goddess: A Way of Initiation for Women.* Toronto: Inner City Books, 1981.

Siegal, B. S. *Love, Medicine and Miracles.* New York: Harper & Row, 1986.

Wohl, A., and Kaufman, B. *Silent Screams and Hidden Cries: An Interpretation of Artwork by Children from Violent Homes.* New York: Brunner/Mazel, 1985.

Woodman, M. *The Pregnant Virgin: A Process of Psychological Transformation.* Toronto: Inner City Books, 1985.

13

Ending the Cycle of Violence: Overcoming Guilt in Incest Survivors

Diane Lépine
Client: "Rebecca"

The issue of guilt comes up with nearly every incest survivor I see in therapy. A client's attempts to cope with the devastating impact of the incest often lead to depression and may involve self-destructive behaviors such as suicide attempts, slashing (self-mutilation), compulsive eating, drug abuse, and alcoholism. Guilt around the incest has a pivotal relationship to these problems, which frequently abate after the issue of the survivor's guilt feelings has been processed in therapy. If the client's guilt is not addressed, however, her deep healing will likely be impeded. For a survivor to progress in her journey toward wholeness and well-being, then, her experiences and feelings around guilt must be accepted by the therapist, her understanding of her experience of guilt must have emerged and been acknowledged, and effective work on the behavioral consequences of guilt must have begun.

Note: I wish to thank my friend Ken Dickson for his support and editing skill in the preparation of this chapter.

The therapist, of course, must understand the dynamics of incest, specifically as they relate to guilt, if her treatment plan is to be effective. There are reasons apart from the obvious for emphasizing the need for this kind of understanding. Like Ariadne's thread, it can guide the therapist through the labyrinth of subtleties described below that occasionally arise in the therapy of incest survivors.

Incest Survivors Who Abuse Others

In my clinical practice, I have found some clients who, despite having worked through guilt around the occurrence of incest, still seem unable to heal. That is, even after having explored such issues as perceived responsibility for the sexual abuse, "manipulatory" behavior within the incestuous relationship, and perhaps even experiences of sexual pleasure during the abuse, some clients find themselves still unable to let go of their crippling guilt. For a *few* of these clients, deeper probing has uncovered additional guilt around their having perpetrated sexual abuse against others subsequent to their own abuse.

While women sometimes act out or offend sexually as children or adolescents, they usually stop (Butler, 1986). This is the case with the women I have seen in my practice. Perhaps it is due to their socialization, which has taught them to emphathize with and nurture others, that women do not usually continue offending as adults. Research by Russell (1986) indicates that the percentage of adult female offenders who persist is small and that they are probably responsible for less serious and traumatic levels of sexual abuse than are male offenders. What is also clear from my experience with this small subgroup of incest survivors is that the frequency of their offending is low. This contrasts sharply with the repeated and ongoing offending of many male perpetrators. However, even though the number of female perpetrators may be small and their offenses less serious and traumatic, it is important to note that some female incest survivors do offend sexually. For the therapist to ignore this fact is to risk impeding a client's deep healing.

There is a potential danger for feminist therapists working with survivors who have also offended sexually. In pursuing their values of advocating on behalf of women, therapists may be inclined to minimize, justify, explain away, or even refuse to consider their clients' offending behaviors. It may be uncomfortable for them to acknowledge an experience that disconfirms an important element of their belief system, that men are the offenders and women the victims. In any case, it is important to note that the guilt around sexual offending is appropriate and should not be dismissed lightly by the therapist in her efforts to advocate for the client. This guilt involves a different therapeutic issue than that experienced by survivors who blame themselves for having been offended against. It is inappropriate (even though well intended) for the therapist to take away the client's guilt around offending. Unless this guilt is recognized and accepted, even if it involves only one incident, a client may find herself unable to progress any further in her healing. However, while the client's guilt around offending should not be minimized, it is also important for the therapist not to join with, support, or exacerbate a disproportionate and disabling sense of guilt. In order to navigate between this Scylla and Charybdis, caring attention must be balanced with clear perspective.

A feminist perspective offers a comprehensive analysis of the phenomenon of incest within the context of patriarchy. The imbalance of power between women and men in a patriarchal society is one of the factors that can contribute to the occurrence of incest (Herman, 1981). In my experience, a therapeutic model based on a feminist consciousness of women's powerlessness has proved useful in working with women who have experienced incest. When survivors can recognize their powerlessness relative to the offender, they can begin to stop blaming themselves for the occurrence of incest. The therapeutic effect is movement from self-blame to the place where true healing can begin.

The Therapist's Role

Clearly, the therapist must understand the phenomenon of incest if she is to be effective in helping clients to work through their incest experience. Less obvious, and perhaps more important, the therapist must be aware of her attitudes, values, and beliefs with respect to sexuality and sexual abuse, as well as to victimization and offending behavior. This is in addition to the issue of feminist values discussed above. Unless she has dealt with her own assumptions about and emotional reactions to incest, she may be unable to effectively assist clients in working through their issues. Hyde (1987) makes the important observation that unacknowledged survivors often become mental health professionals "who have not done their own healing work with a professional" (p. 3). Therapists who have not resolved their own issues may seriously hamper their clients' progress because of their inability to come to terms with their own victimization. This, of course, could include victimization other than by incest. And if, as Dann (1987) suggests, there is a continuum from victim to offender rather than these being two separate categories, therapists' difficulties in dealing with their clients' offending may be even more problematic.

Part of a successful intervention with incest survivors lies in the qualities of the therapist making the intervention. When the client perceives the therapist as trustworthy, the issue of offending will more readily be broached. In my work with survivors, I do not encourage them to trust me, explaining that they have already been betrayed by the very people they should have been able to trust. Rather, I tell them that I will strive to be trustworthy and that part of what this means is that I will never sexualize my relationship with them. This is very important, for two reasons. The first reason is that because of survivors' experiences with incest, the distinction between caring and sexuality gets blurred. Therefore, they can easily misconstrue caring on the part of the therapist as something sexual. Second, some clients *have* experienced instances where therapists or counselors have sexualized the therapeutic relationship. Further, I tell them that I may sometimes say something that will be hurtful or feel unsafe for them and that I will not know this unless they tell me. This is important because clients often feel doubly betrayed if they have begun to trust me and I say or do something that is scary for them.

If the therapist can introduce the topic of offending matter of factly, this often facilitates the client's opening up. For instance, when I suspect the possibility of offending, I may say to a client, "You know, when women have been sexually abused as children, they sometimes act out sexually against others, too." Bringing up the topic in this fashion serves two purposes. First, it lets the client know that she is not the only one to have done this. Second, it tells her that I can deal with the topic. Survivors are typically extremely sensitive to others' feelings and will sometimes strive to protect the therapist. If a client senses that the therapist is uncomfortable with this issue, the client may refrain from bringing it up. Deep healing of the incest trauma cannot occur if this block to self-experiencing guilt over perpetrating sexual abuse remains intact. In this way, therapists who have not come to terms with their own discomfort around sexual abuse or female offending can react in ways that impede the clients' therapeutic progress. This has been the case for many clients that I have seen either who have not broached the subject at all with former therapists or whose concerns have not been addressed by the therapists once they have been disclosed.

Should a client discuss having offended against someone, the therapist's calm acceptance is crucial. It is important for the client to understand that while the offending behavior is unacceptable, the therapist will support her in whatever needs to be done, and without judgment. Clients often expect to be judged as harshly as they judge themselves. Indeed, they have sometimes experienced others' disapprobation as well. If the therapist were not to respond calmly, then the client's worst fears would be confirmed. The possibility of having to report the offense must be discussed sometime at this point.

Therapeutic Interventions

An important part of the work I do with survivors is educational, especially in the areas of feelings and sexuality. Because of their abuse, survivors are often out of touch with their feelings. To illustrate, clients will often tell me either that they don't have feelings or that they can't differentiate between the various ones. It is when survivors repress feelings that the possibility of offending occurs. This has been borne out in my experience with women who have offended; that is, they have been disconnected from their feelings, especially their pain and anger. Once survivors are aware of their feelings and of the options they have in expressing them, they are more able to empathize with others and to meet their own needs appropriately. Consequently, the likelihood of offending usually dissipates.

When clients cannot acknowledge feelings because they don't know when they are having them, it is important to teach them to connect feelings with sensations in their bodies. Whenever I begin work with a client, either individually or in a group, I will say something like, "When I'm meeting someone for the first time, I sometimes feel a little anxious. I can tell because of the butterflies in my stomach. My friend gets tense in her neck and shoulders. How are you feeling about being here? What in your body lets you know that?" A lot of the work I do subsequently with a client is intended to reconnect her feelings with her body. Regarding feelings, the two major points that I stress with clients are (1) the importance of feeling feelings; that is, owning (sensing and feeling) rather than repressing them; and (2) the difference between feeling feelings (once they know how to do that) and expressing or acting on them.

Sexuality is the second major focus of my educational interventions. It is an area of difficulty for survivors and often even more so for those women who have offended. It is crucial for the therapist to realize that even though women may have had many sexual encounters, their knowledge of sexuality may be very limited. For example, one young woman I worked with believed that she masturbated only because she had been offended against and that "normal" girls and women wouldn't do that. When women have offended against others, they often feel disgust at their sexual feelings. It is important for them to increase their knowledge about sexuality and to correct the false notions that they have developed as a result of their experiences. There are some very good books on women's sexuality that can be recommended to clients and that often prove very reassuring to them. The ones I use most often are by Barback (1976), Kitzinger (1983), Loulan (1984), and Maltz and Holman (1987).

One of the things that clients have found useful in dealing with sexuality is a discussion about the issue of owning one's sexuality, much as one owns feelings. Although it seems to be a difficult concept at first, women are very relieved when they realize that their sexual feelings belong to them. Once they have identified and accepted their sexual feelings, they can decide how they will express these feelings, if at all. To illustrate, I worked with a woman who offended against her children when they were babies. As she discussed her sexual feelings, it became evident to me that she didn't differentiate between feeling sexual and acting on those feelings. After we had worked on the difference between feeling sexual and expressing those sexual feelings, we explored various alternatives: just enjoying the feeling and letting it go, pleasuring herself, asking her partner to be sexual, meditating on it, or working out vigorously. It is important to check out the appropriateness of the various coping strategies with the client. In this instance, my client explained that masturbation is considered sinful in her system of religious beliefs and so it is not a viable option for her at this time.

Women who have offended against children in the past are often afraid of repeating the offense. For them to learn to reown their sexuality—in other words, to discover that they are responsible for it—is to free them from some of their fears. At this point, I wish to make clear that if there are any concerns that a female client may be a fixated offender (Groth, 1982), rare though this may be, this issue must be addressed, and the above interventions would be inadequate to deal with such a client's sexual problems.

Another therapeutic strategy that has proved useful in working with clients' guilt is that of chair work, a technique used by Gestalt therapists. Clients are asked to speak to their victims, whom they imagine to be sitting in an empty chair. They may tell them that they are aware of their offense and the suffering they have caused. Often, they wish to apologize and ask for forgiveness. As well, they may tell their victims what has happened to them and recommend that the victims also seek counseling. If this comes up, then whether to approach their victims directly is discussed.

During chair work, I often ask clients to speak from their child self to their adult self, to help put the experience into perspective. Survivors often relate to their experiences as if they have always been adults; that is, they impute adult understanding to and take adult responsibility for events that happened when they were children. Clients' guilt for their behavior often has such a stranglehold on them that the possibility of healing becomes greatly impeded. For them to speak from their child self can create some space for change to take place. This is not intended to take away clients' responsibility for their actions, as it is crucial for them to know that their offending behaviors were inappropriate.

Another possibility for chair work is to have clients speak directly to their guilt and have their guilt address them back. When the client is "being" her guilt, I will often address the guilt and ask it what it is trying to do for the client. I usually take the stance that the guilt is trying to do something useful but suggest that the method employed may have to change, as it is too painful for the client and so may be ineffective. I then get the client and her guilt to negotiate as to how they will work together in future. This can be a very powerful experience for clients. Although clients are often reluctant to do chair work, they almost invariably feel that the work has been useful once they have attempted it.

Hypnotherapy can also be used effectively in working with clients' guilt, in a number of ways. Hypnosis can be useful in helping to bring unconscious guilt into conscious memory. For example, sometimes a client tells me that she wishes to die but is unaware of why she feels that way. Using hypnosis, we can find the guilty feeling that is the basis for the wish to die. Hypnotherapy can also help to uncover the reasons for guilt and, once these reasons come to the fore, to resolve the guilt. For example, a client can be regressed to the episodes related to her guilt, and some work can be done with the feelings that emerge. Another way I use hypnosis in my work with incest survivors is to have clients access and develop the resources they will need in order to deal with their guilt on their own, between sessions. This can be done by creating a safe place, a container to hold difficult feelings and memories, and a guide. The purpose of the safe place is explained by my client Rebecca, whose story accompanies this chapter. She discusses the importance of a safe place "where we could explore our frightening feelings, and face our dark memories, in a place where there was no judgment, no right or wrong." The purpose of the container is to store difficult feelings and memories so that the client has some respite and doesn't become overwhelmed. The guide becomes an internal resource that the client can readily access for support. Finally, it is often useful to end a hypnotherapy session by having the client go in her mind to a future life space where she has resolved her guilt and done some healing. This future orientation provides survivors with a different perspective from the one that they have lived with for so long and creates some hope that things can change. Hypnotherapy lends endless possibilities for counselors who have been trained in its use.

I have found that various writing techniques are useful in helping clients to resolve their guilt. As with hypnotherapy, writing often helps survivors to clarify potential sources of guilt and to resolve it. In my experience, both self-therapeutic writing techniques and therapist-directed writing can be useful. When I lead groups for survivors, I assign a lot of writing, which can be shared or not, as the participants wish. One group writing exercise prompted a woman to disclose her offending. I had asked group members to complete these sentences in their journals: "I can't forgive. . . ." and "I can't forgive myself. . . ." The purpose of this exercise was to have women become aware of some of the issues that might prevent them from healing.

Another writing technique that I often encourage survivors to engage in is keeping a journal (Butler, 1986). These journals may range from a formal process (Progoff, 1975) to an eclectic use of creative methods, including lists, dream work, and visualizations, among other techniques (Rainer, 1978). Clients may write letters to the people they have offended against or dialogues that help them make sense of their experiences and come to some resolution. Although this work is conceptually similar to chair work, it is much less threatening for some clients. It also has the advantage of always being available as a resource. For example, one of my clients gets up and writes in the middle of the night. As with chair work and hypnosis, journal writing is a tool rich in possibilities, and one that the client almost always has at hand. It is very important, however, for clients to feel safe and assured of their privacy if they are to keep a journal that truly reflects their innermost thoughts and feelings. Sometimes, clients have left their journals with me between group sessions because they haven't felt safe taking them home. This is often the case if women are involved in abusive relationships.

Guilt and the Healing Process

In the process of helping a client to deal with guilt, the larger goals of growth, change, and empowerment are also addressed.

Growth is facilitated when a client can deal with her feelings (as opposed to repressing them and acting out inappropriately) and take responsibility for her actions (rather than feeling overwhelmed by circumstances or by others). For example, one of my clients worked on her feelings of guilt, shame, and sorrow with me and accepted the fact that the little girl she had abused could one day confront her. I consider it a sign of growth when my clients can take responsibility for their actions and at the same time stop the self-destructive behaviors that they use in an attempt to mitigate their guilt.

Part of working with guilt involves changing patterns of perception as well as patterns of behavior. For instance, when a client becomes aware of the fact that her sexual feelings belong to her, this allows her to change her sexual behavior. One of my clients reported the feeling of elation she experienced when she chose not to be sexual with a friend, even though she was feeling sexual. She had finally grasped what I meant when I told her that there was a difference between feeling sexual and being sexual. When clients are able to own their feelings and choose whether to express them and in what ways, they have begun to change significantly. Thus, the process of empowerment begins. Empowerment speaks to power over oneself, where one has the freedom to say no and the right to an informed yes.

Conclusion

My experience with incest survivors who have also offended sexually leads me to believe in the importance of resolving their guilt around their abusing behaviors in order to facilitate change, growth, and empowerment. Once these clients have begun to loosen the imprisoning shackles of their guilt, they typically demonstrate freed-up energy that had been diverted into their guilt. With their hard-won freedom, they often tackle such new challenges as upgrading skills, going back to school, and confronting their own offenders and other family members, as well as making such requests of their partners as asking for nurturing. As therapy progresses and the stranglehold of guilt weakens, they gradually allow themselves to give up some of their old coping strategies, such as slashing themselves, attempting suicide, drinking, taking drugs, and eating compulsively.

In the section that follows, my client Rebecca shares the meaning that she has ascribed to her experience of incest and healing.

Client's Voice: Rebecca

I decided three years ago to take a college program that would enable me to work in the "helping" field. Little did I know what kinds of issues would surface. We spent a lot of time on our individual histories, where we had come from and what molded each of us. When we moved into the area of child abuse, I realized there were past issues I needed to deal with. I had a lot of pent-up anger over being verbally and physically abused as a child. I found counseling somewhat helpful in dealing with old memories, but something still nagged at me.

That summer I worked in an agency dealing with families in crisis. One quiet Saturday morning, I began to read a manual that outlined the indicators in mothers, fathers, and children that incest was happening in a family. I felt like someone had just hit me in the chest with a wrecking ball. I had no concrete memories, no way of proving it, but I felt an incredible, horrible realization that my father had molested me when I was a child.

I tried to deny it. I tried to convince myself that I was "making it all up," to excuse all the mistakes I'd made in my life. I told myself I was working with sexually abused children almost every day and was probably "identifying" too much. But I couldn't seem to shake the feeling. I began to have dreams. I began to make connections.

It was another eight months before I could say out loud, "I think my father molested me, but I'm not sure." How crazy that sounded, how ridiculous. Either he did, or he didn't. How can you not be sure about something like that?

It was when I saw a film in one of my classes, where a woman said that she was thirty years old before she remembered that her father had sexually abused her when she was a child, that I went to a telephone and called the Sexual Assault Centre. I talked to an intake worker who assured me that my feelings were normal. She told me that a lot of women deny it happened, think they're crazy, or don't remember actual acts of abuse, so they don't believe their feelings.

Still I denied. I carried on for the rest of the school year, but I found myself bursting into tears in public, becoming increasingly angry, drinking to "numb out," and loathing anything to do with sex.

My marriage was floundering; my children were confused and angry because their mother was depressed one minute and hostile the next. I began to plan my death when memories began to surface—they were never clear enough to actually prove what my father had done but the feelings of disgust and shame were there.

When I noticed my work suffering, I finally went for help. I began individual counseling at the Sexual Assault Centre. My therapist respected me in that she worked with me on whatever surfaced during the session. She didn't *tell* me what I was feeling, she *asked* me. She taught me to trust my feelings, no matter how crazy they seemed. Most important of all, she believed me, even when I couldn't believe myself. She never once questioned that my father had sexually abused me. When I couldn't bring myself to describe the actual acts of abuse as I remembered them she still believed that it had happened. I finally began to believe it myself.

I then entered into a support group run by my therapist. She taught us how to use hypnotic imagery to tap into ourselves and discover our own power. We each created "safe places" for ourselves where we could explore our frightening feelings and face our dark memories, in a place where there was no judgment, no right or wrong, just us, our suffering, our silence slowly being transformed into words that we could understand and accept. We learned that it was all right to nurture and take care of ourselves. Some of us grieved our childhoods. I grieved the relationship I never had with my own mother. I blamed her for "letting it happen." I learned to own my feelings, even the terrible ones, and I finally began to accept my hatred and outrage against my father for the betrayal of trust I had in him.

I began to feel somewhat good about myself, and that resulted in strong guilt feelings. My worst memories surfaced then—memories that prevented me from healing myself. I was disgusted and ashamed to remember how I had "acted out" the abuse I experienced.

When my father began sexually abusing me, I learned to turn off my feelings. I would escape into fantasy worlds and pretend it wasn't happening. I hid myself; I became "invisible." I did whatever I could do with my mind to leave the situation. I learned at a very young age not to be "noticed" too much. As I grew into a young girl, I had isolated myself so much that I had become a loner.

Nobody noticed me; that's the way I wanted it. Being unnoticed meant being untouched. But I was so angry in my silence, so angry, that I took it out on others around me who were less powerful than I. I began to hurt little kids, luring them over to me with promises to play with them, and then pushing them down, kicking them, or slapping them. I helped a little girl get a drink of water from the fountain in the schoolyard. Putting my hand on top of hers, I showed her how to turn on the faucet, then I squeezed and squeezed until she cried out in pain and looked up at me in fear. I felt powerful. But I also felt guilt and disgust for myself.

I baby-sat for a family across the street. When the little boy wouldn't stop crying and go to sleep, I would scream at him to shut up, and I would cover his head with a pillow. I was terrified that I would end up suffocating him, but I couldn't seem to control myself. I stopped "just in time." How dare he cry and make a fuss when I had to be quiet and meek in order to survive. It wasn't fair, and somebody had to pay, but that somebody was far more powerful than me.

I began to act sexually with a little girl I baby-sat, simulating intercourse by lying down on top of her and rubbing myself on her legs. I was totally disgusted with myself but couldn't seem to stop. I believed I was possessed by evil spirits; I knew I had become a destructive person, and I needed help. But I was too ashamed and afraid to tell anyone what I had done.

I had to do something with these crazy feelings, so I stopped acting them out on other children and turned them onto myself. I started shoplifting. When I finally got caught, my parents were disappointed, but they didn't punish me. I began to write black, suicidal poetry. I tried to strangle myself with a scarf, kept a knife in my room, and sometimes sat for long periods of time holding it to my wrist. I took a bottle of aspirin, and once stepped out in front of a moving car and was hit. Nobody ever asked me why—I had become so "invisible" that I was ignored. I finally realized that no one was going to punish me for my sins, so I would have to go on punishing myself.

I denied myself any happiness. I married an abusive man who would treat me the way I thought I deserved to be treated. I let opportunities pass that would have helped me develop and grow, because I felt I didn't deserve to. I wasn't worthy. After my divorce, I walked right into another abusive relationship, which lasted only three months. This man punished me as well.

I got myself into counseling after I recognized my self-destructive patterns, and got to the point where I began to feel some self-worth. I started to get my life on the right track and settled into a marriage with a nonabusive, sensitive man. But I found myself doing things to sabotage my happiness; I started picking away at this relationship, wanting to destroy it because I was not worthy of love. How could I go on lying to myself? I didn't deserve a "normal" life.

It was during group therapy at the Sexual Assault Centre that I realized what I was doing. I would never allow myself to heal because of my guilt for my past. I saw two choices for myself: suicide or risking telling someone about what I had done as a child. I chose the latter, because I had had a taste of self-esteem, and I wanted more. I wanted to heal.

Because of the trust I had in my therapist, I was finally able to share those darkest secrets that hindered my healing. It was the most painful but also the most freeing session of my therapy.

We did some Gestalt work, using the "empty chair." I spoke to each of my victims from the past, explaining what had happened to me and how I had carried the guilt for what I had done to them. I then asked for their forgiveness. I spoke from my childhood to the adult I had become, explaining that I had tried the only way I knew to ask for help, and when I was ignored, I turned everything inward and tried to destroy myself. I then spoke to that little girl from my past, and told her that she had done the best she could to survive.

I hold myself accountable for my past actions, and I know I can never erase them. But now I understand what was behind them.

I still haven't forgiven myself, and I still find myself wanting to sabotage any successes in my life. But now I recognize, I understand. When I feel especially guilt-ridden, I tell myself that I am worthy of forgiveness and that I am willing to forgive myself.

I was surprised to find that therapy helped me to make peace in my heart with my mother. In looking at my childhood, and remembering what she had told me about hers, I realized that she had done the best she could with what she had learned.

I still haven't dealt with my feelings about my father, but I can accept now that I was molested by him. I can believe it and make some sense out of my crazy childhood. Perhaps when I can forgive myself, I may be able to forgive him.

I wrote the following letter to the little girl I lost to sexual abuse. I read it every few months to remind myself that I'm going to be okay. I think I'm healing now.

> Dear little ten-year-old girl:
>
> I speak to you from your future, surrounded by women, strong women, women who have suffered. The thing I want most for you to know is that you are a survivor.
>
> You are now trapped in a family that needs a lot of help. Your family will not seek that help, but you will, later on in your life.
>
> All of the hurts, fears, and anger you are having to store up in that little body of yours will have an outlet some day in the future. Right now it is too unsafe for you to let things out.
>
> Trust your inner self, and do not judge yourself too harshly if you lash out when your burden seems too heavy to carry.
>
> You are learning some very important survival skills that will play a part in molding the strong woman you will become. When you feel your light inside flickering, and you don't think you're going to make it, there will be people who will help you. Some of them you will know, some you won't.
>
> You are stronger than you think. You are

worthy of much love. The people who brought you into this world are hurting you now. Trust that you will be free of them, and will someday come to have compassion and understanding for them. You will make it.

References

Barback, L. *For Yourself: The Fulfillment of Female Sexuality.* Garden City, N.Y.: Anchor Books, 1976.

Butler, S. Taped workshop presented in Edmonton, Alta., 1986.

Dann, D. *Youthful Sexual Abusers.* Unpublished master's degree thesis, University of Calgary, 1987.

Groth, A. N. "The Incest Offender." In S. M. Sgroi (ed.), *Handbook of Clinical Intervention in Child Sexual Abuse.* Lexington, Mass.: Lexington Books, 1982.

Herman, J. S. *Father/Daughter Incest.* Cambridge, Mass.: Harvard University Press, 1981.

Hyde, N. D. "Uncovering the Repression: Some Clinical Considerations in the Psychotherapy of Women Incest Survivors." *Alberta Psychology,* 1987, *16* (3), pp. 3–6.

Kitzinger, S. *Woman's Experience of Sex.* London: Dorling Kindersley, 1983.

Loulan, J. *Lesbian Sex.* San Francisco: spinsters/*aunt lute,* 1984.

Maltz, W., and Holman, B. *Incest and Sexuality.* Lexington, Mass.: Lexington Books, 1987.

Progoff, I. *At a Journal Workshop.* New York: Dialogue House Library, 1975.

Rainer, T. *The New Diary.* Los Angeles: Tarcher, 1978.

Russell, D. E. H. *The Secret Trauma.* New York: Basic Books, 1986.

14

Recreating Equality: A Feminist Approach to Ego-State Therapy

Cheryl Malmo
Client: "Madeleine"

Given that we live in a patriarchal society that has defined a very limited range of behaviors and feelings as appropriate for women and that has devalued women, it is probably safe to conclude that all women to some extent have felt ambivalence or conflict. Feminist therapists have long been aware of how their female clients often feel divided in their daily lives and of the conflict experienced by women in their different roles and as a result of the different demands and expectations placed on them. We are aware, too, of women feeling divided inside as they struggle to meet their own needs while battling old rules or messages that tell them that they should accommodate others, serve, sacrifice, nurture, or be passive and selfless. The result for women of their being constantly ambivalent, in conflict, or divided is that they experience themselves as psychologically split. This phenomenon is explained by John Berger, a British art critic of note. Berger has written about how women typically have been treated as objects rather than as subjects in paintings, this being a reflection of their object status in most societies. He describes the effect of this objectification on women's psyches in his book *Ways of Seeing* (Berger, 1972).

> To be born a woman has been to be born, within an allotted and confined space, into the keeping of men. The social presence of women has developed as a result of their ingenuity in living under such tutelage within such a limited space. But this has been at the cost of a woman's self being split into two. A woman must continually watch herself. While she is walking across a room or while she is weeping at the death of her father, she can scarcely avoid envisaging herself walking or weeping. From earliest childhood she has been taught and persuaded to survey herself continually.
>
> And so she comes to consider the *surveyor* and the *surveyed* within her as the two constituent yet always distinct elements of her identity as a woman [p. 46].

That women's socialization to fit the feminine stereotype has devastating effects on their mental health has been documented by numerous researchers (Albert, 1971; deBeauvoir, 1952; Bernard, 1972, 1974; Broverman and others, 1970). That the socialization of women to be feminine combined with their being devalued results in women feeling ambivalent about their identity was documented by Judith Bardwick and Elizabeth Douvan (1972) in their classic article "Ambivalence: The Socialization of Women." In her article "Accommodation and Resistance in Gender and Gender Development," Jean Anyon (1981) described how women handle their ambivalence and conflict. Anyon determined that while, on one level, girls and women may appear to accommodate to their prescribed roles, on another level, they may be resisting. She gives as an example Doris Lessing's (1973) character Kate in *The Summer Before the Dark*. In one scene, Kate appears on the outside to be a smiling, dutiful, and submissive wife, serving coffee and cake to her husband and his colleague, while on the inside she is bored, turned off, and engrossed in her own thoughts. In another scene, Kate knows that a friend is seeing her as an efficient, high-powered, smiling woman, but inside she feels she is spinning in circles, losing control, and is frightened about the future. The following excerpt describes Kate's discovery of how she might use her ability to split to her own advantage.

> Soon she discovered that if she wanted to be alone, she should sit badly, in a huddled or discouraged posture, and allow her legs to angle themselves unbecomingly. If she did this men did not see her. She could swear they did not. Sitting neatly, alertly, with her legs sleekly disposed, she made a signal. Sagging and slumped, it was only when all the seats in the coffee-room were taken that someone came to sit near her. At which time it was enough to let her face droop to gain her privacy again, and very soon.
>
> It was really extraordinary! There she sat, Kate Brown, just as she had always been, *her* self, *her* mind, *her* awareness, watching the world from behind a facade only very slightly different from the one she had maintained since she was sixteen. It was a matter only of bad posture, breasts allowed to droop, and a look of "Yes, if you *have* to . . ." and people did not see her. It gave her a dislocated feeling, as if something had slipped out of alignment [p. 47].

Many women are aware of feeling divided and acting on different levels, although they may not understand the origin of their conflicts or the pattern of their behaviors as the psychological splitting becomes manifest. Feminist psychologists are gaining greater understanding about the nature of conflict experienced by women. Jessica Heriot (1983) outlines three kinds of conflict experienced by women. She first describes female-identified women, who, as a result of believing that women are less valuable, develop low self-esteem, depression, and anxiety. The second group of women are those who are male-identified—women who have dissociated from their female selves and what is presumed to be feminine and in the process have learned to distrust their emotions. The third group Heriot describes as the women in the middle—the ones who are split, in a double-bind conflict, pulled in different directions by opposing, internalized messages. An example of this kind of division is demonstrated in Margaret Laurence's (1969) character Stacey in *The Fire-Dwellers.* In the opening of the book, Stacey is just getting out of bed and is talking to herself, giving voice to the expectations she perceives and to her own feelings and thoughts. The following is an excerpt (Laurence indicates where Stacey's self-talk begins with a line, ———) :

> Stacey looks at her underwear on the chair but makes no move toward it. Her eyes are drawn back to the mirror.
>
> ———Everything would be all right if only I was better educated. I mean, if I were. Or if I were beautiful. Okay, that's asking too much. Let's say if I took off ten or so pounds. Listen Stacey, at thirty-nine, after four kids, you can't expect to look like a sylph. Maybe not, but for hips like mine there's no excuse. I wish I lived in some country where broad-beamed women were fashionable. Everything will be all right when the kids are older. I'll be more free. Free for what? What in hell is the matter with you, anyway? Everything *is* all right. *Everything is all right.* Come on, fat slob, get up off your ass and get going. There's a sale on downtown, remember? Singing ad on local station—*Dollar Forty-nine Day plink plink.* Funny thing, I never swear in front of my kids. This makes me feel I'm being a good example to them. Example of what? All the things I hate. Hate, but perpetuate [pp. 4–5].

Most women, I think, can identify with Stacey's splitting and with her self-talk. There is a more severe kind of splitting, however, that takes place in women who have suffered from more severe trauma—from having been emotionally neglected and/or psychologically, physically, or sexually abused as children. For these women, dissociation from their feelings and perhaps even from the memory of their abusive experiences has been a coping strategy, a way to deal with their trauma. In dissociation, the psyche splits in such a way that the feelings of pain, guilt, fear, confusion, lack of worth, inadequacy, powerlessness, hopelessness, and so on are separated from the functioning self (who is a dependent child) in order that the traumatic experience can be survived. Sometimes, in severe cases where extreme cruelty and torture are involved, the split occurs many times, the feelings are totally repressed, and the dissociated parts are completely unknown to each other. In the language of hypnosis and ego-state therapy, the ego boundaries become impermeable (Watkins, 1978; Watkins and Watkins, 1979). When this happens, we are seeing the phenomenon of multiple personality disorder. As in the case of *Sybil,* whose story was written by Flora Rheta Schreiber (1973), dissociation is used to protect the person from each new trauma, resulting in the creation of a new personality who is unknown to the original personality and who carries the knowledge and effects of the trauma. The following excerpt demonstrates how some of Sybil's different personalities functioned:

> Sighing, Vicky remarked: "You know, Doctor, I wish Sybil could enjoy life the way I do. I love to go to concerts and art galleries. So does she, but she doesn't go often enough. I'm going to the Metropolitan Museum when I leave here. I mentioned that I have a lunch date with a friend. It's Marion Ludlow. . . ."
>
> "Does Sybil know Marion Ludlow?" the doctor asked.
>
> "I'm afraid not," Vicky replied with faint condescension. "Sybil's not a *femme du monde,* a woman of *esprit.* She saw Mrs. Ludlow in line in the Teacher's College cafeteria and wondered what a fashionable woman like that was doing there. The cafeteria was crowded, and Sybil was sitting alone. Mrs. Ludlow asked if she might sit with her. You know Sybil is always afraid of not being polite enough. So she said, 'Certainly.' But the thought of having to cope with an attractive society woman terrified her. She blacked

> out. So I took over and had a conversation with the *grand dame*. That was the beginning of our friendship. And we're very good friends."
>
> "Does Peggy Lou know Mrs. Ludlow?"
>
> "Oh, I don't think so, Dr. Wilbur. They're worlds apart, you know."
>
> "Vicky, you seem to do many things in which Sybil and Peggy play no part," the doctor observed.
>
> "That's perfectly true," Vicky was quick to say. "I have my own route. I'd be bored if I had to follow theirs." She looked at the doctor with an expression that was part mischievous, part quizzical, and confided: "Doctor, Sybil would like to be I. But she doesn't know how."
>
> "Does Sybil know about you?"
>
> "Of course not," Vicky replied. "She doesn't know about the Peggys. And she doesn't know about me. But that doesn't keep her from having an image of a person like me—an image that she would like to fulfill but that constantly eludes her" [pp. 96–97].

Most dissociation is not this severe; that is, in most cases, the different parts are to some extent known to each other, and they converse, as in the case of Stacey. However, all dissociation is helpful at the time it first happens because it enables the child to survive without feeling the emotional pain, fear, and horror that are a natural reaction to a traumatic experience but that are too great for a child to bear. Over time, however, the dissociation impedes growth, alienating the dominant self from her repressed feelings and the source of her psychic energy. The dominant part of the psyche, which has survived by repressing feelings, maintains inaccurate and destructive beliefs about the feeling part that it is guilty, bad, not good enough, and so on. These beliefs become the basis on which decisions are made and life is lived. Sometimes the repressed part may take over and, acting on its beliefs that it is bad or guilty, may engage in unhealthy or self-destructive behavior. What started out as a survival strategy, born out of fear and desperation, can become a fearful, desperate, and often self-destructive life-style.

Examining Unhealthy Behavior with a Feminist Consciousness

That the behavior of women that on the outside appears to be self-destructive or unhealthy must be understood to be a coping mechanism, a survival strategy, a best attempt to handle a difficult or traumatic experience is one of the principles of feminist therapy, as outlined by Susan Sturdivant (1980). This principle has been widely used by feminist therapists to understand the different problems experienced by their clients. Susie Orbach (1978, 1982) has explained that women who eat compulsively do so in response to numerous negative judgments of themselves that come from others or have been internalized from an earlier time. She outlines how women deal with these criticisms indirectly through compulsive eating behavior while giving indirect messages about their feelings and needs on another level (through body size, posture, gestures, and so on). Orbach maintains that the key to these women achieving mental health is self-acceptance—acceptance of their feelings, their desires, their behaviors, and their own female body. In other words, the overcoming of compulsive eating behavior and the learning of healthy emotional expression and behavior depend on the resolution of internal conflicts arising from self-criticism learned earlier in the family and/or from the culture.

In 1980, I began working with women who eat compulsively, using the approach described by Orbach (1978) in *Fat Is a Feminist Issue*. The more I worked in this area, the clearer it became to me that my clients' judgment of themselves would inevitably lead to a food binge. Having been trained in Gestalt therapy to work with the different parts of a person in order to stimulate growth toward an integrated whole, I began asking my clients to sit in different chairs to assist them to identify, separate, and explore the parts of their conflicts in depth. Consistently, I would hear the voice of a critical, controlling, and punitive part speaking from one chair and the voice of an intimidated, guilty, and hopeless part speaking from another. The criticism might involve feelings ("You shouldn't get angry; it's not nice"), intentions ("You're selfish if you put your needs first"), behaviors ("You're a terrible mother/daughter/friend/wife/lover because . . ."), body image ("You're a fat cow"), and so on. These criticisms were powerful, often causing the guilty part to cower in shame and defeat. The guilty part did have power, too, however. Eventually she would binge, proving to the controlling part that her control was not absolute.

For the first time, transactional analysis (TA) began to make sense to me, and I began to work with the concept of three ego states—parent, child, and adult. The parent part, it seemed, had accepted and internalized society's rules about how women should look and feel and how they should act if they were to be properly feminine, and it criticized the self for her failure to meet these expectations. The child part initially succumbed to the rules, expectations, and criticisms but eventually resisted by having a temper tantrum in the form of a binge, as a way of saying no to the rules and judgments. The adult part seemed to be the wise part who had brought the woman to therapy, was now learning about herself, and could sometimes look at the situation objectively. This part was not often present, however, was typically underdeveloped in relation to the controlling part, and often needed coaching, modeling, or reminding of how she would treat her friends, in order for her to offer understanding, support, and encouragement to the child.

I began to see a similar dynamic in other clients with other problems—drug or alcohol addictions, compulsive buying, phobias, relationship conflicts, and dissociation resulting from childhood trauma and abuse. At one point, I started using props to help clients identify their different parts, cuing them with a cassette tape to represent the parent (with the implication that old, inappropriate messages can be erased and new, appropriate ones can be added), a small, soft doll or stuffed puppy (certain to engender tender feelings) to represent the child, and a calculator to represent the rational adult (reinforcing the idea that it was the newly developing adult that was rational, not the parent, as the client invariably assumed). (I learned about the use of these props from Dr. Brian Gorman at a meeting of the Canadian Society of Clinical Hypnosis–Alberta Division at Devon, Alberta, in February 1984.)

But the TA model did not always fit or seem adequate. Clients identified their different parts with names that were meaningful to them, such as the critic, the controller, the judge, the man behind the desk, or the one in charge for the parent; the little one, the feeling one, the spirit, or the inner one for the child; and the rational one, the wise one, the old one, or the new me for the adult. And often there were more than three parts. I began to understand that I was working with different states of mind that were dissociated from each other and that needed to be explored fully so that they could either learn to work together cooperatively or become integrated. Thus did I discover ego-state therapy, although I did not know at the time that it had been documented and that it had a name.

Origin and Development of Ego-State Therapy

In an explanation of the origin of ego-state therapy, John and Helen Watkins (Watkins and Watkins, 1979) acknowledge that the idea of ego states originated with Paul Federn, a contemporary of Freud. Unlike Freud, who divided the psyche into three states (ego, id, and superego) and explained the dynamic between these states, Federn hypothesized that there were different states within the ego that developed in reaction to the experiences of the individual. Berne's TA reflects this concept of different ego states, which have their own characteristics and motivations and which share the energy of the whole personality. Hilgard also recognized the dynamics of these different ego states, describing them as "cognitive structural systems" and using the term "the hidden observer" to describe a covert ego state (Torem, 1987; Watkins and Watkins, 1979).

It was Helen and Jack Watkins, however, who actually developed two distinct techniques that they called ego-state therapy (Watkins and Watkins, 1979). First, they devised a method of placing several chairs in a circle around a room and asking a client to speak to an issue from all of the different points of view that she could identify within herself. Each ego state was asked to speak as "I," experiencing itself as subject and the other states as object ("you"). Then the client was asked to step outside of the circle and to become cotherapist regarding each of the ego states (its feelings, beliefs, intentions, behaviors) and to assist the parts to negotiate and cooperate in the interest of the whole. In essence, they were applying family therapy techniques to an individual's ego states. The second technique that the Watkinses developed involves hypnotizing the client and then calling forth each ego state in turn to be the "executive," to take control and to speak for itself. Again, each part is worked with as an individual but as if it were in family therapy, having to encounter, relate to, and deal with the feelings, desires, and behaviors of the others. This second method, while commonly used for working with clients with multiple personality disorder, can also be used with clients whose dissociation is less severe.

More recently, Moshe Torem (1986, 1987) has documented his use of ego-state therapy with anorectic and bulimic patients. Building on the Watkins' notion that the separation of ego states involves a kind of dissociation, Torem believes that a dissociated ego state could be responsible for his patients' psychopathology (binge eating, self-induced vomiting, laxative abuse, self-starvation, body image distortion, and fear of food). Once identified, the ego state could be accessed and worked with using hypnosis. Torem states, "These symptoms, which are so typical in eating disorders, may very well be the expression of an underlying disharmony and internal fighting among various dissociated ego-states in the same individual" (1986, p. 138).

On the basis of my experience with numerous clients, I similarly developed a method for working with the different ego states of women who eat compulsively, among others. My method incorporates my feminist values of women's worth and equality, my understanding of how to assist women to regain a sense of worth and personal power, and the feminist therapy principle of viewing a destructive behavior as originating from an earlier attempt to cope with trauma. I have applied this model with success to women who eat compulsively as well as to women (and men) who were psychologically, physically, or sexually abused as children. Like the TA model, my model has as its base three distinct parts, Big Sister (who makes the rules and is the survivor), Little Sister (who carries the feelings and memories connected to the trauma and who has probably been dissociated or repressed in order to be kept safe), and the spirit guide (who is wise, compassionate, and understanding and who gives support and comfort to both sisters). (When I work with men, I use the concepts of Big Brother and Little Brother to describe the same ego states.)

I prefer to work with the dynamic of two sisters (or brothers) rather than with a parent and child, for several reasons. First, the idea of two sisters reinforces the recognition that the problematic behavior or coping strategy, as well as the feelings, originated when the person was a child. Thus, the ego state that makes the rules and then criticizes or punishes is not a parent but only another, somewhat older child. This helps the client to understand that while the behavior seemed to work at the time (and needs to be appreciated as the best attempt of a young child to survive), it may no longer be the best solution. Further, the client can understand that her behavior is no longer appropriate because times have changed and she has learned or can learn new skills. The idea of two sisters also appeals to me because it lends itself easily to teaching the notion of equality among the different ego states. The goal for the two sisters is to become equally responsible and equally respected, to take turns and to cooperate—to be best friends, in fact. When a woman enters therapy, her Big Sister part is often overdeveloped and overworked, and she may be either tense and very much in control or exhausted and depressed. At the same time, her Little Sister part may be repressed, hidden, hopeless, and without a voice, or she may be acting out her hurt and anger indirectly and destructively.

Once each part is identified, the Little Sister will need help finding her voice and learning to speak out, to reclaim her memories, to identify and express her feelings and wants, to act on her own behalf, and, thus, to heal from her trauma. The Big Sister will need to learn how to let go of control, refrain from judging the Little Sister, deal openly with her fears, face the reality of the trauma she experienced, and put the responsibility where it belongs (with the offending adult rather than with Little Sister). She also needs to learn to trust, to take risks, and to become understanding and supportive of Little Sister. For this to happen, the therapist and Little Sister must acknowledge that Big Sister's controlling behavior is motivated by her desire to protect Little Sister and by her fear that Little Sister will be hurt again. Together the sisters will learn new skills and behaviors, taking each other's feelings and needs into account, expressing their own feelings directly, and acting on their new knowledge. Therapists attempting to work with the Big Sister–Little Sister dynamic for the first time need to be aware that when

Little Sister has found her voice and is becoming stronger, she may wish to dispense with Big Sister, believing that she can make it on her own and preferring to leave Big Sister behind. If and when this occurs, Little Sister will need to be told firmly that this is not possible, that they must learn to work together as equals. Neither can be left out. A statement of this kind will be reassuring to Big Sister, who already fears losing control, and will prevent her from sabotaging Little Sister's attempts to become strong by falling back into her old strategies of using criticism and punishment.

The spirit guide is an expanded version of the TA adult concept. It is objective and rational, but in addition it is a wise, compassionate, understanding, comforting, and supportive being, who addresses the spirit as well as the intellect of the client. The spirit guide can take many forms. I have found it best to introduce the idea of the spirit guide to clients by describing its qualities and skills and then to let them determine what form this being will take. Some people experience the spirit guide as a very old woman or man, a peer, a child, or an animal. Some people identify the spirit guide as themselves at a very old age or sometime in the future, or when they were very small and pure, uncontaminated by others. Or it may be experienced as a kind of fairy godmother, a mystical being, a white light, an angel, a goddess or god, or someone dear who has died. Interestingly, I have found that while some clients are very comfortable with the idea of a spirit guide being a separate being, others insist that it must be a part of themselves. I inform my clients that their spirit guide (they may prefer to call it by another name) knows them very well, knows what is best for them, and knows just what to say to make them feel safe, secure, and calm. It recognizes their strengths and can put their problems into perspective.

The purpose of introducing the spirit guide is to assist clients to identify and reinforce or develop the part of them that is (or can learn to be) accepting and self-nurturing. While self-nurturance is an issue for most women, it is especially important for those who have been abused and who have internalized the belief that they somehow deserved the abuse or were responsible for it. Once the concept of the spirit guide has been taught, it can be used to bring a healthy and positive perspective to any problem that has been explored by one or both sisters. In the beginning, a client may not yet have developed the skill of being understanding and compassionate with herself, the Big Sister typically being overdeveloped. When this is the case, I frequently ask the client what she would say to her best friend if her friend had disclosed this problem or feeling or what she would say to her daughter or son, her niece or nephew, or the child she might one day have. If this coaching does not bring forth a positive response (some clients feel as judgmental toward others as they do toward themselves), I might intervene by saying something like, "I'd like to talk to Big Sister now. Would that be all right?" And then I would proceed to say whatever therapeutic things that I thought would be called for and would be helpful to that particular ego state at that time.

The Use of Ego-State Therapy in Feminist Practice

Being an eclectic therapist, I use many strategies and techniques throughout the course of a client's therapy. I use ego-state therapy whenever it appears to me to fit the problem or to instruct the solution. In my experience, ego-state therapy can be of great benefit to clients with conflict and anxiety or with compulsive, addictive, or phobic behavior or who experience psychological splitting or dissociation. Ego-state therapy can be employed in many different ways. I tend to use it in whichever way is most meaningful to a particular client. Sometimes I ask a client to move to different chairs to assist her to identify and explore her different voices; sometimes I use props to assist a client to differentiate her ego states (recently I used a pink quartz crystal to symbolize the spirit guide); or sometimes a client identifies sensations in parts of her body (head, heart, stomach, throat, legs, hands) that hold different feelings and memories, that have different intentions and behaviors, and that appear to me to be different ego states. Recently I have begun to use Guatemalan worry dolls to represent the different ego states of my clients. This is particularly useful with clients who are experiencing some difficulty in owning and speaking for their different ego states—they can speak about the angry doll or the scared doll in the third person and distance themselves somewhat from their intense feelings. Sometimes I assist the exploration of one part or a conflict between parts after a formal hypnotic induction, and often during ego-state therapy a client enters a state of hypnosis spontaneously. Sometimes I become aware that we are working with different ego states when I am assisting a client to work with different parts of a dream, with an image that arises as she explores a feeling, with a metaphor that either of us might develop to describe what is happening to her, or with a photograph of herself that she has brought to therapy. The form that the therapy takes depends on what a client brings to her session and how she wishes to work that day.

As a therapist, I find the concepts of ego states useful in understanding both what has happened to a client to create a particular problem and what the solution to the problem might be. My clients tell me that they, too, find the identification of and working with ego states useful; the concretizing of their internal conflicts, anxieties, dissociations, and so on makes them understandable and accessible and clarifies the changes that the clients need to make to solve their problems. The following are examples of how different problems that clients bring to therapy can be worked on using some form of ego-state therapy.

Conflict Resolution: The Case of Carol. Carol grew up in a home with an alcoholic mother, where she learned early to put others' needs first. She had a history of having been severely depressed after she left home but had not received any help at that time. She came to see me, depressed again following some difficult and abusive relationships with men and the death of an aunt, who had been a major source of support. At the same time, she had been feeling harassed at work (she was a social worker in a supervisory position) by some older male colleagues who were being forced into early retirement and who she was sure resented her. During therapy, Carol's mother died, and her grieving exacerbated her depression. After recovering to some extent, Carol returned to work from a medical leave but soon became depressed again. She was clearly "burned out," and she took another medical leave.

In one therapy session, Carol worried about whether to quit or return to her job. Hearing her describe her concerns, I indicated to her that I could hear a conflict between one part of her, who wanted to leave her job permanently, and another part, who thought that she should stay. She indicated that this was an accurate perception and agreed to further explore the conflict by speaking for each part from different chairs.

Carol decided that the part sitting where she was sitting (usually the strongest or most well-developed part) was the part who wanted to stay in the job and that the part who wanted to quit would sit in the chair opposite. Allowing each part to speak in turn to examine in depth its perceptions, feelings, interpretations, and intentions, Carol gained a greater understanding of the real issues underlying her conflict. It turned out that the part who wanted to stay working at the job was motivated by a desire to be responsible to and for others. This part felt that she owed the people at work her allegiance and that the unit might collapse without her. In addition, the job gave her financial and emotional security. The externally oriented part we called Big Sister. She had developed a pattern of behavior from having grown up in a home with an alcoholic mother, where she learned too early and too well to take responsibility for others—for the adults in her family as well as for her younger siblings. And here she was again, being responsible to others first.

Little Sister, on the other hand, wanted change, a new job, a career move, vitality rather than security. She wanted a sense of energy and lightness that she said she could no longer get at the current job. She was depressed, she said, because Big Sister paid more attention to the needs of others in her wish to stay at work than she did to her inner self, to Little Sister. Little Sister was afraid that she would collapse if she stayed at the job. Carol continued to work with Little Sister and Big Sister over several months. Little Sister had been silent for many years, but as she found her voice, she became stronger and more determined not to be ignored. She insisted on taking another medical leave from work, and Big Sister agreed that this was a good idea. The conflict is not yet resolved, but Little Sister is becoming more of an equal and is learning to speak out and demand the attention of Big Sister. And Big Sister is learning to put Little Sister's needs first, ahead of those of all the others to whom she previously felt responsible.

Fear and Phobias: The Case of Joanne. Joanne first came to me three years ago because she realized that she ate compulsively. I used the chairs and ego-state therapy to demonstrate to Joanne how the critical part of her was vocal prior to her binge eating. We did a lot of work determining how this critical part had internalized her father's criticisms of her and how it now undermined her confidence in her job as a child-care worker, particularly in relation to people in authority. We also dealt with her feelings about the sudden death of her father during this time and her feelings of being responsible for her mother. Six months into therapy, Joanne inadvertently uncovered the memory of having been sexually abused by her father at a young age. Our work together since that time has largely entailed uncovering the memories that she needed in order to make sense of her feelings of hurt, humiliation, and powerlessness. The feelings began to come in floods, and Joanne experienced them as overwhelming at times. She developed panic attacks and phobias, which seemed to provide an outlet for the fears that she was not yet ready to experience directly. At the same time, Joanne is learning to confront and transform the critical and controlling part of herself and is developing confidence both professionally and personally.

For some time, Joanne had been obsessed with various fears. Initially, she panicked at the thought of losing control in public, then she was concerned about her home being broken into, and later she panicked about the weather and the possibility of tornadoes. In one session, when she was expressing anxiety about tornadoes, she acknowledged that her fears were really about not feeling safe with men generally and with her father specifically. I knew from our previous work that this was Big Sister speaking, and I reminded Joanne of this. Then I pulled up another chair and asked her to move and speak for Little Sister.

Little Sister, it turned out, was bored and frustrated. She wanted to be active, not passive; creative, not safe; to try other ways of being and approaching life, not limiting herself to a fearful reaction. She wanted to be in the driver's seat, not always a passenger with Big Sister driving. She wanted to be Big Sister's equal. With all her energy and exuberance (which weren't at all apparent when Joanne entered my office that day), Little Sister quickly wore down

Big Sister (who was tired from always being on guard), and they began to negotiate. They decided that Little Sister could be in the driver's seat for two days, so long as she kept Big Sister safe and answered her questions. Big Sister offered that she would not manipulate Little Sister with her fear and promised to ask questions only when she really needed to. I had not perceived that Big Sister was manipulating with her fear and would never have suggested this, but Big Sister knew and spoke about it quite matter of factly. Big Sister and Little Sister agreed that in two days they would evaluate this experiment, renegotiate on their own if necessary, and continue with Little Sister in charge for two more days if things were going smoothly. (Actually, Little Sister stayed in charge all week.)

At the end of the session, I told Joanne that I was about to give a workshop on ego-state therapy and asked her what it was like for her to do therapy in this way. This is what she said: "It's a very powerful technique, because it brings out inner conversations that until they are verbalized are just feelings inside that I react to. When I identify and speak these feelings, my thoughts become clear. It feels good to feel the strength of the active, Little Sister part of me. Then I feel a synthesis and feel more connected and more whole." Joanne also explained why working this way was hard: "It makes me feel self-conscious. It's like being on stage because I'm talking to myself, not to you. I feel like I'm exposing myself, my private, inner life, and I feel vulnerable. It's also hard because I can't play around; I can't avoid the real issue." Joanne then informed me that I had made her sit on different chairs and talk to the different parts of herself on her first visit to me. She said that she couldn't remember what the issue was, only how powerful the session had been.

Joanne continues to work with her different ego states from time to time. She senses that she has a whole group of little abused girls to take care of, and a whole group of abused teens as well. As the adult part of her becomes stronger and stronger, she becomes more confident of her ability to confront the pain and fear of all these children inside her and to take care of them.

Dissociation and Bulimia: The Case of Maureen. Maureen is a thirty-five-year-old nurse who is divorced from a man who was repeatedly unfaithful to her. She experienced her father as gentle and loving, but he is now dead; she experiences her mother as very controlling, manipulative, and critical of everyone. She has two sisters and a number of friends to whom she is close. Maureen is bulimic; that is, she binges and vomits regularly (several times a week). This behavior was difficult for her to talk about, however—I was the first person she had told—so she chose to begin her therapy by working on current issues, particularly her relationships with her mother and with a boyfriend.

Maureen and I quickly developed the framework of Big Sister and Little Sister from which to work. I acknowledged, accepted, and validated Little Sister, who was angry about her mother's criticism of her father, her sisters, her grandmother, and everyone she encountered or talked about and was hurt about her mother's criticism of herself. I also encouraged Big Sister, who was a timid and good "Mummy's girl," to examine her rules and her fears about allowing Little Sister to speak out about her feelings directly. Maureen realized as she listened to Little Sister that her former husband had been psychologically and sexually abusive to her.

From the beginning, I gave Maureen an ongoing homework assignment to keep a journal about her feelings, present and past. The purpose of the journal was to assist Maureen to become continually aware of and to strengthen Little Sister and to build her confidence. At the same time, the journal writing required Big Sister to explore her past learnings and to trust Little Sister's inner knowledge of her feelings and needs. From time to time, I encouraged Maureen to express her feelings to her friends and family, when she was ready to do so. This was done to encourage Maureen to open up to others and to break her emotional isolation. The spirit guide ego state was further developed by my pointing out to Maureen that she treated her friends and sisters much more kindly and compassionately than she treated herself. I insisted that the double standard had to be fixed, because she, too, was worthwhile. At the same time, I modeled an accepting, nonjudgmental, caring attitude and response.

Maureen made good progress over a six-month period. She was able to confront her mother about not wanting to listen to her criticisms and to set some limits to the frequency and length of their visits. She told two close friends about her bulimia, joined a support group, and told the group about her bulimia as well. She was feeling more comfortable and confident with herself, but she was still binging regularly. It was time for us to talk about the bulimia. Maureen spent one whole session describing her binging and vomiting ritual to me in detail. I asked her to choose one change (from a list of possible changes that we had developed together) in her ritual and to attempt to write about her feelings before binging over the next week.

Maureen returned to therapy the following week feeling very frustrated and hopeless. She had made one change in her ritual (using a different kind of soft drink to binge with) but had not been able to write about her feelings. She had binged desperately all week and didn't know why. At this point, I decided that ego-state therapy was the appropriate intervention. It seemed to me that it was Big Sister who was upset about the desperate binging and who didn't understand what was going on. So I pulled up two chairs, one for the binger and one for the vomiter, and instructed Maureen to talk to these parts. With a great deal of skepticism, she began. The following is a summary of the exchange between Big Sister, the Binger, the Vomiter, and myself.

Big Sister: Why are you so desperate? What's going on?

Binger: You want to bury us, but we're helping you. We're your only way to have control. We let you eat what you want, and we never say no to you like your mother did. But you don't appreciate us—you judge us and call us names.

Me: (to Big Sister) Did you hear her? Can you respond?

Big Sister: I'm really very sorry. I didn't mean to hurt you with criticism and name-calling. I know I'll have to change my attitude toward you.

Me: Did you realize that you were behaving toward them like your mother behaves toward you?

Big Sister: No, but I do now.

Me: (to the Binger) I know you're trying to help, and that your help has been crucial in the past. But this isn't really helping any more. Do you have any new ways to help her?

Binger: We could tell her the feelings if she'd listen.

Me: Okay. What about hearing from the Vomiter?

Vomiter: (in a very angry voice) She hates me and criticizes me the most, and I have to do the dirty work—a job I hate.

Big Sister: It's true, and I'm sorry. I won't judge you if you ever have to do it again.

Vomiter: Well, I don't like doing it, and I just do it because she wants me to. I take care of her because she worries about her weight.

Me: I suppose you could go on strike and refuse to do the dirty work. And then you could take care of her in a different way, nurture her differently.

Vomiter: (Nods)

Big Sister: Whatever happens from now on, I won't criticize them. I have to appreciate what they are trying to do for me.

Maureen was amazed that she could do the exercise, that she could find the voices, and that she really knew what was going on inside herself. She left therapy feeling much more trusting of herself and capable of writing about her feelings the next time she felt like binging. This session turned out to be a turning point in Maureen's therapy. She did not binge at all the following week and then binged only two times in the next two weeks. At the time of this writing, Maureen has gone ten weeks in a row without binging and is working at expressing her feelings as she becomes aware of them. We have had two more sessions using ego-state therapy to work out Maureen's judgment and rejection of her body and her weight. In the first of these sessions, Big Sister talked to and learned to understand and accept her thighs and the many ways they helped her. In the second session, the body made strong arguments about the unfairness of being put on and taken off like clothing, insisting that it become part of the inner-core self.

Dissociation for Survival: The Case of Valerie. Valerie first came to me for help at age forty-five with severe emotional anxiety and outbursts that she experienced in conjunction with premenstrual syndrome. I learned quickly, by asking Valerie to play out her internal conflict around some marital problems (using different chairs), that she had a very highly developed ego state who felt responsible for her husband's and grown-up children's feelings, needs, and happiness. At the same time, she was almost totally unaware of her own feelings and needs with regard to these relationships—this part of her seemed completely repressed. Valerie wondered whether her having been sexually abused by her father, about which she also had no feelings, could be a factor in her difficulties. I indicated that the sexual abuse undoubtedly was a major factor, since it had never been dealt with.

Valerie continued with therapy, often preferring to work under hypnosis to explore body sensations, images, or whatever came into her awareness. Over a period of eighteen months, she uncovered numerous memories of having been sexually, physically, and psychologically abused by her father and physically and psychologically abused by her mother as well. She worked through the stages of reclaiming first her hurt and then her anger about this abuse. She has gained some understanding that the fears, like the hurt and anger, belong in the past but had to be repressed until now, when it was safe enough for them to surface and become known to her.

One day Valerie brought into her therapy session some postcards, a Bible, and a prayer book on which were inscribed messages to her from her father. Valerie and I both perceived that in all of the messages there was the facade of a loving relationship masking an undercurrent of threats, seduction, anger, guilt, and hypocrisy. After some discussion, Valerie identified within herself conflicting feelings of being, on the one hand, a nice, good, and responsible girl and, on the other, an angry, bad, and guilty daredevil. We used ego-state therapy and the chairs to facilitate her further exploration of these two parts. It turned out that the bad girl believed that she was bad for a number of reasons: in relation to the overwhelming abuse, because her mother kept on telling her that she was bad, and because she was energetic and rebellious, not "nice and quiet and ladylike, like Kathy" (her older sister). Valerie recalled, in addition, that her mother had once told her that she was not fit to be loved by God. She also recalled that her father had frequently referred to her, in front of her sisters, as miserable and strange. It appeared that with her parents' identification of her as bad, together with the trauma of the abuse and her hope that the abuse would stop if she were good, Valerie's belief that she was bad and deserved the abuse was created.

Valerie worked with strong feelings of anger and fear over the month that followed. Then, in a session where she was using hypnosis to explore her feelings, she got an image of her father talking to someone named Karen. In the image, she saw her father instructing Karen on how to pose for some pictures that he was going to take of her. Valerie had earlier uncovered memories of her father taking pornographic pictures of her and felt that this new image was connected to that. But she felt that the image was too scary to explore further at this time, so she instead explored some memories about a dog, which seemed less upsetting. The following week, Valerie reported that the idea of Karen still upset her, but she again decided to explore some other issues that seemed more pressing. Two weeks later, however, she was ready to examine Karen. I pulled up another chair for Karen, across from Valerie, and she began a dialogue:

Valerie: Why are you separate from me? That's not fair. Why don't you join me?

Karen: (angrily) I am the part of you who was sexually abused, and I'm bitter because you have ignored me for so long.

Valerie: I didn't know. I think that the abuse caused me so much stress, plus being labeled by Mom as bad, that it was too much for me. So I passed the buck on to you.

Karen: I accepted the job out of love for you, but I won't join you now because I'm still angry with you, and I don't trust you. You judge me the way Mom and Dad did.

Valerie: It's true. I do judge you. But I won't anymore. I realize that I must love and accept you.

After further discussion, the two parts resolved to accept and love each other. This meant that Valerie could now begin to own her sexuality, which previously had belonged to Karen and had been experienced by Valerie only as something that men expected. The session ended with Valerie imagining the two parts within her—the good and the bad, herself and Karen—coming together and walking hand in hand into the future. This was not the end of Valerie's work with Karen—it was simply a resolution of their first encounter. Five weeks later, after my summer holiday, we continued to work with Karen. We learned that while Valerie was asexual and Karen was sexual, Karen felt erotic only in being desired, not because she had any sexual feelings of her own. We would need to develop a third part, who could own and enjoy her own sexual feelings.

Early in therapy, I taught Valerie to image a safe place (see Chapter Ten) and a spirit guide to assist her to feel safe. Valerie found a sense of peace and calm when she sat by (or imagined sitting by) a window where the light or sun was streaming in. In the beginning, we did not know the significance of this safe place. The full meaning emerged months later, when Valerie began uncovering extreme abuse in a satanic cult in which her father and mother were high priest and high priestess. Valerie was compelled to partake in sexual activities and in animal and human mutilations and sacrifices. She realized that the sunlight felt calming to her because the morning marked the end of the ritual abuse, which took place during the night. At this time, Valerie also realized that she had once had a spirit guide in the image of an angel who guarded over her but that she had lost her angel when her mother told her that "your kind of girl isn't fit to be guarded by an angel." Needless to say, we are in the process of uncovering additional ego states that helped Valerie to cope with the extreme abuse.

One of these ego states is Little Valerie, who is four years old and who likes to go out into a sunny garden and pick flowers. She is innocent and escapes the abuse and the horrific scenes of murder she has witnessed by dissociating and imagining herself outside in the sun. Over time, Little Valerie discovered that the garden was not entirely safe, however. She sensed that she must stay away from the left side of the garden or she would fall over the edge of the world, and she must avoid a shadowy place on the right because there was a monster there. What we have learned is that when Little Valerie has been most horrified, by being made to take part in a ritual murder, for example, a part of her falls over the edge into a quiet and still place where she can stay until it is safe for her to return to Valerie. Only a very tiny part of Little Valerie is left at these times.

Recently, Little Valerie decided to find out more about the monster. Under hypnosis, she discovered that he was a man in a yellowish-brown monster suit with a mask and tail, a lionlike devil performing in some sort of ritual. Using the anger that has been raging inside her, she dared to defeat him by refusing to play her part any longer. She decided to put her hands on her hips, stick out her tongue, stamp her feet, and tell him to "back off," which he did. As she did this, she became aware that the monster was her father, who became confused and upset by her lack of cooperation in the ritual. She continued to behave aggressively toward him until he finally collapsed in a heap. In the meantime, her mother, who was also in the image, along with a group of participants, became angry with Little Valerie, telling her that she was a bad girl to disobey and upset her father. Little Valerie told her mother, too, to "back off." Her mother continued to criticize her. Little Valerie reasoned that everyone knew that bad things would happen to anyone who was touched by the monster's tail, so she cut off the monster's tail and hit her mother with it. Now it was her mother's turn to worry about bad things happening to her. Having dealt successfully with both her father and her mother, Little Valerie ended the session by telling the participants, "Go home! There will be no more meetings! There will be no more rituals! There will be no more scaring or hurting little children! There will be no more monsters! There will be no more murders! Go home! It's over! You have to learn to love each other instead of hating!"

The Case of Madeleine. Madeleine's account of her experience in therapy, which follows, describes the experience of ego-state therapy from a client's point of view. It will be clear from Madeleine's writing that ego-state therapy is just one of several methods of working that she found useful. Her account validates my beliefs that ego-state therapy is helpful in assisting clients to achieve emotional health and psychological strength and that it can be meaningfully integrated with numerous other healing techniques.

Client's Voice: "Madeleine"

I had finally agreed to follow the advice of a friend who had been helped by Cheryl. Six or seven months after I'd first called her ("No, nothing that can't wait. Yes, please do put me on your waiting list"), she called saying she now had some time. I said I'd get back to her, got off the phone, curled up in a fetal position, and wondered if I were going to throw up. I was terrified. Journal entry before first visit (September 13, 1985): "Connecting emptiness with wanting—split apart with self-contempt. 'You go ahead and try. I won't have anything to do with it,' says the contempt voice. Cheryl M. will help me. I'm sure of it."

First visit: Cheryl requires me to convince her, to prove (I feel) that I need help. I say that I don't seem to take care of myself well. For proof I cite various dominations by family and friends, and then tell the story of what had driven me to three different shrinks in the past six months: While I was on a holiday in another country, I picked up a man in a bar, something I hadn't done for a decade or more. Ten minutes into the hour's drive out of the city to his place I realized vaguely that I did not want to be there, and said so. He said that since we'd a long drive ahead of us, I'd have lots of time to get worked up about it before we'd arrive. I laughed. We spent much of the night fucking, and next day after he dropped me off in town my skin erupted in oozing blisters. (I'd had various kinds of hives over the years when life was hard.) It was only after I arrived back home that I realized that I had silenced my own self-protective voice, become utterly submissive, and behaved as though this rape were a pleasant social event. (His contempt, rudeness, and so on showed that *he* knew the difference.) It was the blanking out, the refusal to know what was happening to me that scared me. I realized that what I had done in that moment of laughter was to make a survival decision unconsciously, not consciously. And a whole bunch of familiar feelings came with that unconscious choice: You aren't worth fighting for. What do you expect being so stupid? You're only good for being fucked anyway. Don't whine about it; just grit your teeth and take it. That's what you deserve, and so on, and so on. Cheryl was persuaded that I could use some help.

I saw Cheryl once a week for about eighteen months. I felt heard and seen there with her. The power of her attention seemed to provide me with a kind of envelope of safety. My hours (sob, snot, howl, whimper, shriek, moan, rage, whine, roar, weep) seem now wrapped in a harvest light, honey wheat colored (I don't mean to sound like a cereal commercial, but that is the color that comes to mind). Maybe that is what safety feels like to me. I experienced Cheryl's time with me as a warm, intense light. She concentrated intensely on what I was saying, she responded directly, with what seemed like her whole mind and heart.

Although I've studied some psychology, read dozens of pop-psych books, seen various kinds of therapists for various reasons, I never felt that Cheryl's words were predictable. She seemed to be hearing this story for the first time and coming up with a specific and precise and personal response to it. Sometimes that response would be a wry smile of common feeling, or a little tale, or an experience drawn from her own life, or a move across from her chair to sit beside me and hold me. Often it was a keen observation or a musing question: "I wonder if . . ." and light would break through the cloud of my confusion and misery. These are not, I think, merely therapeutic strategies, but rather Cheryl's own self engaging with her clients. Perhaps this is paralleled by the delight I felt in simply *seeing* her—dramatic earrings, brilliant colors, comfortable and beautiful sweaters and shirts and slacks, truly amazing socks. Her pleasure in her own self was apparent and encouraging, no matter how bleak my own spirit seemed to me. The vitality that came from this presentation of self was not merely esthetic. The reds, oranges, purples, greens, golds made an assertion of strength inseparable from joy and seemed to proclaim the right to an enjoyment of life that did not diminish authority. Simply, Cheryl's delight in wonderful clothes did not reduce the sense I had of her as a strong and authoritative woman.

All this warmth was not allowed to confuse the fact of therapist and client. When I attempted, early in our work, to "take care" of her, Cheryl pointed out that my behavior was inappropriate to this setting. (What relief I felt, and what fear—how could I make her care for me if I did not serve as caretaker?) The other inappropriate feeling I had Cheryl also dispelled. I feared that she would succumb to my evil powers as a seductress and thus be victimized by my sexuality. It took some time before I trusted that she would not be vulnerable. Her gentleness and clarity with my exaggerated sense of sexual virulence were the basis for my much later success in facing how deeply sexual power (and powerlessness) was part of my sense of self.

One of the earliest strategies we used was to begin identifying "the voices." I have an image of Cheryl advising me to move physically from one place to another to give each of the voices its own space as I spoke out of it. I'd recognize a "voice"—this was difficult as I had always experienced them as feelings with no way to isolate one from another, no reason to note patterns, rhythms of speech, and so on that made the "voices" distinct from each other and from the person I was calling "me." I sat on the floor of her office, box of tissues beside me, Cheryl very close on a low sofa, leaning in toward me. As a new "voice" spoke, I'd move. Soon I was scrambling around in a circle. Each newly recognized voice would split itself into another, which seemed to provoke a response from yet another. I felt like a loose bundle of shards, and appalled at my discovery of divisions of self against self. And I was frightened.

The grip these old feelings and beliefs had was powerful, and I'd require endless reassurances before taking the next step, before speaking some long-silenced truth about my feelings or experiences. "You can say that to your . . . (fill in the blank—Mommy, Daddy, friend)," she would tell me. "No, no. I can't. I'm too scared." "Yes you can. I'm here; I'll help you." Like a kind teacher guiding a little child's hand, Cheryl traced new possibilities of emotion and of speech with me. Most importantly, she always made sure that an adult (version of?) me was okay before I left her office. I took these exercises away with me, trying to hear myself in everyday life, as Cheryl instructed. Gradually I learned to identify repetitions and patterns, which sifted out of the stuck places and became part of me.

One significant pair seemed to resist our efforts. This was the voice of the cool, intellectual, detached, disdainful, tough self (a male figure in my dreams), which balanced with the helpless, soft, passive, rather dopey me, who was always getting into destructive situations or relationships. I believed that these two needed somehow to embrace each other, to undermine the obvious polarities that were preventing me from "using" the capabilities of the one to protect the other. Cheryl (in a musing way) suggested that the "strong" figure, rather than representing only self-contempt, self-hatred, abandonment, could be seen as a big sister, trying to make a little sister streetwise, to scold her into some survival strategies, to toughen her up. Suddenly "little sister" (which is the voice I identified myself with) had a place from which to speak back to the other voice, which she could never get the best of in a confrontation. She didn't have to live in such shame but could explain to "big sister" that she no longer needed such instruction, that she could keep herself out of trouble now and would manage her own life. The "she" of both figures became me, and I had a way to get past a kind of self-hatred that had been with me since I'd been a child. (What moves me now about this process is the understanding that much of our behavior, though apparently self-destructive, has its roots in the wish to protect ourselves.)

Relaxation-hypnosis seemed to work well for me. I entered the old time (child-time) and found I knew things I did not know I knew. One of my earliest memories (I was not yet three years old) has remained fixed in my mind as a talisman, a "Yes, this is what life is like" feeling. I stand alone in a dusk living room looking out the window down an empty street. I am desolate and silent. Cheryl, soft voice, exquisitely gentle, says, "Where's your mommy?" This question had never entered my mind in all the years I'd held this memory. But I knew. She was in a darkened room with a cold cloth over her head for her headache. "Talk to your mommy. Tell her you are lonely. Tell her you are just a little girl and you need your mommy." I did as Cheryl suggested, with much fear, fighting past the cement block of training that makes "poor mommy" inviolate, not to be disturbed by demands or anger. Although I don't remember this being explicit at this time, my journal makes it clear that Cheryl made herself a mommy, and that gave me in adulthood the safe place for the child still alive in me to speak to *her* mommy. (Journal entry of October 18, 1985: "The little girl [that is, my hurt self] is tenderly cared for by Cheryl—so kind, so gentle, a lovely mommy, and such a trip back to the window—to no-mom. So much sadness and despair. So empty—maybe I needn't be. She gives me hope.")

Image-making (sometimes part of hypnosis, but not invariably) was especially useful for the physical manifestations of misery. I began, for the first time, it seemed, to pay attention to my body and my breathing. I had had, over the years, episodes in which my chest would constrict and I'd be in a lot of pain. When the pain went away, I would forget it (though I had twice been hospitalized for it). As my work with Cheryl became more intense, which is to say as we moved more deeply into the moments of the past and the links between them and my later childhood and adolescence, I became more conscious of my self in the present. I finally began to notice (though the fact had been there for months) that while I was having sex? making love? fucking? having sexual intercourse? I would begin to feel intensely and suddenly lose my breath. My (male) lover described this as having a door slammed in his face. When I brought this to Cheryl, we began tracking the sensation, taking the feeling and going with it back to other, familiar feelings. (Journal of January 31, 1986, reads, "My work with Cheryl is very hard just now. Breathing problems—Father's fist grasping spinal column, lungs, heart. All vital functions slow. Anxiety around women, powerful women. Cheryl says both parents forbade free expression of need. Now fearful of the gasping with *X*. Being in love makes me so vulnerable to displacement—to the shift into a no-place. I fear taking him inside me . . . having him there and not me.")

The constriction of breath took us through various processes of therapy, as well as the image-making. Sometime Cheryl rubbed or pounded on my back to make the breath come; once when I phoned in a panic, choking and gasping, she offered to come (like a fool, I refused) and she said "Write, Write. The feelings want to come." She set up an appointment for a bioenergetic therapist, explaining that since she'd be coming along to learn something, she'd pay the extra. Only later did I learn that the bio. person charged close to twice Cheryl's fee to me. The bio. shrink stood us up, and Cheryl and I kept working away at it on our own. My images of the breathing difficulty got more lurid and more life-and-death fixated. When I felt that the only way I'd ever be able to breathe would be to murder the "mother" who lived in my chest, Cheryl redirected the therapy dramatically and began to focus on the practical matters of everyday survival skills, ego building, self-defense (not against street violence, but against the demands and desires of my nearest and dearest), and affirmation of my work. The intensity of breath constriction was dramatically reduced by this shift. The distance and strengthening that the change in direction gave me (as far as I know at the present) mean that when it is time for me to return to the breathing problems, I will come to the issue with strength, not suicidal despair.

How have I changed? The generalities I could use here don't seem informative. Some comments from others who know me well: "Your voice is so much deeper and stronger. You don't have that tense politeness when you talk about your daughter now"; "You dance so freely. Not so sexual, more movement, more rhythm"; "I don't worry about you any more." That is from the outside. From the inside, my relationship with my daughter is far less frustrating for both of us. I realized that my feelings of guilt crowded out her feelings when she wanted to talk about her problems.

When I started seeing Cheryl, my food dreams (a category I'd had for twenty years) showed me arriving after the food was all gone, or finding no place set for me at the table, or being always pushed to the back of the line at the cafeteria. Then, after we began to work together, I would find food, junk food, dry bread at first. I'd be able to eat it. Then, later, I'd be at the market, buying food, cooking, feeding others. My fridge full of nourishing things. Lots of food. The food dreams have stopped. (I did go through a parallel series late in the therapy about breasts—first dream I had no breasts, then breasts but no milk. I remember with great pleasure Cheryl insisting, urging me to believe her, "You've got what it takes. You *can* feed that baby"—whether the baby was myself or my (now adult) daughter we never bothered to decide.) More than any external indication, these dreams of a lifetime of deprivation and starvation (amazing to me I have no external eating disorder) show that I can now nourish myself and others. I attribute this directly to the work I did with Cheryl.

References

Albert, E. "The Unmothered Mother." In M. H. Garskoff (ed.), *Roles Women Play*. Belmont, Calif.: Brooks/Cole, 1971.

Anyon, J. "Accommodation and Resistance in Gender and Gender Development." Paper presented to the faculty and students of the Ontario Institute for Studies in Education, Toronto, Oct. 1981.

Bardwick, J. M., and Douvan, E. "Ambivalence: The Socialization of Women." In J. M. Bardwick (ed.), *Readings on the Psychology of Women*. New York: Harper & Row, 1972.

Berger, J. *Ways of Seeing*. New York: Penguin Books, 1972.

Bernard, J. *The Future of Marriage*. New York: Bantam Books, 1972.

Bernard, J. *The Future of Motherhood*. New York: Penguin Books, 1974.

Broverman, I. K., and others. "Sex-role Stereotypes and Clinical Judgments of Mental Health." *Journal of Consulting and Clinical Psychology*, 1970, *34* (1), pp. 1–7.

deBeauvoir, S. *The Second Sex*. New York: Bantam Books, 1952.

Heriot, J. "The Double Bind: Healing the Split." In J. H. Robbins and R. J. Siegel (eds.), *Women Changing Therapy*. New York: Haworth Press, 1983.

Laurence, M. *The Fire-Dwellers*. Toronto: McClelland and Stewart, 1969.

Lessing, D. *The Summer Before the Dark*. London: Jonathan Cape, 1973.

Orbach, S. *Fat Is a Feminist Issue: A Self-Help Guide for Compulsive Eaters*. New York: Berkeley Books, 1978.

Orbach, S. *Fat Is a Feminist Issue II: A Program to Conquer Compulsive Eating*. New York: Berkeley Books, 1982.

Schreiber, F. R. *Sybil*. New York: Warner Books, 1973.

Sturdivant, S. *Therapy with Women: A Feminist Philosophy of Treatment*. New York: Springer, 1980.

Torem, M. S. "Dissociative States Presenting as an Eating Disorder." *American Journal of Clinical Hypnosis*, 1986, *29* (2), pp. 137–142.

Torem, M. S. "Ego-State Therapy for Eating Disorder." *American Journal of Hypnosis,* 1987, *30* (2), pp. 94–103.

Watkins, J. G. *The Therapeutic Self.* New York: Human Sciences Press, 1978.

Watkins, J. G., and Watkins, H. H. "Theory and Practice of Ego-State Therapy." In H. Grayson (ed.), *Short Term Approaches to Psychotherapy.* New York: Human Sciences Press, 1979.

Afterword: Empowering Women Through the Healing Process

Cheryl Malmo
Toni Ann Laidlaw

The writings in this book have focused on the healing process as practiced by a selected number of feminist therapists and as experienced by their clients. Through the readings, we discover the richness and diversity of healing practices. We come to know each therapist as she discusses her orientation and the specific techniques that she uses. We come to know each client as she unfolds to the reader her journey toward empowerment.

The methods that enable the healing journey are many and varied. They include dream work, guided and nondirective imagery, body work, massage, drawings, photos, stories, metaphors, ceremonies, rituals, writing, chair work, ego-state therapy, hypnosis, workshops, and group work. All of these methods make use of concrete and creative ways to contact that part of the person that has been judged, denied, or repressed out of necessity as a strategy for survival. While each therapist may conceptualize the healing process somewhat differently, all provide a means by which the inner child or unconscious material can emerge. This inner child is acknowledged and encouraged to speak out and is listened to, accepted, validated, and cared for by the therapist. The feelings and needs of the child are then integrated into the client's adult self with the help of an imagined part of self who is fully developed and who the therapists refer to as spirit guide, guardian spirit, higher self, or crone. For integration to occur, the expression of the child's feelings and needs must be accompanied by a cognitive restructuring of the client's belief system. This restructuring, which is accomplished through the nurturing, wisdom, and unconditional love of the spirit guide, involves a reframing of negative attitudes and beliefs toward oneself and others into constructive and healthy ones. The result of this process is a transformation that is healing, energizing, and empowering for the client.

All of the therapists who have contributed to this book recognize that the transformation process is a natural one—that the client has the innate capacity to heal herself. In therapy, the client is taught to access her inner knowledge and use her inner resources for healing. All therapists (counselors, facilitators, care givers, group leaders, healers, synergizers) perceive that their role is to guide and support their clients through a therapeutic journey. They bring to the relationship an understanding of how the healing process works and the skills to facilitate the process. In addition to providing a safe relationship in which the client can do the necessary psychological work, most emphasize the importance of teaching their clients how to access a safe place in their minds.

Another important issue for the therapists is that their clients assume control of the therapy process by defining their problems, setting goals, making choices and decisions, and determining the timing and pacing of the therapeutic work. Even in group work, where the process is more structured, individuals are encouraged to voice their needs and expectations and to determine the extent to which they participate in any particular exercise. The therapists insist that clients take control in these ways because they recognize that in taking control of their own therapy, clients will begin to develop a trust in themselves and recognize that they are their own best experts.

The relationship between the therapists and clients in the book can best be described as one of equals. Equality in this context does not mean sameness, nor does it mean reciprocity in the relationship. What it does mean is a valuing of individual worth and a mutual respect for the differing expertise of each person, therapist and client, in the relationship. Consequently, the therapist must prove herself trustworthy rather than expect the client to trust her on the basis of her status. Further, because the therapist enters the therapeutic relationship as herself and not as a detached authority, the relationship resonates with genuineness, openness, mutual respect, and warmth. As a result, the therapist knowingly becomes a positive model of self-acceptance, self-nurturance, strength, and empowerment.

As feminists, the therapists in this book have a political consciousness of women's relative powerlessness in the world. As feminist psychologists, they understand the psychological effects on their clients of this powerlessness and of devaluation and stereotyping. They are knowledgeable about various problems experienced by women (incest, abuse, neglect, cancer, growing up in an alcoholic family, and so on) and with the strategies that they use to cope (compulsive eating, addictions, dissociation, self-abuse, and so on). Further, they have developed ways to work on these problems in therapy. Many of the therapists include in their therapy an element of consciousness raising. These therapists recognize the importance of making the client aware that part of her pain is a result of her powerlessness as a woman and not a consequence of personal inadequacy. They recognize that while inner change must take place in psychological healing, clients also need to be active in instigating changes in their relationships and communities. In this way, feminists share with Native cultures a sense of community-mindedness whereby no one is fully healed until all are healed.

Through the clients' creative expressions of their experiences in therapy, we learn of their difficulties prior to entering therapy, of their fears and vulnerabilities, and of their courage in deciding to risk disclosure. Many of the clients describe themselves as having had low self-esteem and little self-worth and as being self-denigrating prior to entering therapy. As they progressed through therapy, many came to recognize that they were psychologically split from their feelings of hurt, anger, sadness, and fear. What the clients valued in their therapeutic relationship echoes what the therapists outlined as important. They wrote of feeling respected, being treated with gentleness, feeling heard, seen, and cared for, experiencing unconditional acceptance, being given total attention, being listened to without judgment, and experiencing the therapist as real and spontaneous. The clients appreciated that the therapists or workshop leaders believed in their ability to define their own problems, speak their own feelings, and make their own decisions. They also valued being given the time and safety in which to find their own voices and explore fully their thoughts and feelings. Finally, they indicate that their therapists were important models to them regarding self-acceptance, self-worth, self-care, strength, and positive action.

As to the therapy itself, clients spoke of the relief that they felt in having their feelings acknowledged and accepted. They learned that they were not to blame for the circumstances that created those feelings, whether they arose from not fitting the stereotyped notions of femininity or from physical, psychological, or sexual abuse. Understanding that many of their problems originated in situations beyond their control enabled the clients to refrain from negatively judging themselves and to begin instead to accept themselves. In addition, the clients emphasized the importance of learning to trust their inner knowledge—their body sensations, feelings, images, thoughts, perceptions. They came to understand how past experiences are carried into the present, often without awareness, and interfere with daily life. Finally, they learned that they could act on behalf of themselves in new and creative ways by implementing new skills and strategies for change. The stories that the clients share reaffirm our basic beliefs about feminist therapy—that the clients are their own best experts and that knowledge is power.

Index

C

D

G

H

I

J

K

L

M

N

T